I0796806

Preparing Tudor Kings and Princes to Rule

Preparing Tudor Kings and Princes to Rule

The Men and Women Who Trained the Royals

Julia A. Hickey

First published in Great Britain in 2025 by
Pen & Sword History
An imprint of Pen & Sword Books Limited
Yorkshire – Philadelphia

ISBN 978 1 39905 255 9

A CIP catalogue record for this book is available from the British Library.

Typeset by Mac Style
Printed in the UK by CPI Group (UK) Ltd, Croydon, CR0 4YY.

The Publisher's authorised representative in the EU for product safety is Authorised Rep Compliance Ltd., Ground Floor, 71 Lower Baggot Street, Dublin D02 P593, Ireland.
www.arccompliance.com

For a complete list of Pen & Sword titles please contact

PEN & SWORD BOOKS LIMITED
47 Church Street, Barnsley, South Yorkshire, S70 2AS, England
E-mail: enquiries@pen-and-sword.co.uk
Website: www.pen-and-sword.co.uk
or
PEN AND SWORD BOOKS
1950 Lawrence Road, Havertown, PA 19083, USA
E-mail: uspen-and-sword@casematepublishers.com
Website: www.penandswordbooks.com

Contents

Illustrations		vi
Introduction: From Knaves to Kings and Renaissance Princes		viii
Chapter 1	The Rise of the Tudors	1
Chapter 2	Battle for the Crown	7
Chapter 3	Henry Tudor – a Fifteenth-Century Aristocratic Education	18
Chapter 4	From Lancastrian 'Imp' to King of England	25
Chapter 5	A Royal Family	33
Chapter 6	Prince Arthur	49
Chapter 7	Henry VIII – The Education of a Christian Prince	65
Chapter 8	Mary Tudor and Henry FitzRoy	76
Chapter 9	Elizabeth and Edward	99
Chapter 10	Hard Lessons	113
Chapter 11	Final Lessons	128
A Who's Who of Lady Mistresses and Governesses Who Raised the Tudors		136
A Who's Who of Governors, Mentors and Household Officers Who Raised the Tudors		169
Table Identifying the Men and Women who Raised Tudor Princes and Princesses		186
Notes		190
Bibliography		204
Index		214

Illustrations

1. Brass rubbing of Edmond Tudor's tomb at St David's Cathedral, Wales.
2. Stained glass window of Lady Margaret Beaufort, Countess of Richmond and Derby, in St Mary's the Virgin Church, Petworth, Sussex.
3. Stained glass window of Jasper Tudor, Earl of Richmond and Duke of Bedford, with his wife Catherine Woodville, Cardiff Castle, Wales
4. Raglan Castle, Wales.
5. Stained glass window in the Cordeliers of Nantes: Francis II, Duke of Brittany praying, 17th century.
6. Bust of Henry VII, after an original by Pietro Torrigiano.
7. The Marriage of Henry VII and Elizabeth of York: print, H. Cook after Jan Gossaert (also known as Jan Mabuse).
8. Elizabeth of York, Queen of England.
9. Three Children of Henry VII and Elizabeth His Queen: Prince Arthur, Prince Henry and Princess Margaret, 1748. George Vertue, 1684–1756.
10. Stained glass window of Prince Arthur in St Laurence's Church, Ludlow.
11. Ludlow Castle, Shropshire.
12. Effigy of Sir Richard Croft at Croft Church, Herefordshire.
13. Effigy of Sir Henry Vernon, St Bartholemew's Church, Tong.
14. Hadden Hall, Derbyshire.
15. The tomb of Arthur, Prince of Wales at Worcester Cathedral.
16. Eltham Palace, London.
17. King James IV of Scotland and Queen Margaret. Print published by John Thane, 1796.
18. Portrait of Henry VIII. Hans Liefrinck after Corenelis Anthonisz, 1539–1547.
19. Henry's reconciliation with Anne Boleyn. George Cruikshank, 1842.
20. Jane Seymour. Wenceslaus Hollar, 1607–1677.
21. Portrait of Edward VI, the future king of England, as a child. Anonymous, 1600–1699.

22. King Edward VI as an infant. Wenceslaus Hollar, 1607–1677 after Hans Holbein.
23. Portrait of 'Mother Jak'. Francesco Bartolozzi after Hans Holbein the Younger, 1797. Now known to be Margaret Giggs (1508–1570), the adopted daughter of Sir Thomas More.
24. Portrait of Edward VI. Anonymous.
25. King Henry VIII with Will Sommers, Edward VI, Mary I and Elizabeth I. Francesco Bartolozzi, 1728–1815, after Hans Holbein the Younger.
26. Sir Thomas More. Jacob Houbraken after Hans Holbein the Younger, 1760.
27. Portrait of Desiderius Erasmus. Quinten Massijs (a copy after) after c.1535.
28. Portrait of John Colet.
29. A man designated as Thomas Linacre. Oil Painting, c.1900(?).
30. Katherine Knollys (née Carey), Lady Knollys, 1562.
31. Plaque dedicated to Elizabeth Calthorpe, Church of St Martin at Palace, Norwich.
32. Stained glass window of Lady Anne Shelton and Sir John Shelton in St Mary's Church, Shelton, Norfolk.
33. Blickling Hall, Norfolk.
34. Ightham Mote, Kent.
35. Blanch Parry, Bacton Church, Herefordshire.
36. Sir Anthony Denny. Wenceslaus Hollar.
37. Hampton Court Palace.
38. The Execution of Lady Jane Grey. Paolo Mercurinaar after Paul Delaroche.
39. An Allegory of the Tudor Succession: The family of Henry VIII. After Lucas de Heere, 1534–1584.
40. King Henry VIII, Edward VI, Queens Mary and Elizabeth. Hendrick Goltzius, 1584.

Introduction

From Knaves to Kings and Renaissance Princes

Henry Tudor was not born to be king. His education, on occasion haphazard, was that of a nobleman placed in the keeping of a guardian. By 1457, the year of Henry's birth, his father, Edmund, was already dead and his mother, Lady Margaret Beaufort, was still a minor herself. And even if this had not been the case, underage heirs could not be in the legal guardianship of their mothers who were regarded, in medieval terms, as being unable to fulfil the feudal duties of a land holder. The monarch automatically held the custody rights over any underage heirs of tenants-in-chief. Wardship was often sold to the highest bidder, or, during times of political unrest, to a guardian that the king could trust. It did not always mean that young children were separated from their mothers. Lady Margaret Beaufort, a wealthy heiress in her own right, became the ward of William de la Pole, 1st Duke of Suffolk following the death of her own father, on her first birthday in 1544, but remained in her mother's day-to-day care. The Tudors were fortunate that Henry VI granted his half-brother, Jasper Tudor, the right to raise their nephew, Henry. After the Battle of Towton in 1461 and the defeat of the Lancastrians and flight of Henry VI, Jasper became an insurgent against the newly established Yorkist regime. King Edward IV passed the responsibility for Henry's upbringing to Sir William Herbert of Raglan.

Guardians were expected to protect and care for their wards until they came of age, which for a male heir was usually 21 years. In return, they assumed custody of the lands and possessions which the child would inherit when they became an adult. During the time of the child's minority the guardian enjoyed all the profits that came from those estates as well as the right to dispose of their ward in marriage. Herbert and his wife Anne Devereux, who fulfilled the role of foster mother or governess, raised Henry alongside their own children and betrothed him to their daughter, Maud, in order to ensure that the Tudor titles and any inheritance he might receive would remain within the Herbert family. It was only thanks to the fortunes of war that Herbert's plans came to nothing in 1469. Henry ended his childhood and adolescence back in the care of Jasper Tudor as a fugitive under the protection of Francis II, Duke of Brittany.

When Henry Tudor claimed the throne after Bosworth, England was changing from a medieval to a modern style of government. G. R. Elton described the coming of the Tudors as a revolution in his 1953 book, *The Tudor Revolution in Government* while Chrimes' text on Henry VII argued that there were no dramatic gear shifts, merely a return to an authoritative monarchy. It is certainly true that Henry VII paid close attention to the way that his realm was administered and gained a reputation for tight-fisted fiscal and financial policies. It was a strategy that ensured that the royal treasury was full by the end of his reign. He gave the same consideration to the way that his heir, Arthur, was raised from the moment of his birth in 1486. However, when Arthur died in 1502, it became clear that Henry VII's second son would inherit the Tudor crown.

Henry VIII was not so well prepared for kingship as his brother had been. While it was Henry who made all the decisions, and supervised even the smallest details of projects that interested him, it was his ministers, famously Cardinal Wolsey and Thomas Cromwell, who were required to come up with the practicalities of implementing the king's wishes for both state and household matters. Unfortunately, and in vivid contrast to his father, Henry VIII made war on his neighbours and implemented magnificent building programmes, the most enduring of which is Hampton Court Palace, finished in about 1540. By then he had also already started to build Nonsuch Palace in Surrey, a brand-new project rather than an adaption of a pre-existing residence, designed to be more lavish than any other royal palace in England and to be the rival of King Francis I of France's palaces at Fontainebleau and Chambord.[1] It was still unfinished in 1547 but by then he had spent £25,000; roughly £7.5 million today.[2]

By the end of the 1530s, with the king spending heavily on the luxuries that identified him as a Renaissance monarch as well as on a new Navy and military campaigns in France and Scotland, there was a need to raise more funds. One strategy that King Henry VIII's ministers adopted was to regularise the way in which orphaned underage heirs and their assets were processed. The Court of Wards and Liveries was established during the 1540s. It was a mechanism to ensure that the king received all the fees, which were a prerogative right, that were due to the Crown. The Court was widely resented by families who were subject to it since the resulting appointments it made could often spell financial disaster. Many guardians were more interested in the profit to be made from asset stripping their ward's possessions than ensuring that the child was properly educated or cared for.

Guardianship of a minority monarch was even more complicated since the kingdom was part of an underage heir's inherited estate. Whenever a child sat upon the throne there was always an anxiety that a guardian might be tempted to seize power for themselves and establish a dynasty of their own. The example of the disappearance of Elizabeth of York's brothers, Edward V and his younger brother Richard, haunted the Tudor imagination, whatever the truth of the matter might have been. Both Henry VII and Henry VIII feared that they would be succeeded by an underage heir, or even worse a female one; an event which could signal a return to the difficult days of the fifteenth century. In the event, Henry VII's thirty-seven page will was drawn up in readiness long before he died and he could rely upon his mother's iron grip on the court and council, to carry out his wishes,[3] thus avoiding the unedifying sight of a power struggle between opposing factions. Henry VIII, who was 17 years of age when he became king, was under the regency of Lady Margaret Beaufort for the few weeks before he achieved his own officially designated majority.

Henry VIII's son, Edward VI, inherited the throne when he was 9 years old, in January 1547. Henry wrote his own will, when he realised that he was dying, to provide a structure for his son's minority government but, without the likes of Margaret Beaufort or a chief minister who could be relied upon, his attempt to order matters from beyond the grave so that no individual guardian was allowed royal power was swiftly overturned. Edward Seymour, the new king's senior maternal uncle, was the natural choice as both guardian and regent so far as the Privy Council were concerned. He took on responsibility for his nephew's education and protection but also wielded royal power, with the advice of the Privy Council, even if it was important to stress the importance of the young king's consent. Guardianship of Edward VI brought with it title, authority and wealth but concluded with ruin and a date with the headsman's axe. His successor, John Dudley, fared no better.

Appointing someone with the desired credentials to manage the wellbeing and education of a royal heir, and their siblings, in a household of their own was usual practice for medieval monarchs and beyond. Kings and their consorts did not have the time to be hands-on parents, no matter how much they might have desired cosy domesticity. Instead, responsibility for ensuring the monarch's wishes on the matter of childrearing and education lay in the hands of men and women trusted for their experience and previous service. Henry VII and his mother, Lady Margaret Beaufort, turned to the ordinances of Edward IV for instruction as to how this was to be best achieved. The Tudors, with their shaky claims to royalty, deliberately created a similar structure for raising their own heirs as their immediate predecessors.

The royal nursery at Eltham transitioned seamlessly from caring for Plantagenet to Tudor royalty. When Prince Arthur was born, Elizabeth Denton, who presided over the nursery of Edward IV's children, was appointed to the post of lady mistress. The chief duty of a lady mistress, or governess, was to supervise the royal nursery, ensure that the child or children were cared for and oversee that the essentials of reading, writing, religion and etiquette were taught. They would report all progress to their royal employers. Women employed within the royal nurseries often tended more than one generation, moved into new roles and were fondly remembered with various gifts and pensions.

Princes left the care of women when they reached the age of 6 or 7 years and were handed into the protection of male guardians. Henry VII, who trusted few men, ensured that no one person possessed overall control of his heir. Instead, Henry appointed a Council of Wales and established a household for his son composed of members of the extended royal family and capable administrators to share the responsibility of caring for and teaching Prince Arthur how to rule. Prince Henry, who was never destined to be king, remained with his sisters at Eltham where he was mentored by William Blount, 4th Baron Mountjoy and Arthur Plantagenet, the base born son of Edward IV.

Henry VIII adopted a combination of models for childcare when it came to raising his own offspring. His illegitimate son, Henry FitzRoy, was placed first under the guardianship of Cardinal Wolsey, who was the boy's godfather. Following FitzRoy's ennoblement in 1525, after which time he was always referred to as a prince in official correspondence, he was provided with a household of his own and sent to Sheriff Hutton as the Lord President of the Council of the North. Sir Thomas Tempest became the comptroller of his household while Sir William Parr was appointed as its chamberlain.

Henry Howard, 3rd Duke of Norfolk took on a supervisory role. When FitzRoy returned from the north and was sent to live at Windsor Castle in 1529, Henry Howard, Earl of Surrey, who was only a year or two older than FitzRoy, was appointed as the boy's mentor, returning to a more medieval concept of princely education.

Princesses, irrespective of whether they were the heir to the throne, remained under the supervision of their lady mistresses until they were granted a place at the royal court to finish their education by serving the queen and learning what was expected of royal wives and aristocratic women. At the end of their education it was anticipated that they would be passed into the care of their husbands. Raising a Tudor princess revolved around the creation of a young woman who would be an ornament to the House of Tudor and a desirable pawn in the game of diplomatic marriage. The women who served as governesses to Tudor females were expected to be teachers, ladies-in-waiting and to safeguard the virtue of the girls they cared for. Consequentially, lady mistresses were usually expected to be married women with children of their own. It was often the case that the lady governess's husband was appointed to a role within the household which held responsibility for financial and estate management.

Guardians, governors and lady governesses fulfilled their royal employer's instructions about the care and education of their wards under the watchful eyes of royal mothers including Elizabeth of York, Katherine of Aragon and Margaret Beaufort, and even, in the case of Katherine Parr, stepmothers. When circumstances allowed they took an active role in raising their sons and daughters but, sadly, little is documented. Chief ministers might also find themselves detailed, within the royal chain of command, to have oversight of royal nurseries and their staff. It was Cardinal Wolsey who orchestrated Princess Mary's removal to Ludlow in 1525 and made the necessary appointments to her household and council. In 1536, it was Thomas Cromwell, who succeeded the cardinal as Henry's chief minister, who addressed Lady Margaret Bryan's complaints about Sir John Shelton's management of the former Princess Elizabeth's household.

Diverse chaplains, tutors and mentors were appointed to attend upon royal Tudors throughout their childhoods to prepare them for the practicalities of life as the progeny of Renaissance kings. As Hilton says, definitions of the Renaissance can be 'notoriously slippery'.[4] Renaissance means 'rebirth' and the Tudors came to the throne when scholars were rediscovering and interrogating classical texts, science was questioning humanity's place in the universe and theologians were reconsidering humankind's relationship with God and the Church.[5] Renaissance princes were men who constructed themselves according to their new found knowledge.[6] And the Tudors were a dynasty who might aptly be said to have fabricated themselves as England's rightful rulers.

It meant, for Henry VII who spent years as an observer of the courts of Brittany and France, that education mattered more than it ever had before. He wanted to be the embodiment of European royalty. To achieve this he selected men who were scholars and advocates of humanism to teach his children rather than settling on aristocratic mentors and royal chaplains as his predecessors had done. He and his successors embraced knowledge, patronised the arts, had their portraits painted, built palaces and grasped the value of scientific innovation.

In Northern Europe the rise of humanism, with an emphasis on classical rhetoric, grammar and history, was closely associated with the development of good moral character. Sir Thomas More asserted that Greek and Latin 'inclined the soul to virtue'[7] as well as the wisdom of the ages. The scope of reading which included study of both Old and New Testaments drew many humanists to question the structures and abuses of the Catholic Church. Humanists with an impact on the early development of royal educational curricula, including Desiderius Erasmus, Thomas More, and Juan Luis Vives, were all Catholic and emphasised the importance of piety. As the sixteenth century progressed, new learning came to be associated with a more radical desire for reform. By the time Henry VIII's long awaited male heir took his place in the classroom the men who were selected to teach him and his chosen companions were described as being 'among the most brilliant scholars of their day'.[8] But they all leaned towards Protestantism, rather than Catholicism, as did Henry's sixth queen, Katherine Parr, who took a close interest in the education of her husband's younger children, Elizabeth and Edward.

Being a Renaissance prince, or princess, required more than following a course of approved academic study. They were expected to be accomplished musicians, dancers, and if they were female, talented needlewomen. Their male counterparts all excelled as sportsmen and knightly pursuits. Juan Luis Vives, the Spanish humanist who wrote a book on the education of girls and could be described as Mary I's director of studies during her childhood, stated that a gentleman needed to 'be instructed in every philosophical and practical discipline to fulfil his social role'.[9] He thought girls should be taught from a narrower palette and pay more attention to domestic skills, whatever their rank. Elizabeth's own tutor, Roger Ascham, did not agree. Unlike Mary, Elizabeth would learn Greek and there would be no restrictions placed on her reading material.

Henry VIII's sisters, Margaret and Mary, benefitted from Lady Margaret Beaufort's interest in learning and her desire to ensure that her granddaughters received a better education than her own. Little is known about the exact nature of their training other than occasional references made to tutors borrowed from their brother. Suffice to say they were to be an enhancement to the Tudor name as befitted their roles as future queens of Scotland and France where they would be defined by their success as wives and mothers. Since Henry and Katherine of Aragon's daughter had no legitimate brothers, Mary was required to have a more formal preparation. By that time English humanists were beginning to both praise and defend the need for women to be educated. The English edition of Erasmus' *Commentaries on the Lord's Prayer* was published in 1524. It was translated by Sir Thomas More's daughter, Margaret Roper and dedicated to Henry VIII's niece, Frances Brandon. Vives' text *The Education of a Christian Woman* at the request of Katherine of Aragon was published the same year.[10] Unlike Sir Thomas More who believed all his children should be taught the same way, Vives argued that Mary was not to be educated in the same manner as her uncle Arthur, or even Henry FitzRoy. If she did inherit the throne, she would marry and the country would be ruled by her husband, as was only natural. Instead, Mary's education should weed out any faults in her character and shape her into a good Christian woman.

Henry VIII's desire for a male heir and the papacy's failure to provide him with the means to put Katherine of Aragon to one side, toppled the Catholic Church in England and set a course for further reform. Princess Mary was demoted and placed in the hands of Anne Shelton who was notable as a lady mistress for her orders to break the will of her charge rather than to nurture her. By the time Anne Boleyn's daughter, Elizabeth, was 3 years old she was an unwanted reminder of her mother. She was the bastard daughter of an adulterous and incestuous mother, rather than her father's darling. There was no formal curriculum planning; being appointed to raise her was not as prestigious as it might otherwise have been and there were no ambassadors lining up to describe her talents. Elizabeth's education and the arrangements for her household were left in the hands of Lady Bryan's replacement, Blanche Herbert, Lady Troy who relied upon Katherine Champernowne to teach the girl and the advice of Sir Anthony Denny, one of the king's favourites. Henry, after his initial antipathy, provided for his daughter appropriate to her station but it was Katherine Parr, Elizabeth's stepmother from 1543, who arranged for her to have lessons from the same circle of humanists who educated Edward VI.

Katherine's influence was not all positive. After Henry's death, Elizabeth moved into her stepmother's household at Chelsea. Who better to supervise a daughter of the late king? However, the dowager's marriage to Edward VI's younger uncle, Thomas Seymour, introduced a new, and dangerous guardian to Elizabeth's life. Even dowager queens were expected to be obedient to their husbands. It meant that Seymour, who was now Elizabeth's stepfather, unless the Council declared otherwise, was in overall charge of Katherine's household. It appears that Edward Seymour and the Privy Council had confidence in Katherine's ability to supervise the upbringing of the young king's sister and her cousin, Lady Jane Grey, who was Thomas Seymour's ward.

The hardest lesson that Elizabeth learned, but perhaps the most important one for Renaissance princes to comprehend, was the importance of self-interest and consequentialism. This is best summarised as 'the end justifies the means' which is in its own turn a simplification of Machiavelli's theory, expressed in *The Prince* and first published in 1532:

> Men judge generally more by the eye than by the hand, because it belongs to everybody to see you, to few to come in touch with you. Everyone sees what you appear to be, few really know what you are, and those few dare not oppose themselves to the opinion of the many, who have the majesty of the state to defend them; and in the actions of all men, and especially of princes, which it is not prudent to challenge, one judges by the result.[11]

It was perhaps the most important lesson Elizabeth ever absorbed. Henry Tudor's granddaughter was never expected to sit upon the throne but her education at the hands of the men and women who raised her equipped her to understand better than most both the uses and limits of power. Thanks to the scandal that surrounded her relationship with her stepfather, she learned to mask her true feelings, avoid inconsistency, and do what was necessary in order to survive. It would stand her in good stead both before she became queen and after.

Chapter 1

The Rise of the Tudors

The family originated from northwest Wales where they served Llywelyn ab Iorwerth, also known as Llywelyn Fawr, who ruled as the King of Gwynedd before establishing himself as the Prince of Wales in 1216. Henry VII's ancestor, Ednyfed Fychan, the prince's seneschal, was rewarded by grants of land, free from feudal dues, across Llywelyn's kingdom in return for his political and military services.

Ednyfed's acquisitions helped to ensure the family's continued prominence in Wales as administrators and soldiers throughout the thirteenth and fourteenth centuries. They have been described as one of the most powerful families in Wales. Wealth, land and lineage were the currency by which Henry's ancestors became 'ministerial aristocracy'.[1] One of Ednyfed's descendants, Goronwy ap Tudur, Lord Penymynydd, from whom the Tudor dynasty takes its name, inherited the family's lands in north Wales in 1331. Goronwy served as a Crown administrator on Anglesey, as a soldier in Edward II's army at Bannockburn and in Edward III's military campaigns against the French. Such was his wealth and position in society that Goronwy was able to take Marged ferch Tomos for his wife. She was descended from the princes of Deheubarth and was aunt to Owain Glyndwr, the last Welshman to claim, and hold, an ancestral title of Prince of Wales.

In about 1407, Owain, or Owen, ap Maredudd ap Tudur, known hereafter as Owen Tudor, became a ward of his father's kinsman, Lord Rhys, in England. He was about 7 years old. Life was not easy for men and women who moved into England either as economic migrants or to begin their lives afresh. Henry IV introduced a series of laws that denied them the ordinary rights of citizenship. They were forbidden from marrying anyone who was English, they could not perform jury service, were unable to hold a Crown office and, most importantly, no Englishman could be convicted on the word of someone from Wales.[2] When he arrived in London the boy was sent to join the household of Sir Walter Hungerford, a member of a powerful family who supported the dukes of Lancaster. It is likely that

Owen was educated first as a page and then as a squire. It is said, with no supporting evidence, that he was one of Hungerford's squires at the Battle of Agincourt in 1415. A man named Owen Meredith is documented in Hungerford's retinue the following year but it is not conclusive proof. It may refer to another man. Owen's name was eventually anglicised to include his grandfather's patronymic rather than his father's, as was more usual, but the surviving documents of the period are not consistent in the form by which Owen is identified.

In 1418 Hungerford was named as steward of the king's household and took part in peace negotiations between the French and English. In 1422 he was one of the executors of Henry V's will and appointed to the Regency Council presided over by the new king's uncle, Humphrey, Duke of Gloucester. Two years later Hungerford, later Baron Hungerford, became steward of the household to the infant Henry VI. It is probably thanks to Owen's position as one of Hungerford's followers that he gained a place in the household of King Henry V's widow, Catherine of Valois, the daughter of King Charles VI of France, at Wallingford Castle.

There is no evidence for Owen's role while he was in service to the queen but it has been stated that during the 1420s he was the keeper of the queen's wardrobe or her sewer, who tasted her food for her before she ate. The first named official, along with the steward, was the most important official within any noble household. He was responsible for the clerks who looked after Catherine's clothes and valuables. The tall, handsome and, no doubt, charming young man caught the dowager's attention. There are various stories about the couple falling in love with one another including the one recounted by Elis Gruffydd, the so-called 'Soldier of Calais', who published his chronicle in 1552. Catherine, who was still only in her twenty-first year when King Henry V died in 1422, caught a glimpse of Owen as he and his friends swam in a river one summer's day and was smitten by the handsome Welshman. In 1597, the poet Michael Drayton explained that the queen's heart was first captured when Owen fell into her lap while he was dancing. The truth of the matter and the duration of the couple's courtship is shrouded in secrecy because, in addition to Owen being Welsh, the pair were of an unequal social status and the remarriage of King Henry VI's mother was a matter of political importance to the Regency Council.

The subterfuge that surrounded the couple was aided by Catherine's isolation from public life. Even though she attended her son's coronation in England in 1429 and was present in 1431 when he was crowned as France's monarch, she lived mainly at Windsor or Wallingford. She was viewed with some suspicion by the English nobility because of her French birth. Gloucester was determined that she should be prevented from playing an active part in either her son's upbringing or the regency for fear that it would impact on his own power. She visited her young son, King Henry VI, on occasion at Westminster but had little to do with his education after he was given into the care of Richard Beauchamp, 13th Earl of Warwick, who was the king's appointed guardian under the terms of King Henry V's will.

An added imperative for secrecy was that since 1427, it was prohibited for anyone to seek a dowager queen's hand without first gaining royal consent:

> Item, it is ordered and established by the authority of this parliament for the preservation of the honour of the most noble estate of queens of England that no man of whatever estate or condition make contract of betrothal or matrimony to marry himself to the queen of England without the special licence and assent of the king, when the latter is of the age of discretion, and he who acts to the contrary and is duly convicted will forfeit for his whole life all his lands and tenements, even those which are or which will be in his own hands as well as those which are or which will be in the hands of others to his use, and also all his goods and chattels in whosoever's hands they are, considering that by the disparagement of the queen the estate and honour of the king will be most greatly damaged, and it will give the greatest comfort and example to other ladies of rank who are of the blood royal that they might not be so lightly disparaged.[3]

The statute arose, according to a contemporary source known as *Chronicon Angliae* or *Giles's Latin Chronicle* after it's nineteenth-century translator, when rumours reached the Regency Council that Edmund Beaufort, the fourth surviving son of John Beaufort, 1st Earl of Somerset, intended to marry Catherine. Any liaison between the queen and Beaufort would have given a potential boost to the political power wielded by the Beaufort family. They were a part of the extended Lancastrian royal family through their descent from Edward III's son, John of Gaunt, and his mistress, Katherine Swynford. Humphrey, Duke of Gloucester, Henry VI's paternal uncle, had no intention that his own position should be weakened by the clan. He was already locked in conflict with Cardinal Henry Beaufort, Edmund's uncle, who was a dominant presence on the Council having served on three occasions as Lord Chancellor.

The law stipulated that permission for a wedding could only be granted by the current monarch when he achieved his majority. At the time of the law's introduction, Henry VI was still only 6 years old. Any man who wished to marry the boy's mother would have to wait at least a decade before royal permission was forthcoming. Beaufort, a younger son, whose inheritance was only £300, aspired to a wealthy bride rather than a penniless queen no matter what her personal attractions might have been. He turned his attentions elsewhere and wed Eleanor Beauchamp, a daughter of the 13th Earl of Warwick, at the beginning of the 1430s.

Catherine of Valois also avoided the penalties aimed at any new spouse by a second marriage made with Owen in either 1428 or 1429. The Welshman had no titles or estates to forfeit and no expectations — an embodiment of 'disparagement'. He did not even have the full rights of an English citizen. In 1432, after his marriage, he sought exemption from the restrictions imposed on the Welsh in England and was granted the franchise although he only became a naturalised citizen in 1434.[4] Catherine, ignoring Henry IV's penal laws, gifted her husband with land in Flint, North Wales at around the same time. The Regency Council must have accepted the marriage when it came to their notice, or chose to turn a blind eye to it, even if they did not approve it.

Modern historians have questioned the paternity of the couple's eldest son, Edmund Tudor, seeking to find evidence that he was actually Beaufort progeny and that Catherine and Owen's marriage was one of convenience from its outset to hide the fact that Henry VI's mother conceived a child out of wedlock. The evidence is based largely on the appearance of Edmund and Jasper Tudors' coat of arms which were granted to them by their half-brother, Henry VI and differenced from his by a bordure.[5] The similarity between the Tudor and the Beaufort arms occurs because they are both based on the royal arms, even though there is no hereditary link between the two families. Besides which, there was no dispute about the paternity, or even the legitimacy, of any of Catherine's sons at the time of their introduction to Henry VI's court or later.

Owen and Catherine's union remained largely secret until after the dowager queen's death on 3 January 1437 at Bermondsey Abbey, shortly after she gave birth to a daughter. The girl was named Margaret, but little more is known, suggesting that the infant may have died shortly after her mother. By then Catherine and Owen were the parents of at least four children. She became pregnant with Edmund Tudor in 1429. He was born at the Bishop of London's palace at Much Hadham in about 1430. Jasper was born the following year at the Bishop of Ely's home in Hatfield. Remarkably, the bishops and their servants seem not to have gossiped about Catherine's growing family. It is difficult to imagine that the two clerics, no matter how sympathetic, would have permitted the king's mother to produce an illegitimate brood under their auspices. The premature birth of Catherine's youngest son, Owen, at Westminster in 1432, meant that the couple's relationship became more commonly known. Owen remained at the abbey where he was raised, educated and, in time, became a Benedictine monk.

It is probable, though not certain, that Humphrey, Duke of Gloucester was restrained from acting against Owen during Catherine's lifetime because of the influence of Humphrey's brother, John, Duke of Bedford.[6] Without Catherine to protect him, Owen's life became more dangerous, even if the king did finally discover that he had a family of younger half-siblings as well as a stepfather. The Duke of Bedford died in 1435 and although Walter Hungerford was still a member of the Regency Council, he did not have the influence that Bedford once possessed. There was no one left to restrain Gloucester, who resented the misalliance of Henry V's widow with Owen, who was both a Welshman and a commoner.

Catherine's widower fled in the direction of north Wales soon after her death leaving his children behind. He was apprehended at Daventry in Northamptonshire. Owen refused to return to London until he was provided with a written declaration that he was free to leave if he chose to do so. On his return to the Capital, perhaps having second thoughts about the value of the promise, Owen evaded his escort and sought sanctuary at Westminster. Maybe he even witnessed Catherine's funeral there on February 8, 1437. He remained in sanctuary, in the company of criminals and felons, until he took the decision to appear before the Regency Council and his 15-year-old stepson.

Owen declared that he had done no wrong and was the king's liege man. He must have been aware that not everyone on the Council supported Gloucester. Some, like Hungerford, were sympathetic to Catherine's widower. Others, including William de la Pole, 3rd Earl of Suffolk, were actively hostile to Gloucester. After some debate, Owen was released and permitted to return to Wales because of the wishes of Henry VI who was also present at the meeting. But Gloucester did not intend for Tudor to escape his clutches and had the king's stepfather re-arrested on trumped up charges, for breaching the terms of the original safe conduct issued at Daventry.

Owen escaped custody at the beginning of 1438 with the aid of his priest but was quickly recaptured and incarcerated once more. He escaped for a second time but was apprehended yet again.. On this occasion, Owen was sent to Windsor where he was placed in the custody of his old master, Walter Hungerford, even though he was accused of harming his gaoler when he made his escape from Newgate. It has been suggested by Welsh chronicler, Robin Dhu, that Owen became alarmed for the safety of his children and this may offer some explanation for his presence at Windsor.

A possible reason for the leniency shown to him on this occasion was that Henry VI attained his majority in November 1437. He had not forgotten about his stepfather or his new minted family of half-brothers. Owen was pardoned by his stepson for all previous offences he might have committed in 1439 and recognised his position within the royal family.[7] The king provided him with a stipend of £100 per annum, official appointments and re-possession of his goods and lands which had been confiscated upon his first incarceration. There was also an annual grant of £40 each year for life drawn from estates in Devon. Edmund and Jasper were already being educated at Barking Abbey at Henry's expense, although on occasion it's abbess, Katherine de la Pole, the eldest of the Earl of Suffolk's three sisters, complained to the treasury that payment for feeding and clothing the boys was in arrears.

Edmund and Jasper assumed places at court as the king's kinsmen. Their half-brother provided for both their continued care and education. In 1449 the two Tudors were knighted and in 1452 they were ennobled as Earl of Richmond and as Earl of Pembroke respectively. In creating Edmund, Earl of Richmond and Jasper, Earl of Pembroke, Henry was showing the court that his brothers were part of the royal family. At that time they adopted the royal coat of arms differenced only by a bordure in recognition of their relationship to the Crown. Not only was the king protecting them, but he was also creating something which had been absent from his own life. Henry was an isolated young man, as well as a pious one, with no close family. His half-siblings provided him with a kinship network on which he could rely. Their allegiance was to him personally and their presence, either at court or in Wales, added strength to Henry's rule.

Chapter 2

Battle for the Crown

Owen was not completely absent from the life of his stepson or children. In 1444 he was part of the retinue that travelled to France to bring Henry's young bride, Margaret of Anjou, back to England. He was appointed captain of Regnéville in France at about the same time.[1] A two-year truce, later extended, negotiated by the Treaty of Tours between England and France was cemented by the wedding. In England, the treaty which required Henry to give up Maine and Anjou to the French was viewed as a disaster when it became public knowledge. The blame was placed with the Earl of Suffolk who was also part of the retinue sent to fetch Margaret back to England. Even worse, Henry's bride arrived without a dowry but the king believed that the treaty and marriage were the first steps towards a lasting peace between England and France.

Instead, in August 1449, the truce failed and open warfare between the two nations resumed. Edmund Beaufort, Catherine of Valois's one-time suitor and now 2nd Duke of Somerset in his brother's stead, was appointed to replace Henry's cousin, Richard, 3rd Duke of York. as commander in France. It was part of a political strategy to defuse Somerset's rejection of the Treaty of Tours rather than a consideration of military merit. York's dismissal from office increased the resentment between the factions at court who either supported York or Somerset. Beaufort's subsequent military failures stoked York's bitterness towards his royal cousin, Margaret of Anjou and the Beaufort family. Suffolk, Henry's favourite and most influential minister since the deaths of Cardinal Beaufort and the Duke of Gloucester in 1447, was blamed both for the policies which resulted in Henry's marriage to Margaret of Anjou and for the humiliating losses in France that followed.

York demanded governmental reform and the prosecution of the commanders who had lost northern France. As the king's nearest male relation, it was felt by many men that York's voice should be listened to but Margaret of Anjou favoured the Duke of Somerset and did not trust York's motives. It was Somerset who was appointed as Constable of England and it was his voice that was heeded while York's advice was ignored. The more exasperated that York and his faction became, the closer Henry VI's kingdom tottered to the edge of civil unrest.

While the opposing factions vied for the upper hand, Edmund and Jasper Tudor remained the king's closest family. He equipped them with rank, property and wealth to befit their status as his brothers and to serve as his instruments in Wales. To this end, in 1453, he granted the brothers joint guardianship of Lady Margaret Beaufort, the only legitimate child and heiress of John Beaufort, 1st Duke of Somerset. Margaret's inheritance included estates in twelve counties. She was a rich prize despite a childhood marriage made to John de la Pole, the murdered Duke of Suffolk's eldest son, while they were both still children. The Church did not approve of marriages made before the age of reason so it was a straightforward matter for the king to have the union annulled before it progressed any further. Canon law stipulated that brides were not bound by marriage contracts entered into before they reached the age of 12 years, at which time they might legally marry. Edmund and Jasper would enjoy Margaret's estates until she came of age and since guardians controlled who their wards might wed it was inevitable that Edmund would secure his fortunes by a marriage to the girl as soon as she was old enough to become his bride. In the meantime, Parliament, which met at Reading in March 1453, determined that the Tudors were legitimate and released them from any restrictions that their Welsh ancestry and Henry IV's anti-Welsh laws may have placed upon them, even though Owen was granted full rights of citizenship after his marriage to Catherine of Valois.

During the spring of 1453 it seemed that the king, or at least his wife and the Duke of Somerset, had the upper hand at court. Margaret of Anjou was pregnant after seven years of marriage. The birth of a prince, or princess, would mean that York would no longer be Henry's heir presumptive. Then, on 17 July 1453, fate took a hand. The Hundred Years War finally concluded in humiliation for the English at the Battle of Castillon. John Talbot, 1st Earl of Shrewsbury, who commanded the army, was killed and his men shattered. It was August before news of the disaster arrived at Clarendon, near Salisbury, where King Henry was staying. When he was told of the loss, the king experienced a complete mental breakdown that left him mute and unresponsive. With the government in flux while Margaret, Somerset and the royal council pretended that nothing was amiss, local magnates took the opportunity to indulge in personal vendettas. In the north of England, for example, a feud between the Neville and the Percy families escalated into a violent confrontation at Heworth Moor on 24 August 1453. Law and order enforced by king's writ was breaking down. Margaret of Anjou and the Duke of Somerset knew that the correct thing to do to prevent the country from spiralling out of control was to invite York, who was still the king's heir, to become protector while Henry was incapacitated. Instead, they sought alternate solutions and ignored York's demands.

Storm clouds continued to gather around the throne. Jasper and Edmund, who had been sent as Henry's representatives to South Wales, watched events unfold from Pembroke. When Margaret of Anjou gave birth and the realm celebrated the birth of Henry's heir, the king remained frozen and failed to acknowledge the arrival of the boy when Margaret took him to his father to receive a traditional blessing. The birth of a male heir bolstered Margaret's position, just as it weakened York's, even though when Somerset was named as Prince Edward's godfather, a rumour spread that he was actually the boy's father. The council continued to have regular meetings, but in November York, and his kinsmen the Nevilles, determined that they would no longer be sidelined by the queen and her faction. By 23 November the Yorkists gained the upper hand and the Duke of Somerset was committed to the Tower as a prisoner.

Parliament did not approve York's appointment as the realm's protector until 27 March 1454 but throughout the winter months, and the subsequent protectorate, the Tudors continued to enforce the rule of law in South Wales, working harmoniously with the duke's appointed ministers including the Neville earls of Warwick and Salisbury. They were not recorded as supporting Margaret's attempt to become regent in January 1454. Nor were they dismissed from their posts by either of the factions because they had no political power beyond that which the State provided them and were not recognisably of any national influence.

In January 1455, the king recovered his senses. The Duke of Somerset was released from custody, York lost the protectorate and his position as the Captain of Calais and his key allies, the Nevilles, were dismissed from the posts which he had granted them. York and his supporters were not imprisoned but they feared what Margaret and Somerset might be planning for them, especially when they were threatened with a Great Council which was due to meet on the 21 May at Leicester.

Jasper Tudor was at court with the king in May 1455 when news arrived that York and his supporters, Warwick and Salisbury, had recruited an army from their northern estates and were intent on a confrontation. Jasper accompanied his half-brother and the hastily gathered royal army commanded by Somerset, to St Albans on 22 May where the first battle of the Wars of the Roses was fought in the town's streets. On this occasion, Richard Neville, 16th Earl of Warwick, was victorious. He did not want unnecessary bloodshed, even though he was determined to rid himself of his enemies. The Tudors had worked alongside York's protectorate and despite the fact that they were the king's half-brothers, they had no claim to the throne so Jasper escaped unscathed. Edmund Beaufort, 2nd Duke of Somerset, was not so fortunate. He was killed during the battle as were other of Warwick's enemies, the most prominent being Henry Percy, 2nd Earl of Northumberland and Thomas Clifford, 8th Baron Clifford of Skipton.

Henry VII was found, with his bodyguard, near Castle Inn on St Peter's Street. The men around him were cut down on Warwick's orders and the king was wounded in the face by a stray arrow. The trauma of the experience may have triggered another mental breakdown, although the written evidence for it is scant. It meant that while York might never be destined to wear a crown himself, that a second protectorate was likely to be a lengthy one. Henry's heir, Edward, was still only 2 years old and York's principal rival, Somerset, was dead, even if his son, Henry, inherited not only his father's titles but also his enmities. When Parliament opened on 9 July 1455 Jasper was among the lords who swore allegiance to the king but continued to serve York and his appointed ministers. Richmond, perhaps recognising the precariousness of his kinship to the king, was a moderate, certainly pragmatic, royal administrator.

Edmund Tudor, who was 24 years of age, married his 12-year-old bride on 1 November 1455 at Bletsoe Castle in Bedfordshire. Although 12 was the age at girls might legally be married, it was usual for couples to delay cohabitation until the bride was deemed physically capable of withstanding the rigours of pregnancy and childbirth. Margaret Beaufort's biographer and chaplain, John Fisher, stated that she was small in stature even as an adult, so was not sufficiently developed at 12 for the burden of motherhood. However, marriage alone did not ensure that Margaret's inheritance fell into Tudor hands. It was essential, according to the law, for a couple to have a child, even a short lived one, in order for the husband to inherit his wife's possessions in the event of her death, otherwise they reverted to the collateral line of her family leaving her widower with nothing. Edmund's concern lay with his new wife's manors and estates rather than his bride's wellbeing. The marriage was consummated and Margaret became pregnant. Edmund gambled on her surviving long enough to present him with an heir even if it, and she, only took a few breaths before dying. Edmund and Jasper returned to South Wales soon after the wedding was celebrated, taking Margaret with them. Jasper resided at Pembroke Castle while Edmund and Margaret either stayed at Caldicot Castle in Monmouthshire, a property once held by Catherine of Valois as part of her dower rights, or at Lamphey Palace near St David's. Both places claim to be the location where the future King Henry VII was conceived.

The Tudors remained in Wales where they continued to work towards the rule of law whether it was embodied by King Henry VI or a designated protector. The uneasy peace established in England after the First Battle of St Albans did not last. Margaret of Anjou filled the political void left by the death of Edmund Beaufort with the support of Henry Beaufort, 3rd Duke of Somerset. She had no intention of permitting York to retain the protectorate or to usurp her own son, Edward's, rights. In February 1456, the duke was dismissed as protector. England's ruling factions were not at war with one another but the atmosphere was tense. The relationship between the Yorkists and the Tudors changed. As York's role in Henry's government declined, he became more determined to exert his rightful authority as a landowner and Crown official in South Wales, even if it was at the expense of the men with whom he worked in earlier times. Jasper and Edmund were now associated, in York's mind, with the royal faction headed by the queen and became a legitimate target for the group of men in South Wales and the Marches who owed their allegiance to him. Always turbulent, the political situation in Wales verged on lawlessness as disputes over land turned violent.

Among the men who disliked the challenge presented by the Tudors to their established authority in South Wales was Gruffydd ap Nicolas of Dinefwr. He lost some of his offices in 1455 when the Yorkists assumed power after the First Battle of St Albans. As it happened, Jasper was needed by the king in London that spring so it was Edmund Tudor who set about bringing ap Nicolas to heel. The earl targeted the castles at Aberystwyth, Carreg Cennen and Carmarthen which all lay in the hands of ap Nicolas despite the fact that he was no longer the constable of the castles following

York's decision to take the offices for himself during the 1455 protectorate. Edmund, whose rationale to establish Crown authority was unaltered despite the change in regime, seized the castles from ap Nicolas by force and occupied Carmarthen. But York, who still saw himself as the castle's legitimate constable, was now determined to remove Edmund. If Carmarthen was returned to royal hands, or even retained by the Tudors, it would compound the duke's loss of status on the national stage.

Men in Wales and the Marches were forced to decide where their loyalties lay. In the summer of 1456, Walter Devereux, a supporter of Richard, Duke of York and Constable of Wigmore Castle, attacked Hereford before taking the castle at Aberystwyth followed by Carmarthen on 10 August. He was assisted in his campaign by his son-in-law Sir William Herbert of Raglan who was a member of Jasper Tudor's council helping to govern South Wales. Herbert, whose loyalty to York was of longer standing than his association with the Tudors (representing the duke in the lordship of Usk, of which Raglan was a part) not only seized Carmarthen but, along with his father-in-law, captured and imprisoned Edmund.

Devereux legitimised his actions by following up his campaign on York's behalf with a commission of oyer and terminer, empowered to hear and determine criminal cases, against men who were hostile to the Yorkist cause. However, Edmund died suddenly on 1 November 1456 leaving a pregnant wife who was still only a child herself. It is unclear whether the earl died from plague, injuries sustained during the defence of Carmarthen or whether his death was a result of starvation. He was buried at the town's priory church before being removed in 1536, on the orders of King Henry VIII, to St David's Cathedral in Pembrokeshire.

Jasper Tudor hurried back to Wales when news of Edmund's death reached him. Edmund's posthumous son, Henry Tudor, was born on 28 January 1457 at Pembroke Castle. The birthing chamber is likely to have been in comfortable freestanding accommodation inside the castle walls, in a dwelling similar to a hall house rather than in one of the castle's towers.[2] The birth was not an easy one and for a while it looked as though Margaret and her infant might die. Henry Tudor's mother was so damaged by his birth that she never bore another child. When she was in a position of power in later life, she was fierce in her protection of the wellbeing of young girls, including her own granddaughter, Margaret Tudor, who was married to James IV of Scotland at the age of 13. For now, as she began a long recovery in the confines of her chamber with only her women for company, Margaret Beaufort focused all her hopes and love on her son. Henry Tudor was named after his uncle and godfather, the king, but there was no suggestion that the boy would inherit anything other than his father's earldom of Richmond and his mother's fortune. Jasper petitioned Henry VI for guardianship of their nephew who remained at Pembroke where he was cared for by a nursery of female servants.

Recognising the volatility of local and national politics, Jasper decided that his sister-in-law, who needed to be protected from fortune hunters, would be safer married into a more powerful family than his own. He, and she, began to negotiate a new match even though Margaret was a widow of only five months. Two months after Henry's birth, Jasper and Margaret travelled to Greenfield, near Newport, in the east of Wales. The manor belonged to Humphrey Stafford, 1st Duke of Buckingham, an important landowner in the Marches. The men in his affinity were drawn largely from the Cheshire gentry and his Midlands heartlands. He was one of the few men powerful enough to rival Richard of York. His service to the Lancastrian kings of England had been both loyal and continuous. During the early 1450s he tried to maintain peaceful relations between the Dukes of Somerset and York. However, in 1455, he was at St Albans on the king's side where he was wounded by three arrows in the face when Warwick ordered his men to attack the king's bodyguard. In short, he was a man Jasper knew and felt able to trust.

Sir Henry Stafford, Buckingham's second son, became Margaret's third husband on 3 January 1458. Since the couple were second cousins, a dispensation was needed before they could wed one another. Although Stafford was Henry Tudor's stepfather during most of the boy's childhood until his own death in October 1471, he had little to do with Henry's education. Stafford was older than Margaret and prone to ill health but it was a good match and the evidence suggests that the union was a happy one even if Margaret, who was 14 years old at the time of the marriage, left her son in the custody of his uncle Jasper at Pembroke Castle when she travelled to Bourne in Lincolnshire to take up her new life. She would hardly see her son again until he became an adult. All she could do was try to protect him from a distance while Jasper took on the role of surrogate father.

Henry grew from infancy into childhood under the supervision of his nursery staff as Jasper sought to control Wales on the king's behalf and to reconcile rebellious Marchers with the Lancastrian cause. In 1457, York relinquished the disputed castles which cost Edmund his life in return for a consideration of £40 per annum. By then Gruffydd ap Nicolas and his sons had also sought a pardon from Jasper. At Pembroke Castle, it is likely that Henry would have become acquainted with his grandfather, Owen, who is known to have fathered a son, David Owen, at Pembroke in around 1459. Much later, in 1485, when Henry Tudor made his own bid for the crown, his half-uncle was by his side.

The Earl of Warwick, who was Captain of Calais, was summoned back to London in the autumn of 1458 to answer charges of piracy perpetrated against Spanish and Hanseatic vessels that traded with England. The earl arrived at Westminster on 9 November 1458 with an armed retinue, wearing the insignia of the bear and ragged staff at his heels. Inevitably supporters of Warwick clashed with the queen's own followers and Warwick, who fought his way back to his barge, became convinced that the attack was a planned attempt on his life. Neither side was interested in the reconciliation advocated by the king. In the summer of 1459 the earls of York, Warwick and Salisbury became convinced that the queen and her supporters were raising a war host to crush them once and for all. The Yorkists gathered at York's Ludlow residence but when the Lancastrian army made camp on the evening of 13 October on the other side of Ludford Bridge, many of Warwick's retinue from the garrison at Calais, led by their commander Andrew Trollope, defected to the king. The duke, his eldest son and their Neville kinsmen were forced to flee into the night leaving their women folk, retinues and the town of Ludlow to face the consequences of stirring the anger of a royal army. Jasper Tudor either did not arrive at the king's camp in time for the confrontation or was strategically positioned to prevent Yorkist sympathisers from Wales reaching Ludlow in time.

On 5 January 1460 Jasper was granted the castle and lordship of Denbigh which had been confiscated by the Crown following Richard of York's attainder for treason subsequent to the events at Ludlow. It once belonged to the Mortimer Earls of March. Richard inherited the lordship from his mother, Anne Mortimer, and visited it on several occasions. Now, his former tenants were reluctant to accept the Earl of Pembroke as the castle's new constable. Jasper was met by armed resistance throughout Denbighshire and had to besiege the castle which was of strategic importance to the control of the region.

The winter of 1459–1460 was a difficult one for ordinary people as trade suffered, lawlessness and feuding between England's noble families became more violent and there were rumours of an invasion by the French. In the spring of 1460, the people of Kent invited Warwick and the Yorkists, holed up in Calais since the previous year, back to England. By the summer, the earl and his supporters were in control of London and of the king. Buckingham, Margaret Beaufort's father-in-law, was dead on the battlefield at Northampton. York arrived back in England on 9 September and marched under the banner of the kings of England as he advanced on London. When the duke arrived in Westminster on 10 October, he expected to be acclaimed king in Henry's place but the best he could achieve was the Act of Accord on 8 November that recognised him as heir apparent to the throne.

The result satisfied no one, least of all Queen Margaret whose son, Edward, had been disinherited by the agreement. Her allies in Yorkshire began to attack estates belonging to prominent Yorkists including York and Salisbury. It did not take long to draw an army north led by the two men. That Christmas a Lancastrian army, commanded by Somerset lured the Yorkists out from the safety of Sandal Castle near Wakefield and met them in battle. Richard of York was killed during the fighting. His 17-year-old son Edmund, Earl of Rutland, was slaughtered on Wakefield Bridge, allegedly by John Clifford the son of Thomas, Lord Clifford, still pleading for his life. Salisbury, injured during the battle, was executed the following day at Pontefract. The way was open for the Lancastrians to retake London.

When news of the disaster at Wakefield reached the Capital, Warwick sent a messenger to Hereford where York's eldest son, Edward, was based with men provided by William Herbert as well as a force sent by Lord Hastings from the Midlands. It was Edward's intention to march on London but Jasper and Owen Tudor raised an army of their own to cut off their advance. The royalist army, led by the Tudors, met the Yorkists on 2 February 1461 at Mortimer's Cross, north-west of Leominster. Before the two armies clashed a perihelion (or mock sun), caused by light refracting from ice crystals in the atmosphere, appeared like a portent in the sky. The 18-year-old Edward seized upon the 'sun in splendour' as a sign that God looked favourably upon his cause. The fighting which followed was brief and ended with the Lancastrians fleeing for their lives.

Jasper was fortunate to escape when his lines broke but Owen, a man of advancing years, was captured as he fled. The old soldier expected, as the king's stepfather, to be taken prisoner and ransomed as was customary but Edward was in no mood for mercy so soon after the deaths of his father and younger brother. Henry Tudor's grandfather was speedily executed at Hereford and his head placed on the market cross. Afterwards his body was placed in the town's Greyfriars Church while Edward took his army east to join with the Earl of Warwick. When Owen's great grandson, Henry VIII, dissolved the monasteries in 1536, the monarch did not give orders to preserve the body of the ancestor who placed the Tudors so close to England's throne by his marriage to Henry V's widow and the last resting place of Owen Tudor was lost.

Jasper, swearing vengeance, returned only briefly to Pembroke before taking war into the north of Wales. He left his nephew, as always, in the care of the women appointed to raise him. Perhaps fortunately for Jasper, he was not present at the Battle of Towton, fought over a period of ten hours during a snowstorm, on 20 March 1461. At the end of the day the Lancastrians broke and threw away their armour as they fled for their lives. Many of them were cut down as they ran or drowned in the swollen waters of the Cock Beck and in the River Wharfe when a bridge collapsed under the weight of men. Margaret of Anjou hurried into exile in Scotland taking her husband and son with her. For the time being, the Yorkists were triumphant.

On 8 May 1461, King Edward IV appointed Sir William Herbert of Raglan as Chamberlain of South Wales with orders to seize the castle and lordship of Pembroke. The men who fought against Edward at Towton were attainted of treason but so was Henry Tudor, 2nd Earl of Richmond who was still only 4 years old. Henry's maternal bloodline and his status as Henry VI's kinsman were risks to be contained in the hands of someone known for their loyalty to the house of York. The honour of Richmond, representative of wealth and power, was given briefly to Richard, Duke of Gloucester before being granted to Edward IV's younger brother, George, the new Duke of Clarence.[3] Henry, still his mother's heir, was placed under the guardianship of William Herbert, who paid the king £1000 for custody of the boy. Henry, still retaining his title as 2nd Earl of Richmond, was sent to Raglan where he was raised by Herbert's wife Anne Devereux. Polydore Vergil would later write that Henry was 'kept as prisoner, but honourably raised'.[4] No one expected him to become king of England but Herbert, who had a large family of daughters, swiftly betrothed Henry to his own eldest daughter, Maud to secure Margaret Beaufort's estates for his own family.

Sir Henry Stafford who took up arms against the Yorkists in 1461 had reason, besides his wife's Lancastrian credentials, to be fearful. Fortunately, Stafford and Edward IV were cousins through their Neville mothers and on 25 June a pardon was issued. Sir Henry and his wife recognised the importance of adapting to the new regime but they were powerless to prevent Henry Tudor from being lodged with the Herberts, or the sequestration of both Jasper and Henry's lands. Margaret remained optimistic that her son would regain what was rightfully his and the surviving records of the period show her tireless efforts to rehabilitate him throughout the reigns of Edward and his brother, Richard III.

The Staffords tried to remain aloof from the continuing conflicts of the civil war and were rewarded in December 1466 with the manor at Woking which belonged to Margaret's Beaufort cousin, the Duke of Somerset, until his execution on 14 May 1464, soon after the Battle of Hexham. The couple made Woking their main home and continued to live quietly. There is every indication that they lived a happy life together and even celebrated their wedding anniversary each year. Lady Margaret Beaufort was not an important political player or even a court lady although she did join her husband in London on occasion.

Chapter 3

Henry Tudor – a Fifteenth-Century Aristocratic Education

The lived experience of Henry's childhood and youth was, on occasion, one of uncertainty and peril. From the age of 5 to 12 years his education was, for the most part, very similar to other nobly born boys of the period, except that his uncle, so far as the Yorkist regime was concerned, was a notorious dissident. It is likely that Jasper Tudor, recognising that King Edward held the upper hand, sailed from either Tenby, Pembroke, or even Harlech during 1461 to join with Margaret of Anjou in exile first in Scotland and then in France. By the end of the year, he was back in Wales, where he was tasked with rallying Lancastrian support, and resisting the new regime.

Almost immediately after Edward IV became king, he set about creating an administrative hierarchy loyal to him in Wales and the Marches. William Herbert was appointed Justiciar and Chamberlain of South Wales for life on 8 May 1461. Herbert and his extended kinship network, including the Devereux and Vaughan families, provided the administrative hierarchy for the Yorkist regime in Wales throughout the 1460s. He was a so-called new man who owed everything to the Yorkists but, unlike the Tudors, he already had an established affinity in South Wales with whom to work. His brothers, Thomas and John, were charged with seizing all of Jasper's lands. A half-brother, William Herbert, was appointed to the commission in August to investigate treasons and insurrections against the Yorkists. Anyone who submitted to the Herbert family would be granted a pardon, with a few notable exceptions including the former Earl of Pembroke[1] and his deputy at Pembroke Castle, Sir John Scudamore, whose lands were sequestered even though Scudamore surrendered Pembroke Castle to the Yorkists in September 1461.

Henry joined the Herberts at Raglan which was in the process of being renovated by its newly ennobled owner. The Great Gatehouse with its elaborate machicolations and towers made an imposing statement of both power and wealth. There was a long history of the Tudors and the Herberts fighting on opposite sides, notably during the Glyndwr rising and most recently in 1456 when William Herbert and Anne's father, Walter Devereux, besieged Carmarthen Castle before capturing it and imprisoning Edmund Tudor. It is difficult to know what Henry, who was still only 5 years old, knew of the animosity between the two families or the extent to which he held William Herbert culpable for the death of a father he never met. Even so, his was not an unusual situation. Noble medieval children were often sent to the homes of their enemies to be educated, in a bid to break a cycle of violence. Nor was it unusual for children to be educated in households other than their own. At Raglan, for instance, Henry Percy, 4th Earl of Northumberland, was another of Herbert's wards. Boys often transitioned from life with their own families at around the age of 7 years when they passed from women's care to male tutors to be prepared for knighthood.

A history of the Herbert family states that Henry's education was entrusted to Anne Devereux, until he reached the age of 7.[2] He shared the Herbert children's schoolroom which, in addition to Anne's ten children and Henry Percy, included Herbert's other wards who were not yet old enough to have assumed their roles as pages and squires. Henry may also have encountered Herbert's illegitimate sons William and Walter[3] as well as children from the local gentry. Information is meagre but it was Anne's duty to appoint nursery staff and oversee the education of the children in her care rather than take an active day-to-day role. By the time Henry was removed from Pembroke it is probable that he already knew his letters and how to say his prayers. The schoolroom at Raglan would have contained a primer, or prayer book, and a Psalter. Part of Anne's task, as a pious mother, was to prepare her charges for confirmation and their first communion so that their souls might be saved. She would have been assisted in the task by Raglan's chaplain who may also have tutored other subjects.

Anne would have overseen lessons that included grammar and logic. Latin was learned by making analysis of the grammar and structure of a sentence before translating it and repeating it. Henry may also have started to learn French while in Anne's care. It was Anne's job to ensure that her charges were capable of running their estates, so mathematics and understanding accounts were also essential components of a nobleman's education but there was no indication of anything more elaborate. Bernard André, who chronicled

Henry VII's life in *Historia Regis Henri Septimi*, stated that Andrew Scotus, an Oxford academic, was retained to teach the children. 'A priest that was the King's schoolmaster' was granted £2 in 1495.[4] He was joined by Edward Haseley, later Dean of St Mary's Collegiate Church, Warwick who taught them grammar. When Henry became king, he awarded Haseley with an annuity of £10 for services to the monarch in his 'tender age'.[5]

A third man, Sir Hugh ap John, also known as Sir Hugh Johnys or Jones, the constable of Oystermouth Castle, Swansea, provided military tuition. Johnys, a member of the Gower's gentry by the time he came into contact with Henry, was part of the extended Herbert kinship network being descended from the Vaughan family.[6] Not much more is known about Henry Tudor's formal education other than that which André recorded and Henry VII rewarded. It is unknown how eventful Henry's life was at Raglan but records from another noble household, that of Richard Duke of Gloucester's son Edward at Middleham in Yorkshire, indicates the likelihood that Henry and his companions made pilgrimages to nearby abbeys and shrines as well as enjoying seasonal festivities and learning how to ride.[7]

As a page, Henry ran errands and helped as he was needed. He acquired social skills and manners by acting as a servant during mealtimes to learn from the earl and his guests while he waited on them, as well as the social status of the countess's guests ranging from the most important at the top of the table to the humbler ones at the lower end of the dining hall. He also learned, by observation, that good food and wine were about much more than eating and drinking. They made a statement about Herbert's wealth and therefore of his power. Evidence from Bristol shows that Thomas, William Herbert's brother, was involved in the wine trade while he served in Spain as one of Edward IV's ambassadors.[8] It is also known that the earl owned a vessel named the *Mary Herbert* which plied its trade between Bristol and Lisbon.[9] From the Herbert family, Henry learned that keeping up appearances was an essential part of being a successful member of the ruling class. Even today Raglan Castle's impressive Great Tower and South Gate reflects the fact that William Herbert was the most important man in the region.

Herbert was responsible for training his male wards for knighthood. Boys from the upper classes learned to ride, mastered the use of different weapons including how to use a bow, about the use and care of armour as well as tactics for the battlefield. Henry's training began with exercises to build his strength. Apart from making himself useful and learning the skills needed to survive as a soldier he would have accompanied Herbert on hunting and falconry expeditions. The ownership of horses and birds of prey was another statement of wealth and power as well as providing meat for the household.

In 1466, William Herbert, Herbert's heir, was married to Mary Woodville, one of the queen's sisters. It was an occasion for celebration, especially as William was made Lord Dunster. Despite the fact that the two earls had worked in harmony for the administration of South Wales in the past, Warwick became steadily more angered by Herbert's domination of the region and by the elevation of his family. Matters were compounded in June when Herbert, who was not often absent from Wales, accompanied the king to visit the Earl of Warwick's brother, Archbishop of York, George Neville at his London residence and witnessed the surrender of the Great Seal following a difference between the king and the Nevilles in the direction of England's foreign policy.[10] In 1468, Warwick's resentment against Herbert was heightened further still, when as well as having possession of Jasper Tudor's lands, Henry's guardian was granted the title Earl of Pembroke. The new earl had an income of £2400 a year[11] and was described as Edward IV's 'master-lock' because of his grip on Wales.

Margaret Beaufort might have noted that her son's guardian made a dramatic ascent from the gentry to the peerage, and part of the king's extended family, within ten years. Throughout much of that time she was determined only to protect her son's interests. All she wished was for him to be recognised as his father's heir as the 2nd Earl of Richmond and permitted to assume his rightful place in society. Henry's betrothal to Maud Herbert was a good match and one she likely approved. It was in Herbert's best interests to rehabilitate Henry Tudor as the 2nd Earl of Richmond.

She remained in regular contact with Henry at Raglan, although little of their correspondence survives, and in 1465 arranged for the boy to be admitted to the Confraternity of the Order of the Holy Trinity near Knaresborough.[12] It's stated purpose was to buy the freedom of Christians taken captive by Turks. A confraternity was a guild of lay people based in a religious institution. It meant that Henry, who was expected to give the order gifts and offering, received religious benefits in return. Margaret's son might not have been close at hand but he was never, it seems, far from her thoughts. In September 1467 Margaret and Henry's stepfather visited Raglan where they stayed for a week as Anne's guests and enjoyed the palatial accommodation that Henry's guardians provided.[13] Anne is likely to have known how worried Henry's mother was about her only child demonstrated by the amount of correspondence that arrived at Raglan for the boy.

In 1468, Margaret was very concerned indeed. Jasper Tudor landed near Harlech on 24 June and struck out with men loyal to the Lancastrian cause into Denbighshire. *Gregory's Chronicle* described the earl holding court session in Henry VI's name before he destroyed the town of Denbigh but failed to capture the castle there. Edward IV initially planned to lead the campaign against Jasper himself but in July he ordered Henry's guardian to secure the region against the Lancastrians and to lay waste Nant Conwy. Herbert raised a royalist army, supported by his brother-in-law Walter Devereux, Lord Ferrers of Chartley. It has been suggested that Henry accompanied his guardian into Wales. At almost 12 years old, Henry was of an age to make the transition from page to squire. The word originally meant shield bearer but fifteenth-century squires as young as Henry were not expected to take part in any real fighting. Just as he watched and learned from Herbert and his guests at mealtimes as a page, it was required as part of the training for knighthood that boys should watch battles from the sidelines as well as to take part in mock battles and tournaments at home so that they could learn by observation. If this was the case, Henry was with Herbert when he caught up with the Lancastrians at Carmarthen on 16 October. Little is known about the Battle of Twt Hill other than Herbert was victorious. Henry watching in safety from Herbert's camp, perhaps with the grooms who cared for Herbert's horses or carrying messages if required, could not have known that his uncle escaped until much later when news filtered back to England that Jasper Tudor was in Ireland where he continued to agitate for his half-brother's cause. For Margaret Beaufort, who had only a mother's concern for what might happen to her child on a battlefield, even if it was little more than a skirmish, it was a time of fear — an emotion with which Anne and all mothers like her must have sympathised as their sons faced similar initiation into the violence of medieval warfare.

Throughout the 1460s, Herbert, who was by far Edward IV's most prominent Welsh supporter, led a number of campaigns against Lancastrian nests in the principality. In 1468, Herbert retook Harlech Castle from its Lancastrian garrison. But trouble was beginning to bubble across Edward IV's realm. Lady Margaret Beaufort and Anne Devereux could only watch as calamity shaped itself from Richard Neville, Earl of Warwick's thwarted hopes. The earl, having assisted his young cousin to the throne, expected to be Edward's principal advisor and to govern policy at home and abroad. Instead, in 1464, the king married Elizabeth Woodville, a Lancastrian widow with a large extended family. The marriages of the new queen's sisters to suitably wealthy and entitled husbands restricted the choice of husband, and associated political advancement, available to Warwick's own daughters. When the king refused to allow his younger brother George, Duke of Clarence to marry Warwick's elder daughter, Isabel, the earl's bitterness overflowed into rebellion.

Early in 1469, surreptitiously encouraged by Warwick, there were a number of uprisings in the north of England led by the shadowy, 'Robin of Redesdale'. By July the king was in Nottingham raising an army to confront the rebels but his brother, George, Duke of Clarence was in Calais with the Earl of Warwick, and the rest of the Neville family, where he married Isabel in defiance of his brother's wishes. The earl and his new son-in-law issued a manifesto listing their grievances against the king which included Edward's reliance on evil advisors, of whom Herbert was one, and returned to England where they raised their standards. England was at war with itself again. The king mustered his supporters including Henry's guardian and the Earl of Devon with instructions that they should bring their men to Northampton to intercept Warwick who had been welcomed into London before his army could join with the rebels in the north.

Problems arose when Warwick's supporters from the north of England bypassed the king's army and an argument erupted between Devon and Pembroke on the evening of 23 July 1469 about accommodation. Devon withdrew, taking his men, composed mainly of archers, with him. Pembroke's men, including 12-year-old Henry, camped on Edgecote Lodge Hill overnight. The following morning the two opposing forces took up their positions but Herbert's lines were weakened by their lack of archers. Henry witnessed the hand to hand fighting after his guardian abandoned his position at the top of the hill on which he positioned himself before the battle because of the lack of archers which weakened the strength of his lines. He saw a closely fought battle beginning to tip in Pembroke's favour until rebel reinforcements arrived and fell on the battered royalist army. The Welshmen under Herbert's levies broke under the onslaught thinking that the new men were the vanguard of Warwick's whole army. During the rout that followed, Herbert and his brother Sir Richard were both captured. They were executed soon afterwards on the orders of Warwick who was not present at the battle. The Earl of Devon, whose absence played a large part in the disastrous outcome, was executed at Bridgewater in August. The decapitations removed the most significant representatives of royal authority in the west of the realm leaving the way open for Warwick.

Henry Tudor was led out of danger at Edgecote by Sir Richard Corbet of Morton Corbet and taken to the home of Anne's brother, Walter Devereux, Lord Ferrers of Weobley in Herefordshire. Corbet, not yet of age when his father died, was Devereux's ward and the following year would marry Elizabeth Devereux, daughter of Walter. The baron was loyal to the House of York even though Edward IV was himself taken prisoner within days of Herbert's death, leaving the Earl of Warwick in effective control of the kingdom. Anne Devereux, widowed Countess of Pembroke, joined Henry or may even have already been with her brother when the fugitives arrived, and continued to care for the boy for the next few weeks. It was a time of uncertainty for the Herberts and for Henry who could only wait upon events as they unfolded around them.

Sir Reginald Bray, a trusted servant of Henry's stepfather, and later of Lady Margaret, found the boy safe and well at Weobley, having first travelled to Raglan to try and locate him. Henry did not return to Raglan but he did not forget the Herberts or Richard Corbet, and they, in their turn, remembered him. On 24 August 1469 Margaret sought to retrieve her son's estates from Clarence and in October, Margaret and Anne's legal advisers met at the Bell on Fleet Street in London to try and reach an agreement about who should have custody of Henry in the future.[14] Herbert's plan for his ward to marry his daughter, Maud, came to nothing when he was handed back into the care of his own family. She subsequently became Henry Percy, 4th Earl of Northumberland's wife.

Chapter 4

From Lancastrian 'Imp' to King of England

The fortunes of the House of Lancaster and their adherents continued, largely, to unravel in the years after Towton. Henry Beaufort, 3rd Duke of Somerset was killed in 1464 having first made his peace with Edward IV in the winter of 1462 when the Lancastrian garrison at Bamburgh surrendered. Jasper received a safe conduct and escaped to Scotland but Beaufort went to London where Edward pardoned him and restored him to his title. Nonetheless, it did not take long for Somerset to return to his old loyalties. He was executed soon after the Battle of Hexham on 15 May 1464. His younger brother, Edmund, was recognised by Lancastrian supporters as the 4th earl although the attainder against the 3rd earl was never reversed.

The Battle of Edgecote, and the death of Henry Tudor's guardian told by chroniclers Polydore Vergil and Edward Hall[1] heralded the beginning of another period of instability for England. The Earl of Warwick's rule did not have popular support and Edward IV was back on the throne within the year when his cousin was forced to release him. The earl, undeterred, came to terms with Henry VI's queen, Margaret of Anjou, and joined forces with the Lancastrians. On 9 September 1470, Warwick and Jasper Tudor left Normandy with a fleet of ships which landed in Dartmouth four days later. Jasper returned to Wales to raise an army while Warwick marched on London. By the beginning of October, Edward IV was in exile with his younger brother, Richard, leaving Warwick to place Henry VI back on the throne in a period known as the Readeption.

Jasper fetched his nephew from Wales (where he had remained in the custody of Anne Devereux since the death of her husband[2]) to London. On 27 October, Reginald Bray is recorded as paying 3d for a barge to take Henry to meet King Henry VI.[3] Lady Margaret Beaufort was briefly reunited with her son and the boy was introduced to his royal uncle. A few weeks later Henry accompanied the Earl of Pembroke back to Wales with a commission of array to gather Welsh troops loyal to the Tudors.[4] His education as a servant of the Lancastrian State offered no allowance for a mother's desire to spend time with her only child.

The Readeption was short lived. On 12 March 1471 Edward IV landed at Ravenspur on the Humber Estuary where Henry of Bolingbroke also landed in 1400. Like Bolingbroke before him, Edward initially claimed that he only sought his father's dukedom. By the night of the 14 April, the victory at the Battle of Barnet was his; Warwick and his brother, the Marquess of Montagu, were dead and Henry VI was once again a prisoner in the Tower. Margaret's husband, Sir Henry Stafford, who chose the winning side, fought in the Yorkists lines but was so badly injured that he never left his bed again. The decisive Battle of Tewkesbury was fought on 4 May 1471 as Margaret of Anjou and Somerset tried to find their way across the River Severn into the comparative safety of Wales where Jasper gathered a Lancastrian army of his own. Among the Lancastrians who died on the field were John Beaufort and the Earl of Devon. The Lancastrian defeat was followed by the death of 17-year-old Prince Edward and the capture of Margaret of Anjou. Edmund Beaufort, 4th Duke of Somerset was among the prominent men dragged from sanctuary in Tewkesbury Abbey on 6 May and executed. King Henry VI was murdered in the Tower of London on the night of 21 May to make Edward's throne secure once and for all.

The deaths meant that Henry Tudor was the most senior male representative remaining to the House of Lancaster. His claim came by right of his mother, Margaret, whose grandfather John Beaufort, 1st Earl of Somerset was the eldest of John of Gaunt's children with Katherine Swynford, who he married in 1396. All the Beaufort children were declared legitimate by Pope Boniface the same year. In 1397 their cousin Richard II confirmed their status as did King Henry IV, their half-brother. The latter amended the terms of their legitimacy by barring them from the throne but failed to enshrine the decision through the parliamentary process. Margaret Beaufort's ancestry, despite its complications, as well as the Tudor uterine relationship with Henry VI, put her son in grave danger.

Jasper Tudor rescued Henry from Pembroke Castle, outwitted Roger Vaughan[5] who had been sent to capture him and sought the comparative safety of France. It was his intention to take his 14-year-old nephew there to seek the protection of his own cousin, King Louis XI. Instead, a violent storm forced the pair to land in Brittany at Le Conquet.[6] Duke Francis II of Brittany welcomed the two earls, gave them shelter and his protection during their exile from 1471 to 1484. King Edward IV was furious when he received news that the Tudors had escaped. Hall described the matter that 'nipped … hardly at the very stomach, as though his mind cast some evil to come after'.[7] Edward demanded that Francis should hand over the fugitives. However, the duke knew the value of his guests as bargaining chips for Edward's assistance against French territorial expansion into Brittany so refused to return them to England, preferring instead to 'entertain them more diligently than they were accustomed'.[8]

Instead, the Tudors remained in Brittany somewhere in the margins between guests and prisoners. They were housed at the Château de Suscinio in Sarzeau near the coast. The chateau had been built so that the dukes of Brittany could indulge their love of hunting and no doubt Henry honed his skills in the company of his uncle. Jasper, back in his role of surrogate father, kept a watchful eye on his nephew afraid that he might be kidnapped by Yorkist agents, intent on eliminating any threat that Henry might pose. The pair would learn that their freedom of movement depended upon the diplomatic relations between Brittany, France and England. Henry and Jasper's freedom became more restricted as their host was pressurised either to return them to the English or, if King Louis XI demanded, that his kinsmen should be given into his own care for their greater safety.

In October 1471 it became clear that Sir Henry Stafford would not survive the injuries of Barnet and made his will. His entirely and best-loved wife was his executor. Without a protector, Margaret was vulnerable once more. She chose a husband who would best be able to shield her own position and be used to the advantage of her son who remained a fugitive. She married for a fourth time[9] in 1472, to Thomas, 2nd Baron Stanley the High Constable of England, and returned to court where she served Elizabeth Woodville and her children. It is thought to have been a political marriage which suited both parties. Henry was never far away from Margaret's thoughts and she aimed, throughout the rest of Edward's reign, to rehabilitate her only child as the Earl of Richmond. She was his best advocate and also his best source of information. Evidence from later letters suggests that there was a sustained correspondence between the pair but given the inherent dangers of committing words to paper it is understandable than little documentary evidence survives.

King Edward IV was a young man with a growing family that included two healthy boys, Edward born at the end of 1470 and Richard born in

1473. There was no reason to suppose that Edward would not live to see them become men. It seemed that the House of York was firmly seated upon the throne. As England and Wales settled into a period of stability, Lady Margaret made a new life for herself. Henry grew to manhood as an exile, reliant on the charity and protection of the Duke of Brittany. In England, there remained a few determined Lancastrians who continued to agitate against the regime of Edward IV. The Yorkists described Henry as the 'only imp now left of Henry VI's brood'.[10] The king and his advisors continued, on occasion, to send ambassadors to the court of Duke Francis II to try and contain the potential threat that Henry posed. It seemed improbable that Margaret Beaufort's son would ever become a king even though the Yorkists viewed him as a potential rallying point for insurgency against Edward's regime.

It was late in 1473 or early in 1474 when Duke Francis decided to separate Henry from his uncle. It eliminated the possibility that both of them would manage to escape at the same time or be secured by Edward IV's agents. Jasper was sent to the Chateau de Josselin while Henry was sent to Largoet, the home of Jean de Rieux near the town of Elven. Rieux had two sons who were of a similar age to Henry and he completed his education there. Henry VII was fluent in both French and Latin, a fact which the Milanese ambassador in England, Ludovico Sforza, was keen to share when Henry became king.[11]

During the winter of 1476, Edward IV decided that the time was right to secure the Earl of Richmond. The Treaty of Picquigny made with the French included a promise that the French would not invade Brittany. The duke would be less vigilant about the welfare of his 'guests' now that their political value was reduced. Accordingly, the king sent the Chester herald, Thomas Whiting, to negotiate on his behalf along with the promise that Henry should marry the king's own eldest daughter, Elizabeth of York. The duke agreed to the terms and Henry was handed over into the custody of the English ambassadors who took him with them to St Malo where they intended to take a vessel home.

Henry who had no warning about his removal from Largoet had learned the hard lessons of his childhood and adolescence. He realised that if he boarded a ship bound for England that 'he was carried to his death'[12] despite the promise of a royal bride. Henry Holland, 3rd Earl of Exeter, Edward IV's brother-in-law, attempted to rehabilitate himself with the Yorkists when he volunteered to serve in the English expedition to France in 1475 that resulted in the Treaty of Picquigny. The king did not trust his brother-in-law who was a staunch Lancastrian as well as being estranged from Anne of York who divorced him in 1472. In September 1475, on their return from France, the earl fell overboard and drowned. Chroniclers and envoys hinted that Exeter's death was not an accident, and Henry may well have heard the tale. At St Malo he feigned illness, escaped his captors and claimed sanctuary in the town's cathedral. It gained Duke Francis's council enough time to persuade the duke to change his mind about releasing Henry into Edward IV's custody.

From St Malo, Henry went to the court at Vannes before being sent to a series of short-term residences. In 1480 he was at the Chateau L'Hermine where he was reunited with his uncle, Jasper Tudor. No doubt when he became king, Henry VII's grasp on the financial necessities of checking waste and making his accounts balance was as a result of his hand to mouth existence during his fourteen years of exile. Equally, Henry's cautiousness, described in some detail by the Milanese ambassador in 1499,[13] was a skill most probably sharpened during the uncertainty of those years. More happily, he also had the opportunity to observe the way in which continental courts and governments functioned. He knew the importance of adornment and clothing which could be described as 'something most rich'.[14] It was certainly not a conventional preparation for the crown but the duke, who protected Henry during his adolescence and early twenties, played an essential part in the first Tudor monarch's education.

On 9 April 1483 fate took a hand when Edward IV unexpectedly died after a week's illness. His heir, Edward V, was just 12 years old and the kingdom faced the familiar uncertainty of a factionalised council. The king's brother, Richard, Duke of Gloucester, became Edward V's sole protector. Within three months the king and his brother had disappeared behind the walls of the Tower of London never to be seen again; they and their sisters were declared illegitimate and Richard ascended the throne as King Richard III. Like his brother before him, Richard hoped to capture Henry and Jasper Tudor to make the crown more secure upon his head.

Whether or not Richard III intended to take the throne when he arrived in London at the beginning of May, in the company of his uncrowned nephew, is a matter of fierce debate. Margaret and Stanley remained in London throughout and were closely involved in the events that put Richard on the throne. Stanley was an active member of the Regency Council and was present on the morning of 13 June 1483 when armed guards attacked Lord Hastings and his supporters during a meeting in the Tower. Sir Thomas More wrote that Margaret's husband escaped serious injury only by falling beneath the meeting table. Hastings was executed without ceremony on a makeshift block while Stanley spent a short time in the Tower. Even so, he and Margaret took honoured places in the double coronation of King Richard III and Queen Anne that followed.

With rumours about the young princes being murdered, Lady Margaret Beaufort demonstrated herself to be the most astute of the fifteenth century's political operators. At the beginning of the year, she aspired only for the safe return of her son to England. Now, in a much-changed climate, she secured the agreement of Elizabeth Woodville, who was in sanctuary at Westminster with her daughters, for Henry to marry her eldest daughter, Elizabeth of York, and unite the two rival houses of Lancaster and York. If the Woodville faction threw their weight behind Henry, a rival claimant to the crown, it might be enough to tip the balance of power in his favour. Some Yorkists, disaffected by the rumours that Edward IV's sons were dead or displaced by Richard III's northern adherents, allied themselves to Henry's cause. At the same time that Jasper advanced his nephew's cause from Brittany, Margaret instructed Sir Reginald Bray to recruit men sympathetic to the House of Lancaster. The view that Henry Tudor might become king became more common. The fact that his claim was slender did not matter.

Henry's mother turned her considerable talents to the practicality of intriguing against Richard III. She sent a trusted servant, Hugh Conway, to Henry with money so that he could invade Wales with the intention of taking the throne. The proposed rebellion gathered pace drawing in Lancastrians, Yorkists unhappy with the disappearance of Edward V as well as members of the extensive Woodville family. Rather than one conspiracy, Margaret made common cause with men whose ultimate aims were not necessarily her own. Henry Stafford, 2nd Duke of Buckingham, Margaret Beaufort's kinsman and nephew by her second marriage took nominal leadership of the plot that came to be known as Buckingham's rebellion. It is unclear why Stafford, a former supporter of Richard III, became involved in the uprising. It is possible that he believed that Edward V was still alive or that he himself had pretensions of sitting upon the throne, as he was also descended from John of Gaunt through his mother who was the daughter of Edmund Beaufort,

2nd Duke of Somerset and also his grandmother who was descended from Gaunt's daughter, Joan Beaufort.

The fast-paced plot of 1483 involved a series of regional risings, which came to be known as Buckingham's rebellion after Stafford, who was the conspirator with the highest profile, foundered in October before Henry Tudor could cross the Channel in a small fleet of ships with 5000 men provided by the Duke of Brittany. Buckingham was executed on 2 November 1483 at Salisbury while Margaret Beaufort was attainted of treason, placed under house arrest and lost control of her property. Margaret was lucky to escape with her life but her marriage to Lord Stanley, who carried the mace at Richard's coronation, may have been a factor in the leniency with which Richard III treated her. She was placed only under house arrest, and in her husband's custody. Margaret was also stripped of her titles and estates to prevent her from sending funds to Henry or becoming involved in new plots. Richard gave all the confiscated property to Stanley in the hope that he would control his wife. But by the time Henry Tudor returned to Vannes, Elizabeth Woodville's son from her first marriage, Thomas Grey, Marquis of Dorset, and several other fugitives from the failed plot were already there and ready to join his cause. That Christmas, at Rennes Cathedral, Henry vowed to marry Edward IV's eldest daughter, Elizabeth of York, after he became England's king.[15]

In 1484 fortune's wheel turned in Henry's favour although he and his uncle narrowly escaped capture by Richard III when the duke's treasurer, Pierre Landais, came to an agreement with the English king.[16] Whether Margaret Beaufort or John Morton, the exiled Bishop of Ely, discovered the plot is uncertain. Margaret's chaplain, Christopher Urswick, arrived at Vannes with the urgent news of Henry's imminent imprisonment having first visited Morton. Henry and his uncle made a daring escape across the border into France where they sought asylum in the court of the new French king, Charles VIII. Duke Francis, whose illness had permitted Landais to conspire with Richard, provided Henry's supporters safe conduct to France. On 9 April 1484, Richard's heir, Edward of Middleham, died. The king's wife, Anne Neville, died the following year on 16 March. There would be no more buds on Richard's branch of the family tree for several years to come, even if he did remarry. Henry, with Jasper by his side, began to appeal more widely for support for his claim to the throne among the nobility of England and Wales. By Christmas, Richard was expecting Henry to launch another attempt to seize the crown and Henry was signing his correspondence in the manner of a monarch with the single letter 'H' rather than as the Earl of Richmond as he had previously.[17]

In 1485 an army compiled of staunch Lancastrians, including John de Vere, 13th Earl of Oxford (who escaped from Hammes Castle near Calais[18]), dissatisfied Yorkists and French mercenaries sailed from Honfleur. Henry and Jasper Tudor's fleet arrived at Milford Haven on 7 August. Henry Tudor's education for monarchy was over at the age of 28 years. Henceforth, he would live or die as England's rightful king.

Chapter 5

A Royal Family

Following the strategic defection of the Stanley family at the Battle of Bosworth, Henry's army defeated Richard III on 22 August 1485, but it took more than winning a battle to establish the Tudors on the throne. Margaret Beaufort planned, well in advance of the physical fighting, that her son would unite the red rose of Lancaster with the white rose of York with a marriage to Edward IV's daughter Elizabeth. The king's mother knew how kings and princes were raised and she intended to be much more closely involved with their upbringing than she had ever been with the day-to-day care of her only child. Her grandchildren's royal credentials would be impeccable. No aspect of their schooling would be left to chance, not only because she assigned herself the role of royal keeper of procedure and protocol but because of her very real interest in the education of talented scholars. She is often associated in this regard with Richard Foxe, Keeper of the Privy Seal, and the founder of Corpus Christi College, Oxford.[1]

Henry married Elizabeth of York on 18 January 1486, nearly six months after his victory at Bosworth and two months after he was crowned king. Edward IV's daughter would have to wait until November 1487 for her own coronation. It was not in the new regime's interest to remind the populace that Elizabeth had a better claim to the throne than Henry VII. The queen would play little public part in national politics and, throughout her life, it would be her mother-in-law, Lady Margaret Beaufort, who would be Henry VII's closest advisor. Instead of signing herself as the Countess of Richmond, she took to signing her name 'Margaret R' hinting at the Latin *regina* rather than Richmond.[2] The king's mother, as she was styled after 1485, was more important than any of the other leading ladies in the land with the exception of her daughter-in-law and Elizabeth Woodville, the dowager queen. Margaret was at the heart of the new royal family and her counsel, from behind the scenes, was essential to Henry for both State and domestic matters. In public, she wore clothes like the queen's and she walked only half a step behind her daughter-in-law.[3] The king ensured that his mother had accommodation near to his own chambers in all his residences and that the household ordinances lodged her close at hand when he was on progress.[4] No one knows what his wife, Elizabeth of York, thought about the arrangement.

Elizabeth was either already pregnant, or conceived during the marriage celebrations given that Henry's longed for heir arrived exactly eight months after the wedding. As soon as it became apparent that Elizabeth was expecting, Margaret Beaufort began to plan for her daughter-in-law's lying-in. She created a set of regulations drawn up from her experiences as part of Elizabeth Woodville's household during the 1470s and from the procedures set out in Edward IV's own book of household guidelines.[5] The result was a treatise on royal ceremonials ensuring that the birth, baptism and care of Tudor princes and princesses was conducted according to customs established by the earlier Medieval kings of England. Modern understanding of the rules relies upon Leland's *Collectanea*[6] which took the material from a manuscript in the Harleian Library.[7] Some modern scholars are cautious about accepting the extent of Margaret's role in the creation of the ordinances because of the lack of contemporary evidence.[8] It is certain though that the Tudors intended to give every appearance of royalty in all they said and did.

As Elizabeth's pregnancy progressed, preparations for her confinement took shape which included purchasing cloths and Arras tapestries to cover all the walls and windows of her chamber, except for one which could be removed to provide the queen with light and air should it be required. Fresh air was not something that was regarded as healthy as it carried miasmas and evil spirits which might steal the unborn soul of the infant. Instead, the air was scented by a mixture of soothing herbs and spices. The tapestries themselves were selected based on the restful nature of their content; anything violent was inappropriate for an expectant mother who might be easily startled or somehow transmit what she saw to the psyche of her unborn child. The chamber was provided with a royal bed, laden with rich fabrics of scarlet and gold upon which the queen could rest but there was a second pallet bed upon which Elizabeth would labour as well as two cradles. One was for ceremonial use while the second, wooden crib, was for the baby to sleep in. In addition, clothing and swaddling bands for the infant were ordered as well as gowns and linens for the queen. When Elizabeth withdrew into the seclusion of the chamber a month before the birth, it would end her contact without the outside world, and with men, until after the arrival of her child. Lady Margaret Beaufort decreed that all male staff in the queen's household should be replaced by women for the duration of her seclusion.

The arrival of an heir would help legitimise Henry VII's rule since a child not only united the blood of the warring houses but also indicated that God smiled upon the Tudors. At the end of August, the royal couple moved to Winchester, the ancient site of King Arthur's court and the home of his round table, which was later adorned with a Tudor rose. Sir Thomas Malory claimed that Winchester was Camelot in his *Morte d'Arthur* and the myth served the Tudor need to legitimise their claim to the throne. King Arthur had been written into history by Geoffrey of Monmouth during the twelfth century and the Tudors claimed descent from ancient British kings. The queen took up residence, having heard Mass and made her confession, in the prior's house at Saint Swithun's Priory with her ladies, Margaret Beaufort and her mother's midwife, Marjory Cobbe.[9] A scant two weeks later, Prince Arthur was born on 20 September 1486. His delighted grandmother recorded the event in her Book of Hours.[10] Four days after his birth, using the formula outlined by the king's mother, the baby was baptised in Canterbury Cathedral's silver font, transported to Winchester. The church was arrayed with Arras tapestries, satin and cloth of gold for the occasion. Margaret Beaufort was absent from the spectacle that she had arranged but Elizabeth's mother, the dowager queen and other members of the Woodville family, including Cecily of York who acted as one of Arthur's godmothers, were present, a confirmation, if one was needed, that they approved of the new monarchy.

Nor was the queen present at the baptism or the celebrations that followed. As a new mother she was expected to remain in her chamber for forty days recovering from the birth. Before she returned to public life, Elizabeth would be churched. Childbirth was associated with Eve's original sin so it was essential that women underwent purification before being accepted back into the Church and society. In October, taper in hand, Elizabeth made her way to the priory church to be blessed and to resume her place under the canopy of state.

A queen's role was to provide her husband with heirs rather than nourishing them after their birth. There was an underlying pressure on all royal wives to produce children and secure the dynasty. Breast feeding was a contraceptive and since weaning did not take place before the age of 2 it was essential that a wetnurse be provided so that Elizabeth could get back to the business of giving her husband more children. Arthur's wetnurse was called Katherine Gibbs and the *Royal Book* stipulated that her health should be monitored by a physician for as long as she cared for the prince. The king also gave orders that her 'meat and drink be essay [for poison] during the time she giveth suck to the child'.[11] Fear of poisoning ensured that the meals provided for the wetnurses of all the queen's children were carefully monitored. In 1490 the king granted Arthur's wetnurse a pension of £20 per year for life but for the most part she remains anonymous.[12]

Wetnurses, ideally, were women of good reputation, healthy and wholesome in appearance who had recently given birth themselves. The search for a thoroughly respectable woman with the right qualities would, no doubt, have been thorough and her own children inspected carefully by royal physicians. It was believed that character was transmitted through breast milk so only a woman whose influence was regarded as positive would be selected for the task of nurturing the heir to the throne. It was equally important to choose a woman who had given birth to a boy because the quality of the milk differed depending on the gender of the child. It was supposed, based on the theories of Aristotle, that a mother's milk was created by heating menstrual blood as it travelled from the womb to the breasts. It was also understood that a male generated more heat than a female who was naturally colder. The idea came from a medical belief in the four humours. The humours were blood, yellow bile, black bile and phlegm. Each of the substances could be either cold, hot, dry or moist. Since breast milk required heat for its creation it was deemed to have masculine qualities. It was naturally thicker and whiter, of better quality, following a male birth because of the associated heat of the infant.

During his first two years Arthur's wetnurse and the female staff of his household were closer to him than his parents. The court moved frequently and there were additional fears that when the court was in London that the prince might be more vulnerable to disease. When he was just three months old, Arthur was established in his own household at Farnham Castle in Surrey under the auspices of Peter Courtenay, Bishop of Winchester. His household included Katherine Gibbs, plus a dry nurse who met the prince's other everyday needs, and three rockers of gentle birth. The rockers at Farnham were Agnes Butler, who received a pension of £3 6s 8d in later years,[13] Eveleyn Hobbes and Alice Bywimble from Wales. Walter de Bibbesworth writing in the thirteenth century explained that a 'rocker' kept a cradle moving and sang lullabies to soothe the child.[14] Tudor rockers were among the staff granted the right to wear Tudor livery of green and white.[15] Fetching, carrying, cooking and cleaning duties were performed by yeomen and grooms. Two male servants, William Wangham and John Hoo, are listed as part of Arthur's household and fulfilled these roles. A sewer was appointed to organise meals and a panter was placed in charge of food supplies. There was also a chamberlain. It was his task to manage the domestic affairs of the household, as well as to receive money and valuables and to pay the household's expenses. He was also accountable for the prince's privy purse. As Arthur grew, his household would mimic more closely the hierarchy of the king's own household from body servants to ushers.

The women that Lady Margaret Beaufort and Elizabeth of York selected to care for Arthur and, later, his younger siblings were familiar faces from the queen's own childhood or transferred straight out of Elizabeth Woodville's royal nursery at Eltham to Farnham. The prince's youngest aunts, Catherine and Bridget of York, were still only 7 and 5 years of age respectively and resident in the long-established royal nursery at Eltham. Henry was aware of the sisters' potential as tools for valuable marriage alliances but also recognised the dangers posed by the little girls who might become the focus for future Yorkist plots now that they, along with their elder sister, were re-legitimised in the eyes of the law. Even so, it was essential that they were well treated if he was to maintain the goodwill, not only of his queen, but of the diverse groups who supported him against Richard III. Margaret Beaufort was also known to be fond of Elizabeth Woodville's daughters. In 1480, it had been Margaret who carried Bridget to her baptism and it is likely she was among the women in the birthing chamber on 9 November when the queen's child was born.[16]

Arthur's household and education while he was still in short skirts was given into the hands of Elizabeth Haute, Lady Darcy who cared for Elizabeth and Edward V during their infancies as well as Edward IV's younger children. She was part of the extended Woodville family through her second marriage to Richard Haute and was also part of the Tyrell family by birth.[17] Henry's accounts show she received £46 as lady mistress of the nursery on 8 June 1487 in addition to a salary of 40 marks (about £26).[18] It was this well-born lady's responsibility to oversee the royal nursery. Henry granted his son's household 1000 marks to meet its necessary expenses which were initially identified in the *Royal Book*.[19] This sum was drawn from lands which belonged to the 3rd Duke of Buckingham, who was Lady Margaret Beaufort's ward as well as being kin to both the king and the queen. Lady Darcy was well used to the routines of a princely nursery. It had been in September 1473 that Edward IV first established the ordinances for 'the virtuous guyding of the person of deerest first begotten son'[20] and which experience she now applied to the care of Henry VII's heir. When the Tudors had all outgrown her ministrations, she received a pension of £20 per year from the Duchy of Cornwall estates as well as grants for 420 gallons of red wine each year.[21]

Farnham Castle was a modern and comfortable building that was improved during Arthur's childhood by the Bishop of Winchester to accommodate the king and queen when they visited their son.[22] Although formal visits by Henry were recorded and evidenced though letters and warrants issued from Farnham, it is less clear how often Elizabeth and Margaret Beaufort visited Arthur. Cunningham notes that Woking, which was Lady Margaret's main residence outside London, was only 9 miles from Farnham. It was a very manageable journey for a woman who might wish to visit her grandson, supervise his care and ensure that he was schooled as a Christian prince should be.[23]

In March 1487 when word of an imminent invasion led by Elizabeth's cousin, John de la Pole, 1st Earl of Lincoln in support of a Yorkist pretender purporting be the Earl of Warwick reached Henry's ears, he gave orders that his queen should go from where she was staying with Margaret Beaufort at Chertsey to the safety of Kenilworth. Elizabeth and the Bishop of Winchester hurried to Farnham to collect Arthur before making their way, along with Margaret Beaufort, to Kenilworth where they remained until the outcome of the Battle of Stoke was decided on 16 June. It was one of the few occasions during Arthur's early years that the queen was able to spend any length of time with her eldest son. That September, writs were issued from Warwick that Elizabeth was finally to have her own coronation on 25 November.

It was not until 29 November 1489 that the queen presented her husband with another child. In October, Elizabeth heard Mass, made her confession and withdrew with great ceremony to the birthing chamber that had been prepared for her at the palace of Westminster on the instruction of Margaret Beaufort and the *Royal Book*. As before the chamber was draped with rich fabrics and blue Arras tapestries adorned with gold fleur-de-lis. For the next forty days the queen would remain in the room with only her ladies, her mother and, of course, Margaret Beaufort, to keep her company. In November, there was a break with tradition when the queen, with her mother and Margaret Beaufort at her side, gave an audience to the French ambassador. Alice Massey was paid £10 to act as the queen's midwife. Elizabeth was delivered of a daughter on 28 November.[24] While the queen was made comfortable the baby, named Margaret, was handed into the care of her wetnurse, Alice Davy, a respectable woman who would care for the baby until she was weaned.

Margaret's baptism followed the ceremonial pattern established in the so-called *Royal Book* and made use of Canterbury Cathedral's solid silver font, transported to Westminster for the occasion. It was John Alcock, Bishop of Ely who immersed the princess in the font. Like many of the men in Henry's regime, he transferred his skills from the service of York to Tudor in 1485, having encouraged the king's marriage to Elizabeth. Margaret's godparents, who had their own responsibility for her spiritual education, were Cardinal John Morton, Archbishop of Canterbury since 1487, Lady Margaret Beaufort and Elizabeth Talbot, the dowager Duchess of Norfolk. Princess Margaret's sponsors promised that the infant would follow the Church's teachings and that they would help to raise the child to know its prayers including the *Pater Noster*, *Ave Maria* and *Credo*. They were also charged with ensuring that the child knew how to make the sign of the cross. A spiritual family relationship was established as well as, in Margaret Beaufort's case, a blood one.[25]

Margaret Tudor was accommodated at Eltham rather than at Farnham with her brother. For the time being the nursery would be on a smaller scale although the regulation of both households followed strictures laid down by Margaret Beaufort in terms of staff and the need for a 'state cradle' decorated with cloth of gold and trimmed with ermine as well as a wooden one more appropriate for an infant.[26] On occasion nursery staff moved between Farnham and Eltham. Lady Darcy returned to Eltham for a time to care for the new princess. Joan Vaux, who had been one of Margaret Beaufort's wards before she entered the queen's household, became Princess Margaret's lady governess. Anne Mayland and Margaret Troughton were listed as Margaret's rockers receiving £3 3s 8d per year.[27] Alice Bywimble also transferred from Prince Arthur's household and was elevated to the role of day-wife, albeit on the same salary as the rockers.[28] King Henry's letter to the treasurer and chamberlains of his Exchequer, for the payment of money to Margaret's attendants, describes Alice Davy, who was Margaret's principal nurse during her childhood, as 'our well beloved'. It is possible that she continued in Margaret's service and cared for her nursling's own daughter, Margaret Douglas.[29] She remained with the royal nursery at Eltham and later joined the household of Katherine of Aragon.

The wages for the nursery staff were generous and always paid promptly at Michaelmas and Easter. When Margaret was 3 years old, orders were issued that nursery staff should not have any of their wages deducted by officials distributing them. It has been suggested that Henry recognised that any delay or loss might have impacted negatively on the loyalty with which the women cared for the next generation of the Tudor dynasty.[30]

Elizabeth fell pregnant again the year after Margaret's birth. Prince Henry arrived on 28 June 1491 at Greenwich. Henry was not provided with his own household. Instead, he joined Margaret at Eltham with the addition of a wetnurse named Anne Oxenbridge. Elizabeth Denton was appointed to be his lady governess, although she continued to draw her salary as one of the queen's ladies, and Margaret Troughton was reassigned from the princess's staff to care for the new prince. When Henry became king in 1508, he granted Elizabeth Denton an annuity of £20, a tun of gascon wine each year and keepership of Lady Margaret Beaufort's home at Coldharbour.[31] Account books and historical records can only hint at the love that must have existed between the women who cared for their royal charges and the princes and princesses who relied upon them from infancy onwards. Re-appointment to care for successive generations and the rewards which were granted years after their terms of office were ended are all that remain of the bonds that grew between the prince and princesses and their surrogate mothers.

As heir, Arthur's education lay in the hands of his father. It is likely that Peter Courtenay advised Henry VII on the selection of Arthur's tutor, John Rede, the former headmaster of Winchester College. The prince's younger siblings remained in the care of their mother until they were old enough to leave their nursery and, unlike Arthur, they would remain accommodated closer to London at Eltham. Following the birth of Margaret and the establishment of the Tudor nursery there, it had become one of the king and queen's favourite residences. It gave both of them, particularly Elizabeth, more of an opportunity to spend time with their children. It meant that the Tudors were less distant from their family than they might otherwise have been. Arthur, however, remained with his household at Farnham.

The location at Eltham, together with the employment of men and women with sound Yorkist credentials, provided an example of the continuity of monarchy. The royal nursery, conveniently close to Greenwich Palace, oversaw the care and education of ten royal infants between Elizabeth's birth in 1466 and Bridget of York's in 1480. The palace had a long association with the Plantagenets. It was one of Henry VI's favourite residences and he made several alterations to it, including the addition of a range of well-lit royal apartments. Edward IV continued the tradition of building work at Eltham in 1475 with a great hall resplendent with a hammerbeam ceiling and the falcon and fetterlock badge. Before that, in 1325, it was home to John of Eltham, a younger son of Edward II and Isabella of France.[32] During the 1490s, Eltham was a luxurious palace, safely located in the countryside away from noxious disease carrying miasmas of London and secure inside its own moat. There was even a flushing toilet. The threat of disease was not an idle fear. During the Christmas season of 1489, several of the queen's ladies died from a measles outbreak.[33] Lady Margaret Beaufort, familiar with the lodgings at Eltham and its parkland from her own time in Elizabeth Woodville's service, must have recognised its attractions as a home as well as approving its symbolic value to the new dynasty.

Margaret Beaufort, widely recognised as the most important person in the kingdom after Henry VII, is very likely to have had a hand in the selection of nursery staff and royal tutors as well as oversight of her grandchildren's progress from infancy to adulthood. In addition to wanting to ensure that Henry's children were raised as princes and princesses, Margaret, whose correspondence showed her to be an attentive grandparent, loved learning and encouraged scholarship. In 1494 she wrote to Oxford University requesting the release of a fellow, Maurice Westbury, to teach her own wards at her home at Collyweston in Northamptonshire. She was a patron of both Oxford and Cambridge universities, founding St John's and re-founding Christ's College in Cambridge, as well as sponsoring gifted scholars throughout her adult life. She was also an avid book collector. John Fisher wrote that she was 'right studious' and that she owned books in English and French.

She patronised the printing press of William Caxton at Westminster Abbey and following his death, in 1492, the press of Wynkyn de Worde. Margaret advised Caxton about which books to print and even leant him some of her own books to copy. Many of the texts were devotional works. There are at least ten books in existence dedicated to Lady Margaret, including the *Mirror of Gold for the Sinful Soul* which she translated from French into English herself and which was printed in 1506.

Princess Margaret was weaned in about 1491 and her wetnurse permitted to return to her own family. The households of Margaret and Henry were more closely amalgamated afterwards. This structure formed the core of the nursery although the young Tudors were joined by new siblings and their associated carers throughout the remainder of the queen's childbearing years. She would bear seven children, of whom three would not survive infancy. The queen was heavily pregnant at Richmond when her own mother, Elizabeth Woodville, died in 1492. The child, when it arrived on 2 July, was named in memory of its maternal grandmother. The princess and her wetnurse, Cecily Burbage, joined the royal family at Eltham where Elizabeth grew into a toddler. It is likely that both Henry and Elizabeth were weaned at the same time, their wetnurses chewing mouth food to feed to their charges. At the start of autumn of 1495, the king paid staff salaries as usual. Then on 14 September, the youngest member of Eltham's royal nursery suddenly died. It is uncertain whether the cause of Elizabeth's 'atrophy' was disease, accidental death or whether there was something more seriously wrong with the princess. She was buried in Westminster Abbey in a ceremony that cost £318, (£160,000 in 2016).[34] The nursery was clad in mourning but there is no evidence to indicate how Margaret and Henry felt about the loss of their little sister.

The queen gave birth to another daughter, named Mary, on 18 March 1496. A new baby took its place in the royal crib. Elizabeth Denton took charge of the child until Anne Cromer was appointed as her lady governess.[35] The routine of the nursery continued but 1497 was punctuated by another Yorkist rising, this time in support of a pretender named Perkin Warbeck purporting to be the younger of the queen's two brothers. In June, Elizabeth hurried her children from Eltham to the security of the Tower of London as Cornish rebels advanced on Blackheath. More pregnancies followed. Edmund was born on 21 February 1499 at Greenwich Palace. He joined his elder siblings at Eltham under the care of his lady governess, Anne Cromer and his wetnurse, Anne Skern, who also suckled the baby Mary.[36] The new prince was created Duke of Somerset but died the following year at the bishop's palace at Bishop's Stortford in Hertfordshire where the nursery had gone to avoid an outbreak of plague. He was given a state funeral and burial in Westminster Abbey, costing £242 11s 8d.[37] A fourth son, Edward, also died soon after his birth.

Margaret, Henry and Mary remained at Eltham where they lived in some state under the governance of their lady governesses, the queen and Lady Margaret Beaufort. The daily routine began at about six in the morning with a Matins service followed by a meal. Dinner, the main meal of the day, was served at eleven. The day's lessons concluded with Evensong in the chapel. They learned practical expectations of piety from the women who surrounded them including their grandmother and mother. Elizabeth gave generous offerings to the Church throughout the year. During the Easter of 1502, for instance, she gave money on Good Friday and Easter Day as well as attending 'high mass' throughout Easter week.[38] On 5 July 1502, as well as making offerings at Windsor to Saint George, the queen also provided an gift of 12d for her daughter Margaret, who was known as the Queen of Scots by that time.[39] In addition to learning their prayers and being able to read and write, the children were expected to look and behave as members of the royal family on all public occasions. They were required to demonstrate regal manners and to impress visiting dignitaries with their appearance, behaviour and graceful dancing. In November 1494, the king bestowed the title Duke of York upon 3-year-old Henry and Margaret was given the responsibility of handing out the prizes at the tournament that followed. She was not quite 5 years old when she attended the lavish celebrations and played a central role in them. The children were taught impeccable table manners and knew how to make conversation with the people that they met. They learned by example and there were etiquette books that could be used for additional guidance if required. Caxton's *The Book of the Knight of the Tower*, completed in 1483 was a tutorial for young women visiting a royal court and warned against the dangers of vanity. Lydgate's text entitled *Table Manners for Children*, printed by Caxton, was a translation of a thirteenth-century poem often attributed to Robert Grosseteste and provided instruction for the table manners of the time including directions for a child not to wipe its mouth on the table cloth, spread butter with their thumbs, or to lick the plate on which their food was served. Any prince or princess picking their nose or spattering themselves with gravy was likely to be severely rebuked by his or her staff. None of the adults who came into contact with the children at Eltham were likely to be receptive to any of the poor behaviour identified by Lydgate, including slouching, scratching, shuffling and failing to look a speaker in the eye.

In addition to looking and behaving like princesses, Margaret and Mary were expected to embroider and sew. It was a demonstration of feminine skill, prevented idleness and was a manifestation of piety, since much of the embroidery created by aristocratic women was destined for the Church in the form of vestments and altar cloths. All textiles of the period were decorated by hand and praise was given to accomplished needlewomen. In later years, Katherine of Aragon's virtue as a wife would be demonstrated by the fact that she decorated her husband's shirts with intricate blackwork embroidery even though she was a queen of England.

Dancing and singing were an essential part of an education for life at court. Prince Henry was a particularly energetic dancer. All the Tudor children played musical instruments. Both Henry VII's daughters could play the lute and the clavichord. In 1501, Margaret, who was 12 years old by then, received a new lute from her father costing 13s 4d.[40] Four years later, on 1 August 1505, Mary received a similar gift.[41] The children also received riding lessons and learned to hunt. Prince Henry might have gone, on occasion, to the royal mews at Charing Cross where the pretender Lambert Simnel, pardoned by the king, worked as a trainer of the hawks there having been promoted from his job in the kitchens.

Elizabeth of York's mother, Elizabeth Woodville, had £400 a year to maintain the nursery of her younger children and it was the queen who managed the small army of gentlewomen and servants who cared for her own children although it was the king who paid their salaries. Elizabeth of York's diary of expenses note the purchase of lutes and lute strings for her children as well as fees to 'Giles the Lute' for tuition he provided for Margaret. In 1499 material was ordered to make clothing for the elder of the two princesses that included 'nine yards of green velvet, edged with purple tinsel, for a gown, and much buckram as will line the same'. In addition, there was damask, linen for smocks, silk ribbons, woollen hose and crimson velvet edged with fur. Margaret was also to be provided with fourteen pairs of double-soled shoes priced at 8d per pair.[42]

Although Elizabeth of York did not care for her children on a daily basis and lady governesses were appointed to fulfil the task, it is thought likely that she taught her younger children to read and write given the similarities in style between mother and children.[43] All of the royal children learned to read either using a horn alphabet tablet to recite their letters or a prayer book known as a primer. Henry VII's accounts show that he paid £1 for 'a book bought for my lord of York'.[44] Like his mother who owned an extensive collection by the time of her death, the king had an interest in books and had developed a taste for French literature during his time in exile. Elizabeth, Henry and Margaret all patronised William Caxton.

The choices for a child learning to read were limited. Most early reading material was religious, even horn alphabets began with a cross so that a young child might learn how to make the sign correctly. Together with Lady Margaret Beaufort, known for her intense piety, the queen would have selected the kinds of books available to the royal children to ensure that they received a Christian education alongside their letters. A book of psalms and a Psalter were essential. The nursery might also have contained devotional Books of Hours like Margaret Beaufort's own famous book which she annotated in much the same manner as an almanac or journal as well as using it as a tool to help her pray. The *Hours of Henry VIII*, illuminated in about 1500 by Jean Poyer, is held by later tradition to have belonged to Margaret's grandson. The *Hours of Henry VII*, at Chatsworth in Derbyshire, was gifted by the king to his daughter Margaret. As well as being educated, the Tudors wanted their children to grow up to be, at the very least, conventionally pious. Presents of Books of Hours were often made as a public display of affection or passed through families. Less enjoyable, so far as the royal children were concerned, were the moralising tales told to them by their grandmother who is known to have had much to do with their day-to-day care and education. Even John Fisher, Margaret's biographer, admitted that the countess was prone to recount the same story 'many a time'[45] and her household was not a joyous one, unlike Elizabeth of York's which Sir Thomas More described as having 'plenty of every pleasant thing' despite her own regular daily attendance at church, a routine which was mirrored by the royal nursery.[46]

Margaret and Mary were expected to be modest, to be pious and, even as princesses, to learn the practical skills of overseeing the household hierarchy rather than to develop academic talents of the kind exhibited by Sir Thomas More's daughter, Margaret Roper. Noble women were also required to be able to run their husband's estates in their absence, or, if they were queens, to act as regents. Elizabeth of York's own aunt, the hated Margaret of Burgundy, impressed the rest of Europe not only with her kindliness but by her capabilities as the wife of Duke Charles the Bold and, when she became dowager, for her skilful political guidance of her stepdaughter, Mary. Unlike Arthur and Henry, neither Margaret or Mary received any documented training for this aspect of their adult lives and were expected, instead, to rely upon the guidance of their counsellors. Margaret Beaufort, who regretted her own lack of Latin, must have approved of humanist educators like Erasmus and Thomas More who wanted girls, as well as boys, to learn it. Both Tudor princesses had some grasp of the language which was essential for scholarship and diplomacy as well as for following church services and communicating with a spouse where there was no other shared language. Most writers believed that girls should be raised to be good Christian wives but that their reading material should be strictly monitored and that there was no need for them to follow the same curriculum as their male counterparts.

In 1495, the business of Henry's education was handed by the queen into the hands of men. The two princesses may have also benefited from the appointment of John Skelton as royal tutor. He was a protégée of the king's mother and Henry VII had given him a laureateship in classical Latin rhetoric on his visit to Oxford University in 1488. He was praised by the most renowned scholar of the age, Erasmus, in 1499. Skelton expanded the curriculum at Eltham to include grammar, religious studies, government, courtesy, astronomy and maths. His work *Speculum Principis* (or *A Mirror of Princes*) was a guide to behaviour that he presented to Prince Henry in 1501. In it he encouraged the prince to not only revere sportsmen but to encourage poets. William Blount, Lord Mountjoy, thirteen years older than Henry, was appointed to mentor the prince. He studied at Cambridge and Paris, as well as learning from Erasmus, who would become the most famous scholar in Europe.

Princesses were as valuable to the Tudor dynasty as princes because they could be used to form alliances through marriage. It made the acquisition of French, an aristocratic *lingua franca*, an essential part of Mary and Margaret's education. In 1498, a Frenchwoman, Jane Popincourt, who was part of the queen's household was instructed to improve Margaret and Mary's grasp of the language. She remained in the royal household for several years but language tuition passed into the hands of Giles D'Ewes, a court musician from Flanders. He also taught Prince Henry, some of whose own musical compositions survive, to play the lute.

In 1498 the king and his advisors began to negotiate a peace treaty with Scotland. The agreement, which included a clause requiring the Scots to yield up the pretender Perkin Warbeck to the English, would culminate in an agreement for Margaret to marry James IV of Scotland. The princess was

9 years old at the time and the king told the Spanish Ambassador she was 'delicate'.[47] He added, 'the queen and my mother are very much against this marriage'.[48] The pair were determined that Margaret should not face the same physical hazards that Margaret Beaufort experienced when she gave birth to Henry Tudor while she was still a child herself. Margaret would not go to Scotland while her mother and grandmother feared that the king, who was a notorious womaniser, would not wait until his bride was mature enough to cohabit with him.[49]

In September 1499, Erasmus, the theologian and educator who popularised humanism, visited England and stayed with Lord Mountjoy. He was taken to visit the royal family at Eltham by his friend, Sir Thomas More. The humanist described seeing the family, including Prince Edmund who was in his nurse's arms, at their games and wrote a poem, *Prosopopoeia Britanniae* in honour of Henry, who at 8 years of age was lively, articulate and confident. The prince demanded a gift from the Dutch scholar when Sir Thomas presented the family with some poems of his own. It was the start of a long friendship between More and Henry that would end in Sir Thomas's death on the block in 1535.

The queen introduced her illegitimate half-brother, Arthur Plantagenet, to the royal nursery. Between 1501 and 1503 he was part of Elizabeth's household and had been part of court life since his own childhood, although his early life is concealed by lack of written records about him.[50] It has been suggested that he may have shared Edward V's education.[51] It is likely, given Elizabeth Denton's continued role as one of the queen's women as well as being lady mistress to Prince Henry, that the queen was often in residence at Eltham but the presence of Arthur, as an informal mentor of chivalrous courtly behaviour for Henry to model himself on, might not have been the queen's own idea. A letter dating from the summer of 1501 from Lady Margaret Beaufort to the king from Calais suggests that Arthur was part of her household prior to transferring to his sister's retinue.[52] This suggests that it was the king and his mother who decided that he was to be trusted and could be a useful role model for Prince Henry who was now in his tenth year. As well as his links to the royal family, his knowledge of royal education and his interest in knightly pursuits, Arthur was described by those who knew him as genial and in later years, Henry VIII described him as 'the gentlest heart living'.[53] Perhaps it was also thought that he could be a good influence on his young nephew?

As the royal children left infancy behind them, the household at Eltham changed to reflect a new focus. In addition to Arthur who was about twenty years older than his nephew, Henry's mother and grandmother chose well-born young men to join the prince to share his education, to be his companions and to serve him. Their number included Joan Vaux's son, Henry Guildford, who shared the prince and Arthur Plantagenet's enjoyment of jousting and sport.

The king celebrated his and Elizabeth's success in establishing a new dynasty by commissioning a portrait of his heir wearing a collar of red and white Tudor roses. Arthur, Margaret, Henry and Mary, always resplendent in garb that marked their status as princes and princesses, were the proof that God smiled upon Henry Tudor — and a reminder to Yorkist sympathisers that the Tudors were on the throne to stay, or so Henry believed as the sixteenth century dawned.

Chapter 6
Prince Arthur

King Henry VII, whose own education had been the haphazard schooling of a fugitive, was determined that Arthur's tuition would be exemplary. It was usual, in addition to academic lessons, for a king's son to be raised to know his manners, to have the prerequisite noble accomplishments and excel at knightly pursuits. While he was at Farnham, Arthur was cared for and taught his letters by the women that Henry VII employed or by his chaplains who also taught him his prayers and to follow church services. As Arthur grew from infancy into childhood the number of females in his household diminished and the king began to send male servants in their place to teach him all that was required of an effective monarch.

Arthur's household staff would prepare him for the rituals and protocols of daily life at court, to understand its hierarchy and management systems and to grasp the roles played by the men who ran it, his government and his personal estates. Thomas Poyntz, an esquire of the body and related by marriage to Joan Vaux, was present at Arthur's baptism, which was followed immediately after by his confirmation in Winchester Cathedral. He also had links with the Devereux family being married to the widow of Lord Ferrers of Chartley and was one of the earliest appointments that Henry VII made. In 1488 he received a gift of 40 marks for his service to the prince but his role in Arthur's household is unspecified.[1] A present of a Book of Hours, dating from about 1495, from Arthur to Poyntz suggests that the relationship was a close one.[2]

In December the same year Robert Knollys was sent to join Poyntz. Knollys was described as a henchman meaning that he was a loyal supporter of the king but of relatively humble birth. He would continue in service to the Crown as an usher of the chamber to both Henry VII and Henry VIII. In January 1490 Richard Howell is listed as marshal of Arthur's household. It was his job to ensure the prince's security. By 1491 eleven yeomen and grooms of the chamber were listed in Arthur's household which now more closely mirrored the structure of Henry's own with cellarers, stewards and an almoner.[3] It was the job of the men that the king appointed to act as mentors so that the prince, young as he was, could begin to learn to manage men, and in return they were rewarded with positions close to the Tudor throne.

It was essential that Arthur learned how to behave as a king as soon as possible. Court politics and international diplomacy went hand-in-hand with ceremony, patronage and long-established concepts of knighthood. Even as a young child Arthur did not remain closeted in the private world of the nursery. On 29 November 1489 he was created a knight and made Prince of Wales and Earl of Chester at Westminster. The following year he took part in a procession of barges on the Thames and met the mayor of London and the Spanish ambassador. On 27 February Arthur rode on a horse to Westminster where he was formally invested with his titles and sat under a cloth of state during the feasting that followed. He was expected to conduct himself as a prince rather than a child barely out of long skirts. The occasion marked the end of Arthur's infancy and was a reminder that the Tudors had an heir to their new dynasty. It was vital that he knew how to maintain the dignity of the Crown.

At Farnham, Lady Darcy understood the importance of exercise and recreation as a preliminary to practise with swords and lances. Henry, who had won his crown on a battlefield and faced repeated Yorkists plots, knew all too well that chivalrous behaviour in the tournament yard was a rehearsal for commanding armies. Edward IV decreed that his own son's routine should incorporate outside recreation and exercise twice a day.[4] It is impossible to know what games Arthur played in his free time but Sir Thomas More's *Pageant Verses* and hangings depicted childhood as a boy playing with a top while the words beneath contained reference to quoits, balls and a 'cock stick' or throwing-stick.[5] And like all boys of the period, the royal princes were required by law to practice archery. Henry VII's accounts show that Prince Arthur received his first bow from his father when he was 5 years old.[6] He was known, like all the Tudor kings and princes, to be fond of hunting and riding. On the day that he was invested as Prince of Wales, before he was 3 years old, he rode to Westminster. It is thought that he was taught to ride by Sir Robert Cotton, the queen's master of horse.[7]

When the prince reached the age of 4 or 5, in about 1490, his formal education began. The king employed professional tutors rather than noble or 'knightly' masters to educate all his children.[8] He was following the model provided by his predecessor, Edward IV, who wanted Elizabeth of York's brother, Edward V, to receive a grounding in the new models of education based on classical texts that was making its way into England at that time. Humanism, or, as it was known in England, New Learning, developed in Italy but spread across northern Europe at the end of the fifteenth and beginning of the sixteenth centuries. Extended study in the schoolroom was an addition to the skills deemed prerequisite for medieval kings, including knowledge about leading families and being able to determine the banners and badges of the men who made up his armies at a glance. To this end, in 1489 Henry VII appointed Thomas Wriothesley, the son of the Garter King of Arms, as Wallingford Pursuivant to teach Arthur about livery, heraldry and the badges that men used as well as about where they came from and their lineage. Wriothesley also shared his knowledge with Arthur's younger brother, Henry. Despite the king's own extensive use of heraldic images to assert the identity of the Tudors, the use of livery and badges other than as decoration was increasingly banned among the aristocracy as a way of dismantling the political allegiances that marked the politics of the Wars of the Roses.

By 1491 Arthur was under the instruction of John Rede, receiving an education that focused on Latin and the acquisition of grammar. In 1496, the blind Frenchman Bernard André, who was rewarded with £3 6s 8d in the same year[9] took over the task, applying humanist principles to the prince's learning. At Eltham, Prince Henry's mentor, Lord Mountjoy, was one of the first advocates of humanism which placed an emphasis on the use of classical texts to systematically teach Latin grammar and rhetoric. The study of Latin language, law and history began with reading from authors chosen for their style and the moral lessons they contained. *Aesop's Fables*, Homer's *Odyssey* and Virgil's *Aeneid* were among the works that should be studied before advancing to Cicero. There was also a focus on history including Thucydides, Livy and Tacitus. The two princes studied more or less the same books under different tutors. By the time he was 16 years old, André boasted that, Arthur had not only read twenty-four of the key texts favoured by humanists but had committed a good chunk of them to memory. Latin was not only the mark of an educated man, for the king's son it resonated with courtly refinement and the need for kings and princes to converse as ambassadors with other nations. Rhetoric would help Arthur with the public speaking requirements of royalty. By the time he was 11 years old the prince was fulfilling his role as an asset to his dynasty. In 1497,

Raimondo, the Milanese ambassador met with the king and his eldest son at Woodstock on an occasion when the Spanish ambassador was also present. Raimondo described Arthur's 'remarkable beauty and grace and very ready in speaking Latin'.[10]

As well as classical authors, Arthur was also directed towards some contemporary writers. Among the books that Arthur owned was Cicero's *De Officilis* which was given to him by his grandmother. It is thought that John Rede is likely to have assisted Lady Margaret Beaufort to acquire an illuminated copy of the book, printed in Mainz in 1465. One of the initials in the text depicts a boy dressed in ermine in a schoolroom being taught by a man in a doctoral bonnet.[11] Arthur also had a copy of the *Aeneid*, in English, printed by William Caxton and dedicated by the printer to his 'natural and souerayn lord'.[12]

Book ownership and patronage went hand in hand. In 1499 Thomas Linacre sent Prince Arthur the manuscript version of his Latin translation of *De sphaera*, which Alda had printed for him in Venice. The work, attributed to the fourth-century Greek philosopher, Proculus, explained the cosmos, the stars and the terrestrial zones of the earth. Not only was he advertising his own qualification to tutor the prince in Greek but encouraging Arthur to recognise Linacre as a scholar who might be patronised as a demonstration of the prince's own accomplishments.

Erasmus, writing down the tale in 1531, described Linacre's presentation of his translation of Proculus at court and that André, jealous of his own position, intervened, announcing that the book had already been translated by someone else and, he added, that it was poorly done. King Henry VII rejected the gift on his son's behalf and Linacre with it. Erasmus's letter indicates that Linacre did not gain preferment in Arthur's household either as a tutor or as a physician at that time. The humanist would also write that André was not the 'best of preceptors'.[13] This was the first time that battle lines between rival methods of teaching would make themselves apparent but it would not be the last occasion that royal tutors would attack and counterattack their peers.

Arthur was aged just 7 years when he left his nursery at Farnham in 1493 for a new home at Ludlow and the next stage of his preparation for the crown, in just the same way that his uncle, Edward, was prepared for kingship. King Edward IV, Earl of March before he won his throne, spent many of his formative years at Ludlow and it was, he decided, where his own son should also be raised. Following the precedent set by the Yorkists, King Henry VII re-established the Council of Wales and the Marches, which Edward IV first used to administer his estates as Earl of March and to enforce royal authority in the region. He envisaged that Prince Arthur, newly enriched with lands throughout the area including much of the former earldom of March, would learn how to manage his estates, dispense justice and navigate his way through the complexities of regional politics.

The prince, who in theory had charge over the Council of Wales, would develop the skills he needed under the guidance of men appointed by his father starting with John Alcock, Bishop of Ely who had served as England's Lord Chancellor in 1475 and again from 1485 to 1487. The bishop also held the presidency of the council. He had the advantage of continuity from the Yorkist to the Tudor regime, having first been named president of the council in 1473. He was a man known for his deeply held religious beliefs, as well as being a champion of education. In addition to founding Jesus College Cambridge, he established a grammar school in his native town of Hull. He was characterised as 'given from his childhood to learning and religion'.[14] The bishop also benefitted, so far as the appointment to Arthur's household was concerned, from being Edward V's tutor during his sojourn at Ludlow.

King Edward IV provided a detailed set of ordinances for the education of his eldest son for both Alcock, who was then Bishop of Rochester, and Anthony Woodville, 2nd Earl Rivers, Elizabeth Woodville's brother, who was appointed as his nephew's 'governor and ruler'.[15] In September 1473 the king set out, in a letter, the way in which the prince's household at Ludlow should be run as well as a timetable for Edward's day. By 10 o'clock in the morning, the prince was to be dressed, have attended divine service, breakfasted and completed his first lessons. Dinner, the main meal of the day, was served at 10 o'clock. No man was to sit beside him apart from his uncle or to disturb him in his private chamber. He was to be served by squires wearing livery. Even while he ate, attention was paid to his education. The king decreed that appropriate books should be read to him at mealtimes. After he had eaten, Edward studied grammar, music, history and the humanities before turning his attention to horsemanship, swordsmanship, tilting and other knightly exercises. Afterward, he attended Vespers before being allowed to play until it was time for him to retire to his bed, at 8 o'clock in the evening. The prince's companions, educated alongside the boy that they also served, as it was intended that they would for the rest of their lives, followed the same punishing schedule. There is no reason to suppose that Arthur's experience was any different when he was sent to Ludlow in his turn.

Under Alcock's tutelage at Ludlow, Edward V applied himself to logic, law, literature, history and philosophy.[16] Anthony Woodville had his own literary and linguistic credentials which fitted him to the task. He was a friend of Caxton's who, in 1477, printed Rivers' translation of the *Sayings of the Philosophers*. He and Alcock were fully equipped to fulfil the king's demands that they should provide Edward with:

> … such noble stories as behoveth to a prince to understand and know; and that the communication at all times in his presence be of virtue, honour, cunning, wisdom, and of deeds of worship, and of nothing that should move or stir him to vice.[17]

Rous described Arthur's uncle as a 'mirabilis ingenii'[18] or wonderful talent, while Sir Thomas More described both the princes many 'gifts of nature … and princely virtues'.[19]

Unlike Edward IV, Henry VII had no intention of investing one man with as much power as Earl Rivers once wielded. The Tudor monarch's determination not to appoint a single governor to oversee his heir's education meant that, in principle, Arthur was master of his own household and of the Council of Wales. In practice the prince was surrounded by men of experience, trusted by the king, who were there to ensure the region ran smoothly and to show Arthur how to govern. Sir Richard Pole, Henry's cousin, already held an assortment of offices in Wales including the 'shrievalty' of Merionethshire and the constableship of both Harlech and Montgomery castles. He was now appointed as Arthur's chamberlain with an annual allowance of 1000 marks for the upkeep of the prince's household.[20] It was Pole's task to oversee the prince's household, to maintain the boy's private living quarters and care for him. It gave Pole direct and immediate access to the prince besides being trusted by the king to receive and pay out money from Arthur's purse. Pole, a member of the gentry rather than the aristocracy, was already matched with Margaret Plantagenet, the daughter of George, Duke of Clarence, whom he married in November 1487. The same year had seen the marriage of Pole's sister, Eleanor, one of the queen's ladies to Ralph Verney who was chamberlain of Elizabeth's household. It was part of Henry's strategy to marry trusted Lancastrian supporters to women of

Yorkist blood, in much the same manner as his own union, to build support for the Tudors and to limit the amount of dissent that might otherwise focus on females of royal birth.

John Argentine, who was Arthur's physician, was also listed in Edward V's Ludlow household as was Arthur's chaplain and theologian, John Burton. Argentine was probably in Ludlow when Edward V was Prince of Wales as he is first listed at court in 1478 and made the transition from a prince's household to a king's household when Edward inherited the throne, as did Alcock, unlike many of the staff who were dismissed.[21] It appears that Argentine left England in October 1483 to join with Henry Tudor. He was one of the last men to see Elizabeth of York's brothers alive according to an account provided by the Italian monk Dominic Mancini, who visited England in 1483.[22] Argentine and Burton were known to the queen, who may have had a hand in their appointment along with Alcock, and trusted to protect Arthur's physical and moral wellbeing.

Sir Henry Vernon was appointed controller of the household. His marriage to Anne Talbot, a daughter of the Earl of Shrewsbury, meant that he had sound Lancastrian connections as well as a family history of Crown administration in the Midlands. He also proved his political adroitness by not committing himself to one side or the other during the conflicts of the fifteenth century despite requests from the Earl of Warwick, George Duke of Clarence and Richard III to take his place on the field of battle alongside them. Instead, his service to the Tudors at the Battle of Stoke in 1487 saw the start of his rise in the service of Prince Arthur. In 1489, he was made a Knight of the Bath when Arthur was created Prince of Wales. His role as treasurer and governor of the prince meant that he was much in Arthur's company. On occasion Arthur stayed at Tong Castle and at Haddon Hall near Bakewell where one of the rooms is known as the Prince's Chamber. And still bears his coat of arms.[23]

Alcock was succeeded, after his death in 1500, by William Smith, Bishop of Lincoln one of the founders of Brasenose College in Oxford who held the post until his own death in 1514. Like so many of the appointments that Henry made, Smith's connections to the Tudors dated from an early association with Margaret Beaufort. He was born in Lancashire, at Farnworth, and it is thought that he was sent to be educated at Knowsley Hall by Thomas Stanley, 1st Earl of Derby. The countess discharged her duties towards promising candidates under her husband's charge by the employment of an Oxford scholar, Westbury, to teach them.[24] His first appointment was to Wimborne in Dorset where Margaret's parents were buried and a month after Bosworth he was appointed to the office of clerk of the hanaper of chancery for life, with a salary of £40. Other preferments quickly followed. In February 1486 he was granted governorship of Catherine and Bridget of York and provided with £200 for 'the keeping and guiding' of his new charges.[25] By 1493 he was a member of the king's council and the Bishop of Coventry and Lichfield. Within three months of his appointment to the latter he was acting on the Council of Wales. He managed to find time to re-found Lichfield's almshouses and to establish a free grammar school there before being translated to the Bishopric of Lincoln in 1496. He spent most of his time with Prince Arthur at Ludlow or Bewdley rather than visiting his see. On 5 November 1500, Smith was nominated as Cardinal Morton's successor to the chancellorship of Oxford University.

Jasper Tudor, restored to his former titles and created Duke of Bedford in 1485, was the Justiciar for South Wales while Sir Rhys Ap Thomas was the region's chamberlain. William Stanley, Margaret Beaufort's brother-in-law, was appointed as Justiciar for North Wales. In total there were ten men on the council, the others being Sir Richard Croft, Sir David Phillips, Sir William Uvedale, Sir Thomas Englefield, Sir Peter Newton (who served as Arthur's clerk of the signet), John Wilson and Henry Marian. Charles Bothe, who became the Bishop of Hereford, acted as both chaplain and chancellor to the council.[26] The king selected men whose past lay with both Lancastrian and Yorkist regimes as well as a new group of men who owed their preferment only to the Tudors. It was this diverse group's task to educate Henry's heir on how to rule a kingdom. The choice of council members was a calculated risk to ensure the future of the realm unified under Tudor rule.

Sir Richard Croft was part of the extended Mortimer family. His wife, Eleanor, was Sir Hugh Mortimer's widow. Mortimer of Kyre Wyard and Martley was the heir of a cadet branch of Richard Duke of York's family. Sir Hugh, part of his kinsman's retinue, was killed at the Battle of Wakefield on 30 December 1460. The following year his widow, Eleanor, married Sir Richard Croft from nearby Leominster. Croft was credited with the capture of Edward of Lancaster at the Battle of Tewkesbury having fought at Mortimer's Cross and Towton on the side of the Yorkists. He was described by the chronicler Edward Hall as a 'wise and valiant knight'[27] who went on to serve as Edward IV's receiver general in the earldom of March and treasurer of Richard III's household. Croft continued in the same roles under King Henry VII as part of the king's policy of reconciliation between the two warring factions. Croft was a loyal servant of the Yorkists and his wife was at the heart of the future Edward V's upbringing. A mother of eight children by Sir Richard, she was appointed lady governess to the prince while he was at Ludlow. Croft was the governor of the castle there at the same time. The pair fulfilled Henry's desire for there to be continuity in the care of royal children from the House of York to the Tudors, as well as ensuring stability for the administration of the region. And Croft, a pragmatist, clearly recognised the benefits of continued loyalty to the Crown, whoever was wearing it. He served Edward IV, was Richard III's household treasurer in 1484 and after Bosworth was quick to make choices to his own advantage, especially since the Corbets, who knew Henry Tudor since his childhood, sought to advance their own family's position in the Marches during the first ten years of Henry's reign.[28]

Sir William Uvedale of Wickham in Hampshire, another Yorkist, was present at King Edward IV's funeral. William's father, Thomas, fought at Northampton, Towton and Barnet but died in 1474 when William was still only 19 years old. Within three years of inheriting, Uvedale was fulfilling his administrative obligations to the county. He sat on a commission to enquire into piracy off the coast at Hampshire and Sussex[29] and on various commissions for peace for Hampshire.[30] By 1483 William commanded the garrison at Porchester Castle and was destined to be knighted at Edward V's coronation. Instead, he was attainted of treason by Richard III and his estates were seized. Like other of Henry VII's supporters he changed sides and was rewarded for his shift in alignment once Henry became king. In 1485 he was pardoned, repossessed his manors and was knighted. Soon afterwards, he was appointed as an esquire of the body, one of the king's personal attendants and resumed his administrative duties in Hampshire where he served as sheriff in 1487 and 1493. He was also present when Prince Henry was created Duke of York in 1494 and took part in the celebratory tournament that followed.[31] In 1486 he was a beneficiary of the will of William Waynflete, the founder of Winchester College, making it plausible that Margaret Beaufort, who was well acquainted with Waynflete, knew of Uvedale prior to his employment in Wales.[32]

By contrast Thomas ap Rhys was from a faithful Lancastrian, as well as a powerful Welsh family. His father was part of the resistance in Wales following Edward IV's victory at Towton in 1461. He and his brother were responsible for the Yorkist defeat at Carreg Cennen Castle but were forced to surrender in 1462. Ap Rhys went into exile in Burgundy with his father but was able to return home in 1467. Even though he took no part in Buckingham's revolt of 1483 and served in the administration of King Richard III, he entered into clandestine correspondence with Henry Tudor and in 1485 made no attempt to prevent him from landing at Milford Haven. Instead, Rhys joined Henry and fought for him at Bosworth. If the poet, Guto'r Glyn, is to be believed it was Thomas ap Rhys who killed Richard III. It is scarcely surprising, if true, that the new king made Rhys Chamberlain of South Wales and steward of both Brecon and Builth Castles in November 1485. Ap Thomas continued to serve Henry on the field, helping to suppress the Brecon rising of 1486, as well as the Yorkist risings of 1487 and 1497. In return he acquired lands and was granted many offices in South Wales. His service on Arthur's council reflected his importance in the region as well as being a reward for his loyalty.

Thomas Englefield, a trained lawyer practising from Middle Temple, came from Berkshire but the family held lands in the Marches although it appears, unlike most of the other men, he had no personal links with the region until Henry appointed him to the council. He was an outsider or 'new man' appointed because of his administrative skills and the loyalty he owed to the Tudors which meant that he had no personal affinity to the Stanley family who dominated Cheshire or to any other of the Marcher families who vied for position in the region. Englefield became JP for Herefordshire, Shropshire, Gloucester and Worcestershire at the same time as being appointed to the council. He also became deputy justice for Chester in 1491 serving under the Stanleys. It was part of his role to ensure that not only was law enforced and peace kept but also that the monarchy received its due in fees, fines and even rights to wardship. His service to the Tudors included acting as executor, along with Margaret Beaufort, to Henry VII's will in 1509. The following year he was the speaker for Henry VIII's first parliament and during the king's absence in France in 1513, he was one of the four men selected to advise Henry's queen. His rise to prominence in the Marches and beyond was thanks to his association with Sir Reginald Bray, who was one of Margaret Beaufort's most trusted associates.[33]

At the same time that Arthur gained practical experience in government, it was essential that the prince, the future king of England, was married to a suitable bride in order to bolster the Tudors' reputation in Europe. Henry VII first sent ambassadors to Spain in 1489 to secure an alliance against France. On 27 March, the Treaty of Medina del Campo was signed but it was only in 1490 that it was ratified. In February 1497 a betrothal was agreed between Arthur and Katherine of Aragon, the daughter of Ferdinand of Aragon and Isabella of Castile. A papal dispensation was issued as the couple were related within the prohibited degrees of consanguinity; both being descended from John of Gaunt. There were other difficulties to be overcome before the wedding could be celebrated. Katherine's parents were all too aware that the Tudor claim to the throne was a weak one and they were concerned about the levels of pro-Yorkist sympathy in England while there were male claimants with better bloodlines to the throne than Henry VII's own. Unsurprisingly the Spanish were apprehensive that the Tudors might be toppled from power. They concluded that Perkin Warbeck, who confessed to being an imposter in 1497 after his capture and who remained in confinement, and Edward Plantagenet, 17th Earl of Warwick, who had been kept a prisoner since the age of ten and was the son of Edward IV's brother, Clarence, were too much of a threat to be permitted to live. Diplomatic pressure and an attempted break out from the Tower during the summer of 1499 resolved the problem of what to do with the pair. Perkin Warbeck was hanged on 23 November 1499 at Tyburn. A week later, Elizabeth of York's cousin went to his death and the direct male line of Richard, 3rd Duke of York was at an end. De Puebla, the Spanish ambassador, reported that 'there does not remain a drop of doubtful Royal blood, the only Royal blood being the true blood of the King, the Queen and, above all, of the Prince of Wales'.[34]

With the removal of the focus of Yorkist dissent, a proxy marriage between Katherine of Aragon took place at Tickenhill Manor in Bewdley, Worcestershire, where Arthur was then living. The Spanish ambassador, Roderigo de Puebla took the bride's place while the Bishop of Lincoln officiated at the ceremony. Sir Henry Vernon witnessed the marriage contract.[35] Arthur was able to write in Latin to his betrothed bride as his 'dearest spouse'[36] and express 'an earnest desire to see her'.[37] Two letters survive demonstrating the use to which Arthur put John Rede and Bernard André's schooling. The rhetoric of love sent across the seas to Spain was copied piecemeal from Pliny and Cicero. The letters were not the missives of a young man writing to a young woman, they were diplomatic correspondence confirming a marriage treaty.

During 1501 there were also rumours that the queen, who had only recently suffered the loss of her youngest child, was pregnant again. There were enough whispers for the Portuguese ambassador to report that 'the queen was supposed to be with child; her apothecary told me that a Genoese physician affirmed that she was pregnant, yet it was not so; she is plump and has large breasts'.[38] The magnificent State cradle would remain empty. Lady Guildford was recalled to the queen's service from the royal nursery at Eltham in time for the arrival of Katherine of Aragon in England on 2 October 1501, at Plymouth.

'Mother Guildford' would continue to play an important role in Princess Mary's life but the royal children were increasingly of an age where they were deemed old enough to take their place in the world. On 24 January 1502, England and Scotland signed the Treaty of Perpetual Peace and agreed the terms of Margaret Tudor's marriage to James IV who was twice the age of the bride. The proxy marriage, conducted by the Archbishop of Glasgow, took place in the queen's chamber. Margaret, still a child of 12 years, would remain in England for the time being but would be referred to as the Queen of Scots and leave her childhood home for the court at Westminster or Windsor where she was provided with a household of her own and her education as a queen in waiting would be finished in an adult environment, learning from the way Elizabeth of York ran her household and behaved at court.

It took a month for Katherine of Aragon's retinue to arrive in London from the West Country. Arthur first met his bride at Dogmersfield in Hampshire on 4 November 1501, having travelled there from Ludlow, but neither the king nor Katherine's husband escorted her for the rest of the journey as it would have been against etiquette to do so. The princess entered London on 12 November, accompanied by Prince Henry who would act as the Spanish princess's attendant throughout the coming days, amid much celebration and pageantry. On 14 November, it was Henry, aged 10 years, who conducted the bride to St Paul's Cathedral, where Katherine and Arthur, who was 15 years old, were publicly married to one another. Afterwards it was Henry who led the procession back to the Archbishop of Canterbury's palace at Lambeth. The wedding had been a long time coming to fruition but it swiftly become apparent that despite sharing Latin as a common language, the bride and groom's tutors took different views on the correct pronunciation of Latin, complicating communication between the pair.

At the end of the wedding celebrations there was a bedding ceremony. The couple were escorted to a bed which they shared as husband and wife. It would turn out to be one of the most argued about wedding nights in history. Arthur boasted the next morning 'bring me a cup of ale for I have been this night in the midst of Spain!'[39] When her second husband, Henry, sought to annul their marriage on the grounds that Katherine was his brother's widow and that the union, was therefore incestuous, according to Leviticus 20:21, she insisted that her marriage to Arthur had never been consummated. The men and women present at the wedding celebrations would be summoned to testify on the matter. For now, as the end of the year approached, the newly married couple went to Ludlow to live. They travelled first to Woodstock where the household celebrated Christmas before spending a month at Tickenhill.

The year turned, and on 24 January 1502, the marriage treaty between James IV of Scotland and Princess Margaret was finalised at Richmond. The royal children were all present for the occasion to witness Margaret's confirmation that there was no impediment to the wedding and to take her proxy vows with the Earl of Bothwell. The ceremony was followed by feasting, processions and a tournament. Soon afterwards, Henry VII commissioned a portrait of his daughter while the queen set about purchasing a wardrobe of new clothes for the young bride who continued to practise her lute and learn about life at court.

Elizabeth's account books for the year show that she took charge of her sister, Catherine's, children at the beginning of February. She set up a new nursery for her niece Margaret and nephews Henry and Edward at Dagenham Manor in Essex. They too were provided with a governess, Margaret Cotton,[40] who was already employed by the queen to care for another of her charges, as well as rockers and servants. Catherine and her husband, William Courtenay, attended the wedding celebrations of both Arthur and Margaret but during that same year, Edmund de la Pole, Duke of Suffolk, one of Elizabeth and Catherine's cousins, fled England with the intention of seizing the throne for himself. In February 1502 it came to the king's attention that Courtenay, a descendant of King Edward I, was implicated in the plot having dined with de la Pole shortly before the earl departed from England and there being some evidence of continued correspondence. Catherine's husband was imprisoned in the Tower of London and deprived of his property.

Dispossessed, his wife and children became dependent on the kindness of the queen for their food and shelter.

Disaster struck the Tudors on 2 April 1502 when Prince Arthur died from an unknown illness having made a will which left all his belongings to his sister Margaret.[41] There are many different theories about what caused Arthur's death from tuberculosis to sweating sickness but the prince became increasingly unwell in the seven weeks before his death suggesting that the cause was unlikely to have been either sweating sickness or plague, both of which killed their victims quickly.

According to Leland, Arthur's chamberlain, Sir Richard Pole, sent the letter announcing the death of Henry VII's heir to Greenwich where it was opened by the king's councillors. It was Henry's confessor who broke the news to the king the following morning with the words, 'If we receive good things at the hands of God, who may not endure evil things'?[42] Elizabeth comforted her husband as best she could, reminding him that they still had a son as well as two daughters, before returning to her own chamber where, according to the *Croyland Chronicle*, she collapsed and was comforted in her turn by Henry.[43] The care that the couple exhibited for one another in their grief does much to disprove the notion that the marriage was a political one only. Henry and Elizabeth had lost the living symbol of their dynastic security as well as their eldest son. Instead of heralding a new Arthurian golden age, the throne would now pass to Arthur's brother, Henry, who was unprepared for kingship.

Arthur's body remained at Ludlow until 23 April. His internal organs were removed and buried in St Laurence's Church and his body embalmed in preparation for its last journey. The queen paid John Cope of London for the black velvet and black cloth that covered Arthur's coffin as it was carried from Ludlow to Worcester via Bewdley.[44]. Gruffydd ap Rhys ap Thomas who was raised with the prince at Ludlow and had been made a Knight of the Garter as part of the ceremony that surrounded Arthur's wedding, was with Arthur and Katherine when they returned to the Marches. He had only recently become even closer to the prince, through his own marriage to Catherine St John, a cousin of Margaret Beaufort's, who had been appointed as one of Katherine of Aragon's ladies-in-waiting. Now it was his task to ride in front of Arthur's coffin bearing the Prince of Wales's banner. After his own death, in 1521, Gruffydd, resumed his place by the prince's side being buried near Arthur's chapel at Worcester.

Sir Richard Croft and Sir William Uvedale, the steward of Arthur's household, rode ahead of the cortege to Worcester to ensure that protocols were observed at the city gates prior to the arrival of the procession.[45] William Smith, Bishop of Lincoln conducted the funeral service at the end of which Croft, Uvedale and the rest of Arthur's household broke their white staffs of office and threw them down into the prince's grave. Henry VII, who did not attend the burial, ensured that his son's tomb and chantry chapel was filled with visual symbols of the Tudors.

Arthur's widow, Katherine of Aragon, was destined to spend the next seven years in limbo at Durham House, on the Strand, and in rooms set aside for her at court, either at Richmond or Windsor, while her father-in-law and her father, Ferdinand of Aragon, squabbled about her future and her dowry. The queen, compassionate in her own grief, was kinder to her daughter-in-law and sent her regular gifts while she lived.

Within a short time of her eldest child's death, Elizabeth, who told Henry that they were still young enough to have more children, was pregnant but would be reminded of the frailty of infant life when her young nephew, Edward Courtenay, died suddenly on 13 June 1502. The queen paid for his funeral as his parents were unable to do so. That summer Elizabeth made many offerings to shrines around the country having travelled through Oxfordshire to Monmouth and Raglan where Henry VII spent some of the formative years of his own childhood.[46] It is unclear whether the offerings were made for Arthur's soul or for her own safe delivery of another child. The queen might also have felt the need to give alms in the name of her two missing brothers. Sir James Tyrell confessed to the murder of Edward and Richard before his execution for treason on 6 May 1502. By September the queen's household were concerned about her health and an apothecary, John Grice, was in attendance to ensure that Elizabeth had a safe journey back to London where she began to prepare for another lying-in.

The Tudor dynasty, which a short time before possessed both an heir and a spare, hung by a single thread. Elizabeth planned to give birth at Richmond but, at the beginning of February, she joined her husband in the royal apartments at The Tower. Her baby was not due for at least another month. Fortunately, Alice Massey, her midwife, was already present in the queen's household when she went into early labour. Henry hurriedly ordered a cradle for the newest addition to the royal family, a girl named Katherine. Elizabeth became ill a week later, on 9 February, from complications arising from either the pregnancy or the difficult birth that followed. She died aged 37 years, on 11 February 1503. The infant lived only a few more days before joining its mother.

Henry retired to his private chambers to mourn for Elizabeth having arranged for Masses to be said for her soul but, as was traditional, he did not attend the burial in Westminster. Instead, Catherine, Lady Courtenay, the queen's sister was chief mourner. Ordinances for the way a royal funeral should be conducted were written in 1494 but it was Lady Margaret Beaufort who decided what all Elizabeth's ladies should be required to wear and took control of the arrangements that followed. Henry VII, prostrate with grief, did consider a new marriage, including with Katherine of Aragon, but remained a widower for the rest of his life.

Chapter 7

Henry VIII – The Education of a Christian Prince

Henry VII lost his wife and the eldest son upon whom so much care was lavished within a year of one another but he had another son, Henry, who was now required to step into his brother's shoes. The king had no intention of risking Henry to the dangerous air at Ludlow or to the tuition of other men. For a time, while he was still Duke of York, the king had contemplated providing Henry with a home at Codnor Castle in Derbyshire. He even agreed to pay Lord Grey's executors £1000 for the castle there as well as other of the baron's estates shortly after Grey's death without legitimate children in 1496.[1] Now though, the king determined that he would teach his 11-year-old son the art of kingship when the time was right; in the meantime Henry would remain in the safety of Eltham. To the prince it must have seemed unlikely that he would ever excel at his studies as much as Arthur who swiftly acquired a reputation for excellence thanks to André's flattering self-publicity and the king's grief for the loss of his treasured first-born son.

Prince Arthur was a distant figure for much of Henry's early life, although they met at Christmas when Arthur joined the rest of the royal family and for important ceremonial events. When the Duke of York became heir to the throne in April 1502, he was already coping with a loss much closer to him than a brother who never shared his nursery. On 23 February, Elizabeth Denton was dismissed as the prince's governess and transferred into the household of Lady Margaret Beaufort. Henry was at an age where his education would be supervised by men. Even so, it was not a household entirely devoid of gentlewomen. Frideswide Puttenham remained. She had rocked the prince's cradle and Margery Gower, who performed the same office for Princess Margaret, was also listed as were Jane Chace, Elizabeth Bailey and Avice Skidmore. The fact that they stayed demonstrates the bonds between Henry and the women who cared for him. In 1509, when Henry ascended the throne, he provided a personal invitation for his former wetnurse, Anne Oxenbridge, who was now Anne Luke, to attend his coronation as well as paying for a new gown for the occasion. He also increased her pension by £20 per year and, on occasion, he sent her gifts, including cheese in December 1519.[2] She was already in receipt of fees accruing to the office of bailiff of the town of Winchelsea which were given to her in 1496 following the death of her husband, Godfrey Oxenbridge.[3]

All that can really be certain of Henry's tuition is that he was educated as a Renaissance prince and likely according to the same model as his elder brother and Plantagenet uncles. Like Arthur, he was provided with companions to learn alongside him and to serve him. Lady Guildford's son, Henry, became the prince's cupbearer with four other esquires of the body. William Thomas, who previously served Prince Arthur as a groom of the privy chamber, and Ralph Pudsey, a groom of the king's privy chamber, joined the prince's household. Sir Henry Marney, part of the Essex gentry and another veteran of Bosworth and Stoke, was placed in charge of the prince's household as its chamberlain. Like so many of the other men and women who cared for Henry VII's children, he held office in the household of Lady Margaret Beaufort prior to his service to the Tudor Crown. Later he would serve as one of the executors of the countess's will.[4] As captain of the Yeoman of the Guard, his focus was on his charge's security. His care of the prince, and advancement in the service of the Tudors, would ensure that Sir Henry was able to build Layer Marney House in Essex, with its eight-storey towers. And it was something of a family affair, as Marney's son, Thomas, and daughter, Grace, were also part of the household at Eltham.[5]

John Skelton, a graduate of rhetoric, or the art of persuasion, from the universities of Oxford, Cambridge and Louvain was another of Lady Margaret Beaufort's protégées. He was made Poet Laureate in about 1488, and appointed as Prince Henry's tutor in about 1500. Skelton, who appears to have taken holy orders in 1498 by which time he was in his thirties,[6] held a parish at the abbey of St Mary of Graces, near to the Tower of London. It is likely that his perceived piety and growing reputation as a translator and poetic orator won him his place in the schoolroom at Eltham. Erasmus described Henry's tutor as the 'light and ornament of British letters', who would 'kindle' the prince's studies.[7] Besides Latin and grammar, Skelton taught Henry history from works such as the *Chronicle of France*. The *Speculum Principis* (*A Mirror of Princes*),[8] written in 1501, gifted by the poet to Henry, argued that wisdom came from study of the past. Virtue, learning and honest counsel went hand in hand. He added that princes should employ men such as himself and when they had finished with their education to reappoint them. It was not so much advice for a student nearing the end of his study as a plea for future patronage. Skelton would later write that he taught the prince to spell as well as 'acquainting him with the Muses nine'[9] but while his advice to Henry contained information about learning and virtue, the advice that the prince should prize his wife was clearly not something that the boy committed to memory.

Skeleton, best known for his satire, would be succeeded as Henry's tutor in 1502 by John Holt, a humanist scholar from Magdalen College, Oxford. Skelton, who may have been briefly imprisoned at about the same time for unknown reasons, withdrew from court, taking with him a gift of 40s from Henry VII, and became the rector of Diss in Norfolk[10] at the instigation of Lady Margaret Beaufort, where he caused considerable scandal when he secretly married and had several children. Skelton developed his poetry during his sojourn in Norfolk and returned to court as the King's Orator in 1512.

The speed with which another tutor was found for Henry when he became heir presumptive suggests that either Skelton's behaviour was too scandalous for him to remain or that the king did not value Skelton in the way that he lionised Bernard André. William Blount, Lord Mountjoy, who continued to mentor Prince Henry but who was also required to fulfil other duties in Calais, may have had a hand in ensuring that André's influence over Henry's education was limited. After all, it was the Augustinian who had prevented Blount's fellow humanist, Linacre, from gaining a position as a tutor in Arthur's household.

Henry's next tutor was John Holt, another of Blount, Thomas More and Erasmus's friends and a fellow humanist who wanted to transform education by stripping it back to the original classical sources for a purer form of language and rhetoric. Humanists believed that a more effective scholarship would lead to a deeper view of Christ and the Church Fathers which in turn would bring about a reform of corruption within the Church. Holt wrote a text for schoolboys, in about 1489, on Latin grammar entitled *Lac Puerorum* (*Milk for Children*) which used pictures and aid memoires, one of which taught a method to help remember the different declensions of nouns and pronouns using the fingers and thumb of one hand. In his foreword to the text Sir Thomas explained that *Milk for Children* was an introduction to prepare pupils, like Henry, for the works of great men. Holt's grounding in the classics lay in his own education at the Cathedral School in Chichester and Oxford where he became a fellow at Magdalen in 1490. Afterwards, Holt entered the service of Cardinal Morton where he taught boys under the cleric's guardianship, providing them with a preparation in Latin and grammar. It was during his time at Lambeth that Holt first met Sir Thomas More, soon after More had been a pupil there himself.[11] Holt's connections with Morton, who was at the heart of Henry VII's government, is the most likely reason that it was he who was appointed as a royal tutor rather than the task being given solely into the hands of William Blount, Lord Mountjoy who is known to have mentored the prince before Holt's appointment and possessed impressive academic credentials of his own, as well as connections to the Woodvilles and to the household of Elizabeth of York. When Holt died unexpectedly[12] he was replaced by William Hone, another Latin scholar from Magdalen who was also Princess Mary's tutor. It has been suggested that Lady Margaret Beaufort, with the advice of John Fisher, found likely candidates from among the scholars at Cambridge as tutors for her grandchildren.[13] Hone continued lessons using the humanist principles of Henry's earlier tutors.

In 1506, Prince Henry sent a letter to Erasmus that was so polished that the Dutchman could not believe that the prince had written it. Only when Henry Parker, Lord Morley, who had grown up in the household of Margaret Beaufort and who was a scholar of some repute confirmed that he had seen the prince's drafts and corrections of letters like the one to Erasmus did the scholar believe that Henry could have written it rather than Hone.[14] Prince Henry was proficient in Latin and French, which he was likely to have been tutored in by Giles D'Ewes, and was able to hold some conversation in Italian.

Like his brother before him, the prince was provided with works deemed to be appropriate for study including *De Officis* by Cicero, in which he inscribed, 'Thys boke is myne.'[15] The book contains notes and summaries in the prince's hand as well as additional remarks made by his first tutor, John Skelton. The prince never did grow out of his childhood habit of writing in books. The *Henry VIII Psalter,*[16] commissioned in about 1540, which depicts him as the biblical David playing his harp, contains a series of handwritten notes in the margins vindicating his break from Rome. He also marked up books written by Erasmus and Martin Luther as well as many other theological texts in his possession, so much so that he has been described as a 'compulsive annotator'.[17] The habit of questioning texts was one Henry learned from a very early age, although what his grandmother would have thought about him writing love notes to Anne Boleyn in the margins of his Book of Hours, albeit in French, in 1528, when he should have been paying attention in church, is best left unexplored.

Music was also an important part of Henry's education. He could play the lute, the virginals and the pipes. The prince was taught how to sing and to compose music. Giles D'Ewes, who was selected to tutor Henry and his sister Mary, remained a constant in the life of the royal family. As well as tutoring French and music he was also appointed keeper of the prince's wardrobe and was later appointed as the king's librarian at Richmond with a salary of £10 per year. An inventory of Henry VIII's belongings made after his death in 1547 showed that his love of music continued throughout his life. He owned a harpsichord, a flute, handheld pipe organs, virginals, cornets, viols and a set of bagpipes.[18]

Like his brother and uncles before him, the daily routine began with Matins and Mass before a morning spent studying. Dinner was served at 10 a.m. and this was followed by an afternoon of martial training, more studying and music lessons. It was not all hard work. Henry VII's accounts show that during the Christmas festivities of 1501–1502, the 9-year-old prince was given £3 6s 8d to play at dice.[19]

Henry VII and Lady Margaret Beaufort trusted the prince's tutors and household staff, including Marney, a strong male role model, to educate Henry but, in 1504 when he was 13 years old, the prince's household changed again. The king decided to absorb Henry's household into his own. Rather than equipping his heir with a council in either Wales or in the north of England to learn how to govern, Henry VII, whose health was deteriorating, decided that his own counsellors, including men like Richard Foxe, Bishop of Winchester, should mentor the prince while he retained oversight of the boy's development as the future king of England. In July 1504, the prince was moved with his household to the royal court at Greenwich, where he enjoyed sports and chivalric pursuits more than his books. These were the skills that turned him from a boy into a medieval monarch honed for war. The king joined his son on horseback for that summer's hunting and hawking and even employed a professional tennis coach.[20] It was an opportunity for the two Henrys to become better acquainted with one another. Like Arthur, the prince could ride almost before he could walk. On 1 January 1494, the king paid 14s for a pony for Henry.[21] As well as hunting and hawking the king ensured that his son learned how to wrestle, to fight with a sword and with a quarterstaff. He was also taught how to fight on foot, in armour, and with an axe by Thomas Simpson. By 1505 Henry, an ardent admirer of chivalric knighthood, was practising in the lists although his father prohibited anything so dangerous as an actual opponent armed with a lance. He was restricted to running rings, or quintain, with his companions. The first involved riding at full speed towards a suspended ring with a lance. The aim was to hook the ring onto the weapon. The quintain was another training tool requiring the competitor to strike a shield or board with his lance. The prince's passion for jousting was a long lasting one. He saw his first tournament as part of the entertainments that followed the ceremony creating him Duke of York when he was just 3 years old at Westminster. The king might have been alarmed that his precious heir was endangering himself needlessly, even if he watched his son in the tiltyard on occasion, but Lady Margaret Beaufort gave her remaining grandson a horse, saddle and harness. It has also been hypothesised that it was Henry's uncle, Arthur Plantagenet, who taught him the art of chivalry. Untroubled by the burdens of state, Edward IV's illegitimate son had more time to spend on the prince's interests in sports, tournaments and deeds of valour than the king. Soon after he became king, Henry VIII ordered a gravel tiltyard to be built at Whitehall so that he could practise and replaced the old one at Greenwich, in 1514, with a yard that was provided with purpose-built viewing towers.[22]

Henry learned to ride and hunt while he was still under his mother's care. The prince, who read *The Mayster of Game* by Edward, 2nd Duke of York, also enjoyed hunting throughout his life. The book, dedicated to another Prince of Wales, was a set of instructions about how to hunt effectively. Henry received his first hawk as a gift from his father when he was 9 years old. In the summer of 1500, his father's accounts included a set of hawk bells costing 8s, paid while Henry stayed at Hatfield to avoid the plague.[23] Hawking was a popular sport for medieval kings and he was taught by Sir William Tyler, who was one of the king's gentlemen of the privy chamber who had been appointed as Captain of Berwick in 1498. Like many of the king's other appointments, Tyler had fled England during the reign of Richard III, joined Henry Tudor in exile and been knighted shortly after Henry's landing at Milford Haven in 1485.[24] Sebastian Giustinian, the Venetian ambassador, writing in 1519, declared that the king tired 'eight or ten horses' whenever he went hunting.[25] During the summer of 1525, Henry almost drowned in Hertfordshire while he was out hawking but was saved by a footman who leapt in the water after him.[26] Prince Henry's love of sports and knightly pursuits became well known once he was king and he could indulge them without limits being imposed upon him.

So great was Henry's passion for playing tennis that he gave orders when he was king, in about 1532, for the Great Close Tennis Court to be built at Hampton Court. Henry VIII shared his father's love of the game[27] and was keen to show off his prowess to visiting dignitaries. In 1519, the Venetian ambassador described the sight of the king playing as 'the prettiest sight in the world'.[28] Until the sixteenth century kings and prince exercised to be ready for war but attitudes changed during Henry VIII's lifetime. Castiglione's *Book of the Courtier* written in 1527 regarded it as one of the social accompaniments of a gentleman.[29]

In 1503 preparations were made for Henry's sister, Margaret, now second in line for the throne, to join her husband, James IV, in Scotland. The king's mother had successfully delayed the wedding celebrations until Margaret was in her fourteenth year, and perhaps more physically prepared for the rigours of married life than her grandmother had been when she was married off to Edmund Tudor as a child. Margaret, titled Queen of Scots, said her farewells and departed from Richmond on 27 June for Lady Margaret Beaufort's home at Collyweston in Northamptonshire accompanied by a household of ladies and servants. The *Great Chronicle of London* recorded that Lady Margaret ensured that their reception there was a joyous one. In the train were three royal mistresses of the nursery: Lady Darcy, Lady Guildford and Elizabeth Denton.

On 23 June 1503, the king agreed to a new marriage treaty with the Spanish. Arthur's widow, Katherine, would marry Prince Henry who was now 11 years old but still too young, the king argued, for a ceremony. She moved to Durham House on the Strand while Henry VII awaited the arrival of the balance of Katherine's 200,000 crown dowry from Spain. In 1505, when it failed to materialise, Prince Henry was required to make a formal protest about the proposed union to Richard Foxe, Bishop of Winchester and to swear that the marriage would never take place. The king also ensured that Henry was unable to communicate with the princess who lived in a poverty-stricken limbo created by her father and father-in-law, although by then both Henry and Katherine were resident at Richmond.

Henry's behaviour was strictly monitored. He lived in chambers adjoining his father's and was not permitted to leave the palace except by a door into the grounds and, even then, he was accompanied by men appointed by the king.[30] The prince was only seen on public occasions with his father and Henry VII commissioned projects in both their names, including the fan vaulted ceiling at St George's Chapel, Windsor Castle.[31] Fuensalida, Ferdinand of Aragon's ambassador, noted that the king was eager for visiting dignitaries to see his son but added that Henry was kept as closely confined as a maiden.[32] There was no opportunity to sound out the Tudor heir or to hear his opinion on the matter of the proposed Anglo-Spanish marriage. The prince answered only to his father. Henry was not to be given a taste of independence either because the king was afraid of losing his remaining heir or because he feared the prince was not sufficiently schooled. It is also possible that Henry VII wished to ensure that the Spanish ambassador did not gain unsupervised access to the Prince of Wales.

During 1508, Henry VII's health failed but he continued with his policy of keeping his son under strict supervision and refusing to allow him to shoulder any of the royal responsibilities that he had been eager that Arthur should learn. On occasion it must have seemed to the king that Fate intended to rob the Tudor dynasty of its remaining prince. During the summer months, four of Prince Henry's servants succumbed to sweating sickness. The disease first appeared in England in 1485, some said with Henry Tudor's army. Symptoms, including cold shivers, headache, breathlessness and dizziness, materialised suddenly and in the final stage, which took place less than twenty-four hours after the disease's onset, the patient fell into a deep sleep before dying. The king's obsession with the health of his remaining son perhaps added to Prince Henry's own personal interest in medicine.

When he assumed the throne, King Henry VIII appointed Thomas Linacre as his royal physician. More and Erasmus lauded Linacre's abilities as a humanist scholar and he was noted for a translation of Galen's theory about the four humours. Henry's friend, Sir Thomas More, had his own interests in medicine as evidenced in his description of Utopia's public health system. It made sense for a Renaissance prince to be interested in medicine and to modernise his kingdom to reflect the learning of its monarch. As king, not only was he able to demonstrate his own learning but in supporting innovative ideas of Tudor physicians and imposing a legal structure upon the practice of medicine in Tudor England he was reinforcing his own wisdom.

It was Thomas Linacre, who initially aspired to being Arthur's tutor, who persuaded the king to found the College of Physicians in 1518 to help regulate medical practice. In 1540, Henry's court painter, Hans Holbein, depicted the king head and shoulders above the Company of Barbers and Surgeons, all commoners, who shared the same space as him only because of royal interest in their work. Medicine was an area of importance that never diminished for Henry VIII. As a young man he began a collection of medical texts and medicinal plants and with the passage of years, hypochondria aside, the king suffered from many complains that needed continued care, from recurring migraine headaches (probably caused when his friend Charles Brandon struck his head above the eye during a jousting contest in 1524), a painful leg ulcer and various other complaints. *Henry VIII's Book of Medicines*,[33] contains nearly 200 recipes, many concocted by Henry himself. Inevitably, the passage of time meant he became more preoccupied with his health and the cure of his ailments rather than as a demonstration of his superior learning.

King Henry VII died on 21 April 1509. His passing was witnessed by only a handful of trusted men. He had been monarch for nearly twenty-four years and his mother, Lady Margaret Beaufort, was at hand to ensure that her grandson, Henry, now a strapping 17-year-old, would inherit her beloved son's throne without any difficulties. For the next two days, the Countess of Richmond controlled her grief as the Royal Council went through the charade of normal government and court protocol as though Henry VII was struggling to draw breath in his private apartments. On St George's day, England learned it had a new king. By then Henry VII's hated tax collectors, Sir Richard Empson and Edmund Dudley, were behind bars. It signalled the beginning of a new era.

When Henry became king in 1509, he was praised for his ability as a linguist and a musician as well as for his knowledge of the humanities. He was also described as being a talented mathematician. Lord Mountjoy wrote to Erasmus, encouraging the Dutch scholar to come to England. He claimed some understanding of the new monarch's education and attitude to learning but there is little in the way of detail. The letter states that the king's heart was 'set not upon gold or jewels or mines of ore, but upon virtue, reputation, and eternal renown' and that the 18-year-old longed to be a better scholar.[34] Thomas More wrote that Henry 'has more learning than any English monarch possessed before him'.[35] In 1511 Edward Hall, the Tudor chronicler, stated that Henry shone 'in shooting, singing, dancing, wrestling, casting of the bar, playing at the recorders, flute, virginals, and in the setting of songs, making of ballads, and did set two Godly Masses'.[36]

Henry VIII's interests were both many and varied throughout his life, as reflected in his collection of books, many of them stemming from his formative education including astronomy and philosophy. He also took an interest in map making and owned many maps and map making tools. He was introduced to Nicholas Kratzer by Sir Thomas More when he stayed in England, in 1516, and tutored More's children. Henry VIII appointed him as the court's own astronomer and watchmaker. For the king, learning was a lifelong passion, for which he spared no expense, and he appointed tutors as he required them.

It is thought that John Robins, the mathematician and astrologer, taught the king about both subjects following his appointment as one of Henry's chaplains. Robins was born in about 1500 and went to Oxford where he was elected a fellow of All Souls' College in 1520. He was made a canon of Christ Church and of Windsor in 1543. He continued to hold his offices during the reign of Henry's daughter, Mary, and was buried in St George's Chapel following his death in 1558. He wrote several treatises, including *De Portentosisis Cometia* and *Accidentibus futuria* both dedicated to the king, on the subject of astronomy and was regarded as 'the ablest person of his time'.[37] Henry invested in state-of-the-art technology to continue his interests as well as appointing men he wished to patronise. The British Museum holds an astrolabe dated 1545, while the astronomical clock at Hampton Court, depicting the month, phase of the moon, day and hour, was commissioned by the king in 1540.

Throughout his reign, Henry was a collector and a patron of the arts which filled the 60 or so residences that he called home. Like his father before him, he used art and literature to create an image of how he wanted to be viewed by the rest of the world. From Guido Mazzoni who created the terracotta sculpture of a boy believed to be the young Henry, to Hans Holbein's rendering of King Henry VIII and his family, the Tudors were determined to make use of Europe's most sophisticated sculptures, paintings and even tapestries to create a story that placed them at the heart of their realm. Like his father before him, Henry VIII understood that patronage helped to shape the way that the world perceived the Tudors. Whereas Henry VII used it to legitimise his rule, Henry VIII used it to demonstrate that he was one of Europe's most cultured kings, not to mention one of the wealthiest.[38] Henry's answer to Francis I's employment of Leonardo de Vinci was to go one better by appointing Hans Holbein, known for his realistic portraits, in 1526 as his own court painter as well as men like the Spanish swordsmith, Diego de Çaias, who left France to come and work for Henry. The king's use of culture from the start of his reign until its end made a statement about his level of refinement. The lesson was one that Henry Tudor learned while he was in exile and observed the way in which the French and Bretton courts operated.

In short, at the start of his reign King Henry VIII's education turned him into an almost ideal Renaissance man, gifted with intelligence as well as a being superb physical specimen standing at 6 ft. 1 in. tall, when the average was 5ft. 6 ins., and an all-round sportsman as well as a collector of magnificent artworks that rivalled his peers across the Channel.

Chapter 8

Mary Tudor and Henry FitzRoy

Henry VIII married his brother's widow Katherine of Aragon, the daughter of Ferdinand of Aragon and Isabella of Castile, on 11 June 1509 in a quiet ceremony at Greenwich because he wanted his bride to be crowned alongside him at a joint coronation. Pope Julius II granted a dispensation for the wedding in 1503 so there was no need for further delay.

Lady Margaret Beaufort acted as the new king's unofficial regent until he came of age with his eighteenth birthday. She managed the first peaceful change of monarch in thirty years; she also helped to arrange Henry VII's funeral and the double coronation of Henry VIII and Katherine of Aragon. It was said that Henry's formidable grandmother cried on the day of his coronation on 24 June 1509, whether from relief that a second generation of Tudor monarchs sat upon the throne or through some foresight of what was to come, is another matter entirely. Her grandson was the fifth king who had sat on the throne during her lifetime and the coronation, which she viewed in private, was the third she had witnessed. When she became ill during the festivities at Westminster that followed the crowning ceremony she was moved to the abbot's house where she remained for the next week until she died on 29 June 1509. It was the day after Henry VIII celebrated his eighteenth birthday and was officially of age to rule in his own right. Her job was done. With typical attention to detail, Margaret had commissioned Renaissance sculptor, Pietro Torrigiano, to build her tomb in 1506. Her effigy rests with its feet on the Beaufort yale surrounded by heraldic symbols of the Tudor kings of England and of her husbands in the south aisle of King Henry VII's chapel.

In January 1510, seven months after the 18-year-old king married his 23-year-old bride, the queen gave birth to a premature stillborn daughter. In 1511, on New Year's Day, Katherine was at Richmond when she presented her husband with a son. The boy was named Henry, immediately created Prince of Wales, and London celebrated with bonfires and free wine when the news was proclaimed. The prince was baptised in the same solid silver font as his father according to the established protocol of the *Royal Book*. God, it seemed, was smiling upon the handsome young king who was not ungrateful for divine confirmation of his right to wear the crown. He went on pilgrimage to Walsingham in Norfolk to give thanks for the arrival of an heir so soon after his own accession before returning to hold a celebratory tournament. But seven weeks after the birth, on 22 February 1511, the court was plunged into mourning when the baby unexpectedly died. The next few years repeated a similar tragic pattern with Katherine becoming pregnant, retiring to her birthing chamber and delivering a stillborn child or an infant who did not survive beyond the first few weeks of its life.

In 1514 Henry's younger sister, Mary, left the secluded world of Eltham and life at her brother's court behind her to become a royal bride. The king and his chief minister, Cardinal Thomas Wolsey, had secured a treaty with France. The final clause specified that Mary, sometimes described as the most beautiful princess in Europe, would marry King Louis XII. She was 18 years old when she finally crossed the Channel to wed her 52-year-old syphilis-riddled spouse. Among the eighty men and women who accompanied her was Joan Vaux, Mary's former lady mistress. Jane Popincourt, who taught the princess French until John Palsgrave took over the role in 1512,[1] should also have been part of the retinue but she was absent. Jane was the mistress of Charles d'Orleans, Duc de Longueville who was captured by Henry at Tournai in 1513. The duke's ransom was paid and he would return to France with Mary having acted as his cousin's proxy at her wedding. Unfortunately for Jane, when Louis XII was presented with a list of women who would accompany his new wife, he struck her name from the list claiming that she was an immoral woman.[2] It may have been at around this time, when Jane left Mary's retinue and became part of Katherine of Aragon's household, that she briefly became Henry's mistress.

Joan Vaux, Lady Guildford, who was part of Margaret Beaufort's household until the countess's death, scarcely fared any better when Louis insisted that she return to England. The new queen of France, who was distressed by Mother Guildford's removal, wrote letters to her brother[3] and to Wolsey protesting that her old governess was essential to her wellbeing.[4] Joan had been persuaded out of retirement to accompany Mary to France; she spoke French and was an experienced older woman who could smooth the queen's path through her new life. Wolsey responded with a letter of his own to Louis stating that Joan was 'a wise, honourable and discreet lady',[5] but it did no good, probably because the king thought that Mother Guildford was trying to restrict his access to Mary when he wished to 'be merry'[6] with his bride. He agreed only that his wife's younger, less experienced women might remain. Joan was sent home despite Mary's protests where Henry VIII granted her a pension of £20 per year. In 1515 he added £40 per year to her annuity.[7]

Mary was left to fend off the unwanted advances of the French king for herself but Louis died after only three months of marriage, exhausted, it was rumoured, by his exertions in the bedchamber. His young widow, clad in white mourning attire, was shut away for forty days, as tradition demanded, to establish whether she was pregnant or not. Believing that her brother had agreed that she might take who she wished as a second husband, Mary, who had no wish to be a pawn on a diplomatic marriage board, quickly wedded Henry's handsome friend, Charles Brandon, who had been sent to fetch her, and as much of the princess's jewels and plate as possible, back to England. One of the witnesses to the union was King Francis, who was the husband of Louis' daughter, Claude. Mary, who might not have enjoyed the classical education of her brother, knew how to get what she wanted and she decided that Brandon, a man with a complicated marriage history and who she had known since childhood, was going to become her second husband whether or not she really had Henry's permission to marry. The couple would go on to have four children together. A son, named Henry after the king, was born the year after she and Brandon married and another son, also named Henry, was born in 1523. Both boys died while they were still young but Mary's daughters — Frances born 1517, and Eleanor, born 1519 — would both survive to adulthood and have their own part to play in the Tudor story.

On 18 February 1516 Katherine of Aragon gave birth to a daughter named Mary at Eltham. Unlike her four older siblings, the princess thrived. After so much disappointment, the king did not give orders for any tournaments, feasts or celebrations, and besides which, the baby was a girl. When the Venetian ambassador congratulated Henry on the safe arrival of the infant, the king responded that while 'it was a daughter this time, by the Grace of God the sons will follow'.[8]

Mary was baptised at Greenwich two days after her birth. It was usual for a girl to have one godfather and two godmothers. Cardinal Wolsey fulfilled the former role while her great aunt, Catherine, Lady Courtenay and the Duchess of Norfolk were selected for the latter. At Mary's confirmation, or 'bishopping' as it was then known, which followed immediately after the baptism her kinswoman, the queen's friend Margaret Pole, the daughter of Edward IV's brother, George Duke of Clarence, became the third of Mary's godmothers.

Katherine, after so much loss, was eager to care for her daughter herself but Henry insisted that his daughter's education should follow royal customary procedures and besides which, if sons were to follow the arrival of their sister, the queen would have to remain by the king's side as he travelled from residence to residence. The only compromise was that the princess would not be sent to Eltham, she would remain close to her parents so that Katherine, and Henry, could visit their daughter whenever they wished. She and her household, including her wetnurse, Catherine Pole,[9] the daughter of Sir Giles Brydges of Coberley, accompanied her parents on their travels. In 1520 Mary is known to have spent time at Richmond and at Greenwich. If the residence was too small to accommodate the queen and her daughter, the princess would be housed nearby with her staff. Katherine would remain close to Mary until 1525, making her an influential figure in her daughter's early life.

The princess had her own nursery and staff. As well as Catherine Pole, whose husband was one of the king's gentleman ushers, there was another nurse to care for her everyday needs, four rockers and a governess to oversee the whole. Henry appointed Elizabeth Denton, his own former lady governess, even though Mary's household was initially quartered in the queen's apartments. As she grew the princess was allocated two rooms, one where she lived and slept and a second, outer chamber where guests might be received. Like the other Tudor infants, she slept in an ordinary wooden cradle but was also provided with a magnificent state cradle so that visiting dignitaries could admire the new addition to the dynasty.

Elizabeth Denton, whose death the king anticipated because of her increasing infirmity,[10] was soon replaced by one of Katherine's ladies, Lady Margaret Bryan.[11] The Yorkshire woman, from Beningbrough, became the focus of consistency in the early lives of all of Henry VIII's recognised offspring. At the same time that she was appointed to the task in 1518, the king created her a baroness in her own right, perhaps to counter the influence of Elizabeth Denton or even Mary's own mother. Margaret was the mother of Henry's friend Sir Francis Bryan, known to the monarch and later Thomas Cromwell, as the Vicar of Hell because of his rakish ways.

More respectably, Lady Bryan was the sister of John, 2nd Baron Berners who was a respected translator of histories including *Froissart's Chronicles*. She ensured that Mary and the rest of Henry's children were schooled in their prayers, manners and literacy skills from infancy onwards. She was assisted in her task by Mary's chaplain, Henry Rowle.[12]

In 1518 the queen, then aged 32 years, became pregnant for the final time. By June, Giustinian was able to write to the Doge that the pregnancy was 'most earnestly desired by the whole kingdom'.[13] A plan took shape to marry 2-year-old Mary to Francis I's eldest son, born in April 1518. The betrothal cemented an Anglo-French alliance agreed in October. The agreement stipulated that in the event of Henry having no sons, that Mary and her husband would live in England. Katherine gave birth to a daughter who lived only a few days. The Venetian ambassador wrote, in November, that the nation feared Mary's union with France lest they should find themselves in foreign hands 'through marriage'.[14] For Mary it became essential to learn to speak French. John Palsgrave, who had taught Henry's sister, held benefices in Suffolk and Leicestershire at the time but Giles D'Ewes, who was the librarian at Richmond, and received various grants and licenses for the importation of wine during Mary's early years, was formally appointed her tutor in 1527.

By 1518 Elizabeth Blount, better known as Bessie, was Henry's mistress. William Blount, Lord Mountjoy, the king's childhood mentor and Latin coach was Katherine of Aragon's chamberlain and Bessie, who was one of his cousins, was given a place as one of the queen's ladies. While Katherine struggled to come to terms with the loss of yet another child, her failure to fulfil her duty to provide the Tudors with a male heir, and her husband's disappointment, Bessie blossomed. In June 1519, she gave birth to a son at a house belonging to Henry, at Blackmore near Chelmsford. Delighted, the king named the boy Henry FitzRoy. The boy was proof, if proof was needed, that it was the queen's fault not his own that the kingdom lacked a male heir. King Henry, who like his subjects was both devout and superstitious, interpreted his lack of legitimate sons as a sign of divine displeasure. He began to fear that his marriage to Katherine was cursed because he was married, contrary to God's law, to Arthur's widow. Bessie, meanwhile, was swiftly married off to Gilbert Tailboys of Kyme in Lincolnshire. FitzRoy, Henry's first acknowledged surviving son, became the Duke of Richmond and Somerset and Earl of Nottingham. Only Mary had pre-eminence over the boy. Even so, the arrival of FitzRoy set the king thinking that illegitimacy need not be a reason for a son to be denied the crown. It was almost impossible for Henry to imagine a female sitting upon England's throne. The last active female claimant to the throne, Empress Matilda, caused a protracted civil war between her supporters and those of her cousin, King Stephen, during the twelfth century remembered as the Anarchy. While there was no law prohibiting a woman from sitting upon the throne, no one supported the claims of either Elizabeth of York or Lady Margaret Beaufort, and both were passed over in favour of Henry Tudor even though many people regarded Henry VIII's mother as the true heiress to the throne. Traditionally a woman might transmit a claim to the crown but not rule. One of the reasons for the delay in Elizabeth of York's coronation was so that no one could mistake her and Henry VII for joint sovereigns.

During FitzRoy's infancy, Lady Bryan, Princess Mary's governess, was sent to care for him while Henry's own kinswoman, Margaret Pole, Countess of Salisbury became Mary's governess. She was a friend of the queen's as well as one of Mary's godmothers. Descended from the Plantagenet kings of England and Richard Neville, Earl of Warwick, Margaret understood etiquette, courtly behaviour and court life, as well as its perils, better than most. Margaret followed a model of education for Mary laid down by Sir Thomas More for his own daughters. In addition to a humanist education and learning the behaviour of a pious Catholic, Mary began to learn to play the virginals, the clavichord and the spinet. By 1520 she was able to play for a party of French diplomats. It is also plausible that, during her early years, Thomas Linacre, the classicist who was now more than 60 years old, had a hand in Mary's education when he sent her the *Rudiments of the Latin Language*, dedicated to the princess, which paved the way to a thorough grounding in the language.

Despite the Treaty of London made in 1518 which arranged Mary's marriage to the dauphin of France, 1520 saw negotiations open between Katherine of Aragon's nephew, Charles V of Spain, and the English to form an alliance against the French. Among the discussions was the idea that Mary, now 4 years old, should marry Charles. It was a proposal that Katherine of Aragon approved. The betrothal was confirmed in 1522. It was increasingly apparent that her dowry would one day include her father's kingdom and Mary's potential as a bride was a valuable diplomatic tool for Henry and his ministers. Even so, it was essential that the English princess, young as she was, demonstrated her aptitude for learning, music and dancing for the ambassadors who came to inspect her during the various marriage negotiations of which she was part.

The first sign that the French might have had in 1520 that the proposed union between England and France was destined to failure was when Mary did not accompany her parents to France for the Field of the Cloth of Gold. During their absence the king was kept informed of his daughter's progress at Richmond. Mary, the Lords of the Council, said 'Is right merry and in prosperous health and state, daily exercising herself in virtuous pasttimes and occupations'.[15]

In 1521 the smooth running of Mary's household was unexpectedly disrupted when Margaret Pole was dismissed from her office as Mary's governess. The difficulty lay in the countess's Yorkist ancestry; her father was George, Duke of Clarence and, more importantly, so far as the king was concerned, Margaret's daughter Ursula was married to Edward Stafford, 3rd Duke of Buckingham, who was executed for treason on 17 May. In addition to listening to prophecies which predicted the death of the king, the duke proclaimed that the death of Henry and Katherine of Aragon's son, Henry, in 1511 was divine retribution for the judicial murder of Margaret's brother, Edward 17th Earl of Warwick in 1499. The boy was the last direct male descendent of King Edward III and his claim to the throne, and by implication the Countess of Salisbury's, was stronger than that of the Tudors. His death was made an essential requirement by the Spanish who refused to allow Katherine to travel to England to marry Henry's brother, Arthur, until the threat he presented was removed. Margaret Pole's exclusion from Mary's household signalled the king's growing suspicion of families with a Yorkist heritage who might present an alternative to Tudor rule while he was without a legitimate male heir.

After Margaret Pole's removal, Mary was sent to Windsor where she remained until a new governess could be found for her. Elizabeth Trussell, the dowager Countess of Oxford, declined the office giving ill health as a reason for her refusal. Instead, Cardinal Wolsey, acting on the king's instruction, appointed Lady Calthorpe and her husband Sir Philip, who became Mary's chamberlain on an annual salary of £40. Jane, Lady Calthorpe assumed the role on 24 July 1521.[16] Jane, or Amata, a sister of Thomas Boleyn, married Sir Philip in 1518. The couple had a daughter, Elizabeth, who may have accompanied them even though there is no extant record of Mary having companions or being educated alongside other children. Although accounts show that her cousin, Frances Brandon, spent time in the princess's company.

Mary left Windsor Castle with her new guardians and went to Ditton Park in Berkshire where she celebrated Christmas without her parents. This was an important element of transitioning away from childhood for royal children. The king sent Mary a gift but Katherine, who missed her daughter, took an opportunity to leave court to spend a few hours with her. The queen's attention remained focused on her only surviving child while her husband became more distant from both their lives. Katherine determined that Mary would have the kind of education that she and her sisters enjoyed as infantas of Spain. Katherine is recorded as having started to read and write at 6 years old. The following year she began to learn Latin from Beatriz Galindo.[17] Katherine's mother, Isabella of Castile, whose own education was limited, valued learning and as well as collecting an extensive library, taught herself Latin as an adult in order to rule more effectively. She employed Italian brothers, Alessandro and Antonio Geraldini, to oversee her daughters' education and they added French to the curriculum. The end result was that Erasmus credited Mary's mother with being one of the best educated women in Europe as well as one of the most pious. Now, she had every intention of ensuring that Mary was similarly equipped. However, she must have hoped to avoid the practical lessons in warfare provided to Isabella's daughters when they accompanied their mother and her army on campaign in Granada against the Moors.

Sir Thomas More, who provided a model of how daughters might be educated, recommended the humanist scholar Juan Luis Vives, from Valencia in Spain, as a potential tutor for Mary. More first met Vives, who was another associate of Erasmus, in 1521 in Bruges and was impressed by his knowledge. At More's instigation, Katherine commissioned Vives to write a book, in Latin, about the education of women entitled *The Education of a Christian Woman*. The book, which was a bestseller of its time, was dedicated to Katherine and divided a woman's life into three parts: maiden, married woman and widow. The scholar, who did not believe in female independence let alone sovereignty, wanted the queen's patronage to promote his own views about society, and women in particular. Katherine arranged for Wolsey to interview him for the post as Mary's tutor but rather than appointing him to the role, offered him a position at Oxford University instead.

In 1523, Vives sent the queen a syllabus for the princess, dedicated to her, focusing on Latin tuition but he observed women should not be prepared in the art of rhetoric as they had no need to make speeches, given that it was not they but their husbands who governed. It was widely accepted that women, the descendants of Eve, were weaker and more sinful than their male counterparts. Taking the Bible as its moral source, the theory of natural order gave men authority over women. Vives suggested instead that Mary's Latin should begin with domestic paraphernalia, clothes and musical instruments and progress from there to useful conversational Latin of the kind that might be useful with a husband who spoke a different language — in much the same way that Katherine and Arthur had conversed when they first met one another. Even so, by the time the princess was 9 years old, the queen was teaching her Latin, French and Spanish. Mary was also able to understand Italian. By the time she was 11 years old, in 1527, she could write to Francis I, in French, and was much praised for her translation from Latin into English of a prayer by St Thomas Aquinas which also reflected the importance of religion to her education.[18] The prayer's topic was about the ordering of a pious life. It was both traditional and popular but was a basic work rather than a work of literature in its own right.

Vives was less concerned by Mary's grasp of language and more anxious that an appropriate Christian education for a girl, even a princess, focused on establishing a proper religious and moral character. It was inconceivable to him that a woman would not marry. If Mary should become queen, then it would be her spouse who ruled on her behalf. Vives and Erasmus shared in common the idea that an excellent education weeded out bad characteristics from a child, and in the case of a girl, turned them into a good Christian. Vives placed an emphasis on modest behaviour and instructed that Mary's guardians should maintain a careful watch for moral laxity. The belief that women were more naturally sinful than their male counterparts stemmed from Eve's consumption of the apple in the Garden of Eden and humanity's subsequent fall from grace. Girls, put quite simply, were more vulnerable to temptation than boys. The reading matter he recommended was directed towards virtue. Romances were to be discouraged as were any texts containing an excess of violence.[19] He did not approve of the tales of King Arthur or the poems of Ovid which he believed to be morally destructive. Even Virgil's *Aeneid* was deemed improper reading material for a princess because of its focus on war. Instead, Vives offered Katherine a selection of serious Christian alternatives to share with Mary. Sidonius, for example, was a fifth-century bishop. He also thought that Plato and Cicero were acceptable, even though they were pre-Christian. And, if the princess had to read history, she could 'with no great trouble, learn history from Justinus, Florus, and Valerius Maximus'.[20]

He also recommended that Mary should read the New Testament and reflect upon the applicable passages from scripture after attending Mass. He suggested that the Old Testament should be confined to carefully chosen passages because the content of the whole was not for female eyes. He added the recommendation that when the queen was in doubt about the suitability of any text, a responsible male should be consulted. He most certainly did not think that Mary or the queen should use their own initiative when it came to selecting reading matter, rather he endorsed the idea of careful regulation. Mary's chaplain, Richard Featherstone, was the man he most likely had in mind, as it was his task to provide the practicalities of Mary's tuition. Vives' only concessions to the princess's status as the king's heir was to suggest that she read Sir Thomas More's *Utopia* and Erasmus's *Education of a Christian Prince*.

The strategy for learning required Mary to read a passage and memorise it. The princess should use phrases from the texts she learned to practise her conversational Latin. Vives advised that it would be useful to keep a glossary of words and phrases that might come in useful. The scholar thought that Erasmus's *Colloquies* was a readymade book of this type since it contained proverbs and elegant phrasing as well as an emphasis on piety.

Vives also stressed the importance of traditional aristocratic feminine occupations for Mary including music and embroidery. He noted that as a girl, she should keep her hands busy with domestic tasks, including cooking, even if she was a princess. Idleness, he concluded, led to vice or, even worse, to chatter without any real direction. He noted that Katherine, and all of Queen Isabella's daughters, learned spinning, sewing, and needlepoint. It was the queen's duty to educate Mary to become a conventionally virtuous wife and mother rather than a monarch. Katherine's own religious commitment and charitable acts provided a model for Mary to follow.

While Katherine was attending to the words of Vives and ensuring that Mary had the kind of education required by a sovereign, the king found time in August 1522 to send his daughter the gift of a goshawk. Hunting was as much part of a noblewoman's education as it was for a man. The princess's instruction included falconry and horse riding, just as it did for all aristocratic children. In the same month as she received the hawk, George Neville, 3rd Baron Bergavenny, sent her a horse.[21] Having just been released from prison on suspicion of treason, it appears that Neville's gift was an attempt to buy his way back into the king's favour. Mary's musical education and dancing lessons also continued. Both Katherine and Henry shared a passion for music and dancing that Vives is unlikely to have approved. The princess learned the lute and the regal, a portable pipe organ with a single set of reed pipes, as well as other keyboard instruments.[22]

Meanwhile, Mary's half-brother, Henry FitzRoy, was educated under the directorship of their shared godfather, Cardinal Wolsey. He and the king selected humanist tutors for the boy with a plan of study following a curriculum suggested by the king's friend, Sir Thomas More, and the cleric Stephen Gardiner. The latter was a student of Erasmus as well as being a classics graduate from Cambridge before becoming one of Cardinal Wolsey's secretaries. In May 1525, the king gifted his son with a royal coat of arms and, on 18 June, the boy was created the Earl of Nottingham, Duke of Richmond and Duke of Somerset with pre-eminence over all the other dukes, except for any legitimate sons that the king might sire. He was also provided with a household of his own, headed by his nurse, Agnes Partridge, at Durham House on the Strand.

During the August of his seventh year, FitzRoy was sent north to Sheriff Hutton having been made keeper of the city and castle of Carlisle and Lord Lieutenant of Ireland and Warden of the Cinque Ports. He was given charge, in theory at least, of administering lands worth £4000 per year and the Council of the North which governed England's borders with Scotland. John Palsgrave, who had been Henry's sister Mary's French tutor, and who was regarded as one of the foremost proponents of humanism alongside Thomas More, accompanied FitzRoy to provide him with a classical education of the kind his father and uncle enjoyed. He was thwarted in his attempts due to the way that some members of FitzRoy's household threw obstacles in his path and encouraged Henry's son to rebel against Palsgrave's lessons in favour of outdoor activities, including hunting and knightly pursuits. He complained to both Wolsey[23] and to Thomas More about both his lack of funds and the way FitzRoy's household treated him.[24]

By June 1526 Palsgrave was recalled to London and Richard Croke, another classical scholar, was sent in his place to teach the boy Latin and Greek. He proved no more successful than Palsgrave. It did not help that FitzRoy was more interested in hunting and jousting than the fine italic hand he was taught to write or Latin and Greek. As an incentive, the king announced that as soon as Richmond could translate Caesar's *Commentaries*, that he would buy the boy his first suit of armour.[25] Croke's surviving letters, sent to Wolsey, provide an insight to FitzRoy's schoolroom and the companions taught alongside him. They were supposed to provide him with role models of excellence and to be used as examples for punishment when they failed to attain their goals. The 8-year-old did not learn the lessons his companions were there to provide, instead FitzRoy's household, George Cotton and Sir William Parr were identified in particular, conspired to undermine Croke's authority. Parr roused Croke's wrath when he told FitzRoy that he no longer needed to repeat his lessons back to his teacher after his supper or to attend to him in other matters.[26]

The queen was furious with Henry's determination to promote FitzRoy. By 1525, Katherine knew she would have no more children besides Mary and that the king's son was being gifted with titles and roles that were within the rights of a legitimate heir. Two years later, Mendoza reported the rumour that the king wished to make his son the King of Ireland.[27] Henry's decision to ennoble FitzRoy and provide him with estates to support his new status was akin to announcing that Henry intended to make the boy his heir. The Venetian ambassador, Ohio, wrote that the king blamed three of Katherine's women for her behaviour following the ennoblement of FitzRoy and arranged for them to be dismissed.[28]

However, the queen's anger did have an unexpected outcome. Cardinal Wolsey was charged by the king with arranging for Mary and her household to travel to Wales.[29] Mary, now 9 years old, was sent to Ludlow with her own household headed by Lady Margaret Pole who was back in favour once more. It was a symbolic location and suggested that the princess, rather than Richmond, was Henry's heir apparent. She was accompanied there by John Veysey (sometimes Voysey), Bishop of Exeter, who was Lord President of the princess's council in Wales. Veysey has been described as the princess's tutor but this was a later confusion. It is unclear exactly how much Mary was expected to learn about the day-to-day running of the council as she did not attend their meetings as her uncle Arthur had done. Her chief gentlewoman was Lady Katherine Cradock, previously Katherine Gordon, the wife of a Glamorganshire knight who had once been married to Perkin Warbeck.[30]

Also among Mary's household was her former nurse, Alice Baker, and the Calthorpes.

The king laid out a set of detailed instructions for Margaret Pole to follow at Ludlow. Mary was to learn Latin, play musical instruments and to dance. Giles D'Ewes accompanied the household to ensure that Mary continued to learn French. Unlike her half-brother, princess Mary was not taught to write in the new italic style and, while Croke was a noted Greek scholar, Mary had to make do with her chaplain, Richard Featherstone, who had no experience as a schoolmaster, no background in Greek nor links with Erasmus or Thomas More. He was an archdeacon at St David's in Brecknock, South Wales and like Mary's mother a staunch Catholic. Piety remained at the heart of Mary's curriculum. Particular attention was be given to 'training' the princess in 'all virtuous demeanour. That is to say, at due times to serve God'.[31] Mary's physical recreation should take the form of moderate exercise, walks and dancing.

In April 1527 French envoys arrived at Ludlow to meet Henry VIII's daughter. They were in England to sign a treaty between England and France that would be cemented by another betrothal. Mary would marry Henry Duc d'Orleans who was three years younger than her. Diplomatic channels filled with speculation whether or not Mary would marry her Spanish or her French suitor.[32] The princess who was betrothed many times during her childhood had met Charles V in 1522 when she was 6 years old. On that occasion she had danced for her cousin and played the spinet. Now, she met with the French and fulfilled her father's desire that she should once again impress the French. The Viscount de Turenne reported that the 11-year-old spoke French, Latin and Italian and that she had danced and played for him. He added that she was very intelligent and would grow into a beautiful woman.[33] Mary's education, it seemed, was paying off. She was an asset to her father's foreign negotiations as a potential wife.

By 1527 Henry VIII was in love with Anne Boleyn. Katherine was seven years older than the king and had become steadily stouter with each pregnancy. It was increasingly obvious that she would never have any more children. The Tudor dynasty remained invested in a solitary auburn-haired princess. Henry had already persuaded himself that the queen was not his lawful wife and Anne promised him a son, if he discarded Mary's mother and married her instead. Katherine was officially informed of her husband's decision on 22 June 1527. Mary, in Ludlow, remained, officially at least, in ignorance of the situation. In time, when she discovered what her father intended, Mary, her own status in doubt, was obdurate in her opposition to the divorce.

In November 1528, Mary returned from Wales but she was not permitted to re-join the queen's household. Instead, she continued to live separately under the supervision of Margaret Pole. Katherine of Aragon remained determined to argue her case against the annulment of her marriage with Henry. She tried to enlist Vives to represent her at the papal court which would decide the matter. The scholar excused himself from the role but when the king discovered Vives' potential involvement, he had him detained in the Tower for six weeks before exiling him from England. It meant that the queen lost someone upon whom she had come to rely.

Mary was not the only Tudor whose legitimacy was being challenged. Margaret Douglas, the daughter of Henry's sister, Margaret and her second husband Archibald Douglas, Earl of Angus, faced even more uncertainty than Mary. Until she reached the age of 10 or thereabouts, Margaret Douglas had remained in her mother's care with Scottish as her first language. The exact nature of her education is uncertain but as an adult she wrote poetry and an abundance of her written correspondence is preserved. In 1527, her parents' marriage was annulled by the Pope but Margaret remained legitimate because of a clause in the document. In Scotland this factor was often ignored and Margaret was described as base born. Katherine of Aragon, who had her own matrimonial worries, wrote to her sister-in-law, chiding her for not thinking of her daughter's status. The year after the divorce, the Earl of Angus effectively kidnapped his daughter from Margaret Tudor. He took her to Tantallon Castle and placed her in the care of Isabel Hoppar, the daughter of an Edinburgh Merchant, who was both lady-in-waiting to the girl and governess. James V declared Angus a traitor and demanded the return of his half-sister to their mother. By then Margaret was 13 years old and part of the squabble between Angus and his former wife was about whether their daughter should marry Patrick Hepburn, Earl of Bothwell or James Stewart, the younger brother of Margaret Tudor's third husband, Henry. Angus moved his daughter and her governess to Coldingham and from there to Norham on the English side of the border where he knew she would be safe in the hands of her royal uncle. She was third in line to the throne, having been born in England rather than Scotland, after her cousin Mary and her mother Margaret. In 1529, while Margaret remained in the care of Sir Thomas Strangeways, comptroller of Berwick Castle, her father hurried south to seek the support of his former brother-in-law, King Henry.

The king had his own problems. He was pre-occupied by the so-called Great Matter — divorce from Katherine and marriage to Anne Boleyn. Mary was 13 years old when a public trial, presided over by the papal legate Cardinal Campeggio at Blackfriars, was held to decide the case of her parents' marriage. Whether or not her return from Ludlow that year was initially supposed to be a temporary one is unclear. Mary's life as the beloved daughter of Henry VIII was about to change. She remained Henry's heir but he could not envisage a woman sitting upon England's throne and besides which, if he divorced Katherine, with no special clause saying otherwise, Mary would be rendered as illegitimate as her half-brother, FitzRoy.

Failure to resolve the King's Great Matter and the revocation of Katherine's appeal for justice to Rome saw the ruin of Mary's godfather, Cardinal Wolsey, whose success had arisen from providing the king with what he wanted. It meant that Henry FitzRoy lost the man who had supervised his education from afar. More practically, Croke retired as FitzRoy's tutor in 1528 having had little success in installing a love of the classics in the king's son who much preferred hunting to reading. From 1530 onward, FitzRoy was mentored by Henry Howard, Earl of Surrey, returning to the more medieval model of the knightly educator. It was intended that Howard, who was only a couple of years older than FitzRoy and who had received a classical education from the best tutors available, would act as a companion and friend to the king's son, rather than as a teacher. The express intention was that he would encourage FitzRoy to emulate the model he provided.[34] It helped that Surrey excelled at riding, hunting, jousting and tennis. The pair of them spent many hours in the tiltyard at Windsor practising their skills in the same way that the king had once done, either running their lances at rings or at the quintain. Later, the earl would recall, in a poem written during 1542, how both he and FitzRoy bonded over their desire to impress the bevies of court beauties and compared notes over their conquests. While Mary was being taught the value of modesty and chastity, FitzRoy was being encouraged to consider chivalric themes including King Arthur as well as the story of Paris and Helen of Troy.

In May 1530 Margaret Douglas finally travelled south from Berwick to London in the company of Sir Thomas Strangeways. The king provided his niece with a splendid new wardrobe before sending her to join her aunt

Mary, Countess of Suffolk, at Westhorpe in Suffolk where she became better acquainted with her Brandon cousins. The following year she was sent to join her cousin Princess Mary at Richmond. The cousins were able to sympathise with one another, as both of them were now of questionable birth. But, unlike Mary, Margaret was able to maintain silence on the subject of Henry's marriage and remained in favour with him while Mary's life became more and more troubled by her father's determination to set her mother aside.

Katherine and Henry maintained a public show of cordial relations as their marriage deteriorated. In June, Scarpinello, the Milanese Ambassador, described Henry and Katherine living alongside one another as though 'there had never been any dispute whatever between them. Yet, the affair has not slackened in the least'.[35] He was also able to report that Mary was occupied with her studies.[36] A similar report that December placed the king and queen at Hampton Court but 'the princess is always apart, some ten or fifteen miles away with a suitable establishment. We hear that she is already advanced in wisdom and stature'.[37] As Mary prepared to fulfil her duties as a Tudor, Europe's courts speculated about her parents' relationship and whether or not the Pope would capitulate to Henry's wishes for a divorce.

In July 1531 Henry was hunting at Windsor. Mary joined her mother there on 23 July.[38] Shortly after their daughter arrived, the king left the queen at Windsor without first saying goodbye. It was rumoured that he did not mean to permit Katherine to live with him again. Mary must have witnessed the queen's private distress. In August, the king ordered that she should leave Katherine's side for Richmond Palace while her mother was to go to The Moor in Hertfordshire. It was the last time that Mary saw her mother, although they continued to write to one another.

By December 1532, Anne Boleyn became pregnant and in January 1533, the king married her in a secret ceremony. In April, Henry sent a message to Mary stating that he was no longer married to Katherine and that Anne Boleyn, a niece of Mary's governess Jane Calthorpe, was his new queen. The Archbishop of Canterbury, Thomas Cranmer, was called upon to judge the matter of Henry VIII's union with Katherine of Aragon, at a court held in Dunstable. Inevitably he announced their marriage was never valid and annulled it. Mary was declared illegitimate. She went from being Henry's heir to another illegitimate daughter with less value than FitzRoy, who had the advantage of being male. Lord Mountjoy, Katherine's chamberlain since 1512, was given the task of informing the queen that she was Arthur's widow rather than the king's wife. Henceforth, she was to be called the princess dowager. She was moved from her residence at Ampthill to Buckden in Cambridgeshire.

At the end of August 1533, Anne Boleyn retired to her chamber following the ceremonial stipulated by the king's grandmother at the start of the Tudor era and on 7 September she gave birth to a living child. But it was not the promised male heir — it was a red-haired girl, who was named Elizabeth after Henry's mother. The rules laid out in the *Royal Book* continued to be followed despite the king's disappointment and the cancellation of a celebratory two-day tournament. Emperor Charles V's ambassador, Eustace Chapuys, did not bother to hide his delight and even refused to attend Elizabeth's baptism which was held at the Franciscan friary church at Greenwich where the king had himself been baptised. Andreasio, the Milanese Ambassador of Rome gleefully informed his master, Francesco Sforza, that the arrival of a daughter signified God's disapproval of Henry's 'unholy designs and appetites'.[39]

Anne, who doted on her daughter, desired to breastfeed the child for herself but Elizabeth, like her half-sister before her, was provided with a wetnurse and a nursery at Greenwich in the first instance. Anne may have been inspired by Jacques Guillemeau's book that advised mothers to breastfeed their own children.[40] Elizabeth was sent to Hatfield at the insistence of the king who expected his wife to follow the usual patterns of royal childcare. It was essential that the queen regained her fertility as soon as possible and provided Henry with his promised heir. In the meantime, Elizabeth was proclaimed Princess of Wales in Mary's place.

Katherine wrote to her daughter advising her how to handle the situation in which she found herself, urging her to avoid any proposal of marriage and to obey the king in all things unless it offended God to do so.[41] Henry sent the earls of Oxford, Sussex and Essex to tell Mary that she was no longer a princess and to dissolve her household. She refused to resign her title of princess even though her servants were instructed to remove the gold from their uniforms[42] as well as Mary's livery badge and forbidden to address her by her former title. Cromwell wrote to Sir John Hussey, who replaced Philip Calthorpe as chamberlain of Mary's household, ordering him to audit all of her plate and jewels. The latter were to be given to her infant half-sister; anything unsuitable for a baby was to be returned to the Jewel House. Margaret Pole, who remained with Mary, refused to comply with the order stating that she would not do so until she received written instructions from the king. Her loyalty was to her charge and to Katherine rather than Henry who was her cousin and who had made her Countess of Salisbury in her own right in 1512, restoring part of her grandfather's titles and lands to her.

On 26 November, a papal dispensation was issued so that FitzRoy could marry Mary Howard, daughter of the Duke of Norfolk. Now that Henry VIII was married to Anne Boleyn, FitzRoy and Anne's cousin were related within prohibited degrees of consanguinity. The Duke of Norfolk maintained that the union was the king's idea rather than an example of the Howard family's soaring ambition. Mary Howard's mother believed that the wedding was the product of Anne Boleyn's intrigues.[43] The marriage between the 14-year-olds went ahead on 28 November 1533. Mary Howard returned with her mother to Kenninghall in Norfolk but FitzRoy, whose status as a son made him more important than Mary Tudor now that they were both illegitimate, spent Christmas at court. He did not suffer from being a potential rival to Princess Elizabeth nor were he or his servants defying his royal parent. Instead, Henry showered gifts upon his son and continued to ensure that he was treated as a prince of the realm.

Mary's festive celebrations were less enjoyable. On 14 December the Duke of Norfolk and Earl of Oxford arrived at Newhall in Essex where Mary was staying with instructions that she was to move to Hatfield, with only two of her own attendants[44] and join the household of Princess Elizabeth — she was no longer a princess, instead she was to serve Anne's daughter who was Henry's heir to the throne. Mary replied that the title belonged to her and no one else, and that the request was both 'strange and dishonourable'[45] but Norfolk was unyielding. Margaret Douglas, Mary's cousin, was told that she could not stay with Mary any longer, instead she went to court to become one of Anne Boleyn's ladies where she would learn her position as an aristocrat and as part of the Tudor family by observing the queen and serving her. Margaret Pole, Countess of Salisbury was summarily dismissed from her post although she offered to pay the wages for Mary's entire household from her own purse. Richard Featherstone, Mary's tutor and another loyal supporter of Katherine's was also discharged. Featherstone would later be imprisoned on charges of treason and executed for failing to acquiesce to the Act of Succession or to take the Oath of Supremacy; the first of which declared the king's first marriage to be invalid and Mary illegitimate while the second accepted that Henry was the Head of the Church of England rather than the Pope.

Mary's formal lessons were finished but she faced an education in adversity when she arrived at Hatfield. Norfolk enquired whether she would go to visit the princess and pay her respects to which Mary responded that she 'knew no other Princess in England except herself'.[46] Chapuys added that Mary also noted that since the king chose to recognise the baby, just as he recognised Henry FitzRoy, she might call the girl, sister in the same way that she named FitzRoy, brother. When Norfolk reported back to his king, Henry accused the duke of being too soft in his treatment of Mary. If the king thought he could break his daughter to his will, he was sadly mistaken.

Princess Elizabeth's household was overseen by Anne Boleyn's aunt, Lady Shelton, who was now instructed to break the former princess's spirit. She was to serve her half-sister. Henry even told her to beat Mary if she was troublesome. Lady Shelton never did hit Katherine's daughter and on one occasion even accused the Duke of Norfolk of being too harsh in his approach. However, Mary was surrounded by men and women who were hostile to both her and her mother. Her servants whom she had known since childhood were all gone and she was not permitted to spend any time with her mother. Without her attendants, ignored by her father, Mary was on her own. When the king visited Elizabeth, he refused to see Mary and issued orders that she was to be confined to her chamber until he departed. On occasion the girl's windows were boarded shut and guards placed outside her door to prevent her from finding a way of reaching her father.

Henry was intent on humbling Mary. Instead of eating in her own chamber she was expected to eat with everyone else and her room was in the worst part of the house. As her money dwindled, she found herself lacking the means to buy new clothes. Lady Shelton picked fault with her and followed Anne Boleyn's instructions to break her but even then, in February 1534, Anne's brother, George Boleyn, announced that she was being too sympathetic to the former princess.

Lady Shelton had other problems besides taming the king's obdurate daughter. Anne Boleyn was pregnant once again and fearful that one of her ladies from a court faction hostile to her might become the subject of royal affection in her absence from the king's bed. It seems that Anne decided that it would be politically advisable if women from her own family satisfied Henry's appetites until she was able to resume her wifely duties. There were rumours that Henry was enamoured of Lady Shelton's elder daughter, Madge, or perhaps a younger daughter Mary; it is impossible to know which of the girls attracted the king's attention. They were part of their cousin's household in order to find suitable husbands, not to be smeared by rumours of immorality let alone to become a short-term royal mistress. No wonder Lady Shelton was waspish about the difficult situation in which she found herself and the painfully proud girl who refused to give an inch of her rights.

Mary was required to yield precedence to her half-sister at home and whenever the household moved from residence to residence. When Mary refused, in March 1534, to travel behind Elizabeth, Lady Shelton ordered some gentlemen of the household to force her charge into the litter that would travel behind the infant and her nurse and then to hold the girl there for the entirety of the journey. When she arrived at her destination, Mary wrote in secret to Chapuys to ask what she should do when the situation arose again, as she knew it would. The ambassador told her to protest but not go to the extreme of being held captive as it was both undignified and dangerous. For many of those difficult years it felt to the princess that Chapuys was one of the few friends who remained to her and she valued his advice which was smuggled to her through sympathetic hands. Lady Shelton dismissed Mary's lady-in-waiting, Lady Anne Hussey, who was also suspected of passing correspondence. Anne was imprisoned in the Tower after a visit to Mary made in December 1533. Her statement, given on 3 August 1534,[47] still survives.

In 1534, after having refused to sign the Act of Succession or to acknowledge her father as the Head of the Church, Lady Shelton told Mary that no one cared if she lived or died. She added that perhaps the king would execute her for her disobedience. So great was Mary's fear at that time that she seized an opportunity to tell Elizabeth's doctor, in Latin knowing that no one else in the room could speak the language, what had happened and pleaded for help. She completed her entreaty by saying, in English, that she no longer had the opportunity to practise Latin and that her skills were rusty. The doctor agreed that her Latin was not as good as it should be but made it his business to inform Chapuys of Mary's plight.

That summer Mary became ill and Lady Shelton arranged for an apothecary to treat her rather than her usual doctor. Mary's condition worsened. Anne Boleyn's aunt found herself fearing for the wellbeing of the girl. She may also have been counselled by Lady Alice Clere, another member of the Boleyn family, placed in charge of Mary. Alice was fearful that she and her sister would be accused of poisoning Katherine's daughter. The idea was not so far-fetched, after all the king's own uncles had disappeared into the Tower and were presumed murdered. Henry VIII sent his own physician, Dr Butts, to tend her as well as her mother's doctor to ensure that she was properly cared for. Butts, whose wife had been part of Mary's household in happier times, believed that Mary's illness was caused by the hostile conditions in which she lived and suggested that she could reside with her mother. By then Katherine and Mary had not seen one another for two years. Henry refused to permit this or even to allow Margaret Pole to return to his daughter's side.

It is probable though, despite her subsequent recovery, that Mary became more anxious than ever when rumours reached her ears that her father really did intend to have her executed if she did not swear the Oath of Succession that cut her out of her inheritance in favour of her half-sister. The king's old friend, Sir Thomas More, refused to take the oath and was sent to the Tower in April, tried for treason and executed on 6 July. Mary, who feared that she might be poisoned now that there were no ladies in the household to care for her, began to plan her escape from the nightmare in which she found herself. Chapuys and Emperor Charles V were less encouraging of Mary's intended flight from her father's kingdom and at Christmas, when Katherine of Aragon fell ill at Kimbolton, the idea was dropped.

Katherine died on 7 January 1536. Four days later, with scant regard to ceremony or the feelings of the former princess, Lady Shelton told Mary, who was now 20 years old, that her mother was dead. At about the same time Lady Clere tried to convince Mary to accept Anne Boleyn's offer of friendship. The queen was pregnant again and if she produced the king's longed for son, her crown would be safe upon her head. It would better for Mary if she acquiesced to her father's wishes before rather than after that happened. But on 29 January, as Katherine was buried at Peterborough, Anne miscarried the baby boy who might have been her salvation. The queen's failure was one too many as far as Henry was concerned. In May she was arrested and charged with adultery with five men, including her own brother. When Anne arrived at the Tower, one of the women sent there to serve her was Lady Anne Shelton. Her task was to report everything that Anne Boleyn said and did in the days leading up to her execution on 19 May.

1536 would be known as the year of the three queens. The day before Anne's execution Cranmer annulled Henry's marriage on the grounds that Mary Boleyn, Anne's sister, had been a royal mistress before he married Anne. 3-year-old Elizabeth was now illegitimate. In July, Sir John Shelton, Anne Shelton's husband, was made comptroller of both Elizabeth and Mary's household, with Anne and Lady Alice Clere being identified as lady governesses in charge of the former princesses. Elizabeth, who was precocious, famously asked Lady Bryan, 'how happs it yesterday Lady Princess and today but Lady Elizabeth?' Mary might have felt some sympathy for her half-sister having already undergone the same bitter experience. For a brief time, it was even openly suggested that Elizabeth was not the king's child. Chapuys reported that Archbishop Cranmer thought she was Henry Norris's daughter. On occasion, Mary speculated that her half-sister was the daughter of the musician Mark Smeaton rather than the king.

Mary's own situation initially showed little sign of improving despite the removal of Anne Boleyn. At Hunsdon, in Hertfordshire, where both Elizabeth and Mary were now housed, she was threatened with violence but still she refused to sign the document declaring that she accepted the Oath of Supremacy or to recognise her reduced status. Thomas Cromwell, Henry's minister, proved unexpectedly conciliatory as he tried to ameliorate the situation between the king and his elder daughter who stubbornly refused to accept that she was the Lady Mary rather than Princess Mary. The minister explained that her supporters would suffer if she continued to defy her father's wishes. Chapuys offered his own advice, that Mary 'must dissemble for some time'.[48] He added that God would recognise the intention rather than the act and it was essential that Mary save herself from her own father's anger. On 22 June, Mary finally submitted to her father's will and took the oath. By August, the Milanese were able to report that:

> … the princess is well, thank God. The king, her father, has treated her much better than he used, and I hope that in a few days they will agree to the thing with which she will be content.[49]

On 5 July, Cromwell wrote to Bishop Gardiner describing Mary as 'a most obedient child'.[50] Six months later Lady Mary was permitted to return to court. She wrote, in secret, to Charles V asking for him to gain a papal dispensation which would permit her to break the oath that she gave the

Privy Council. Reconciled with her father, Mary was provided with her own household which was larger and better staffed than Elizabeth's even if they were accommodated in the same building. By then the king was feeling more optimistic about the future of the Tudor dynasty. Henry's new queen, Jane Seymour, whom he married eleven days after Anne's execution was pregnant.

Chapter 9

Elizabeth and Edward

During October 1536 an uprising against Henry's reformation of the Church and dissolution of the monasteries began to spread through Lincolnshire. The rebellion which extended across the north of England became known as the Pilgrimage of Grace. Sir John Hussey, Mary's former chamberlain, remained neutral rather than rounding up rebels near his home at Sleaford, opening himself up to charges of treason. His wife, Anne, was confined to the Tower for a time during 1534 for having continued to use Mary's royal title and afterwards she continued to visit the girl, carrying correspondence from her mother and Chapuys. Sir John, who was once a favoured member of Henry VIII's court, was a prominent supporter of Katherine of Aragon and Mary and even discussed the potential of an uprising against King Henry with Chapuys. The Pilgrimage of Grace and the news that Anne Hussey offered refreshment to the rebels was too much for the increasingly angry monarch. Hussey, who denied involvement in the rebellion, was executed on 29 June 1537 and his cousin, Thomas Darcy, who delivered the royal castle at Pontefract to the rebels was beheaded the following day. Even so, John Hussey's family retained its anti-Church of England stance.

All three of Henry VIII's acknowledged children were now illegitimate. The heir to the throne, for the time being, was Lady Margaret Douglas, daughter of Margaret Tudor but she betrothed herself to the Duke of Norfolk's son, Thomas Howard, without royal permission in 1535. When, in July 1536, the king learned of the matter the couple were sent to the Tower.[1] Margaret renounced the union and was permitted to travel to Syon Abbey from where she was quietly released. In October 1537, Thomas Howard, who was accused of attempting to interrupt the succession of the crown, became ill and died in the Tower before he could be either executed or pardoned.

It seemed that God really had turned his back on King Henry. By the time of Margaret's disgrace, Henry FitzRoy was dead. It must have seemed to Henry, who had lavished love and affection upon the boy, that he was unable to father a son. There was no indication that FitzRoy was ill before the summer of 1536. He died suddenly on 23 July at St James' Palace. Chapuys, who took a more pragmatic view than FitzRoy's father, wrote that 'it was not a bad thing for the interests of the princess'.[2] Henry's son was buried quietly at Thetford Priory in Norfolk on the orders of his father-in-law, Thomas Howard, 3rd Duke of Norfolk. The remains would be relocated to Framlingham in Suffolk following the priory's dissolution.

Elizabeth's governess, Lady Bryan, who had recently been widowed for the second time, faced upheaval in the nursery and took Sir John Shelton to task about the way in which the former princesses' income was divided after her elder sister was granted a household of her own but without the resources to fund it. Lady Bryan was a woman who took her employment and the care of her charges seriously. The toddler, an inconvenient reminder of Anne Boleyn, could not simply be ignored or forgotten. Margaret wrote to Thomas Cromwell saying that she did not know how to order Elizabeth's household or to treat the former princess.[3] This was somewhat disingenuous as she was a royal governess with many years' experience, but it made the point. She went on to observe that the 3-year-old did not have clothes that fitted her and there was no money to buy more. She was also fed unsuitable foods in the great hall because Shelton would not permit the child to eat in her own rooms. While it would have been more appropriate, the staffing costs of feeding Elizabeth separately to everyone else would have been detrimental to Shelton's planned economies. Lady Bryan was more concerned that because Elizabeth was teething, it was difficult to correct her behaviour in public when she reached for foods, and for wine, which were all too rich for a child of her years. Chastising a member of the royal family, even a bastardised one, in a formal setting was not something to be done unless the king approved it first. Part of the problem arose from the lack of official instructions that Elizabeth's household received about the child's status and the way in which she was to be treated. For the time being, it was left to Lady Bryan who emphasised the child was a 'toward' one. She would, Margaret told Cromwell, do the king proud if she was seen in public.[4] Lady Bryan was not the only one in the household to plead Elizabeth's cause. Mary, newly restored to their father's favour, wrote to Henry VIII on 21 July stating that her half-sister would give the king 'cause to rejoice'.[5]

Cromwell, with his customary efficiency, wrote to Sir John Shelton addressing Lady Bryan's immediate concerns, ensuring that Shelton understood the ordering of the household as well as providing a sufficient income for all of the former princess's necessities.[6] There was nothing he could do about the king's desire to forget his younger daughter's existence. Henry was removing any sign of Anne Boleyn from his life. In the royal palaces, workmen were busy eradicating her initials as well as her emblem of a white falcon holding a sceptre.

On 12 October 1537, Jane Seymour gave birth to Henry's longed for heir. The king gave orders for free wine to be distributed in London, bonfires were lit and bells rang. The *Royal Book* provided guidance on the prince's baptism which took place three days later. Lady Bryan's son, Sir Francis, carried the towels; Mary was Edward's godmother; and 4-year-old Elizabeth, carried by Edward Seymour the queen's brother, held the chrism or baptismal cloth. Nine days later joy turned to sorrow when Jane died from complications arising from childbirth. Mary, whose return to court had been welcomed by the queen who had been one of Katherine of Aragon's ladies-in-waiting, was her stepmother's chief mourner at the funeral which took place at Windsor on 12 November 1537.

Lady Bryan, still Elizabeth's governess, took charge of the new prince who remained at Hampton Court in a magnificent new suite of rooms ordered by the king before his son's birth. Elizabeth stayed in her care, so the two were often in one another's company. Edward flourished and his proud father invited ambassadors and foreign dignitaries to come and admire his heir from February 1538 onwards. Lady Bryan was only formally transferred to Prince Edward's household, which was established by Thomas Cromwell, in March 1538. The lady governess sent reports on the prince's development to the king's chief minister including the news that he was teething.[7] It is to be wondered if either the writer or recipient reflected on the previous letter that the lady governess wrote on the subject of teeth.

Sir John Cornwallis of Brome Hall in Suffolk, part of East Anglia's network of gentry, became Edward's steward.[8] He was knighted by Henry Howard, FitzRoy's mentor, in 1523 during the king's French campaign. Sir William Sidney was appointed as the prince's chamberlain, having previously been one of the king's esquires of the body since 1517. Sidney was part of the Kent gentry but is likely to have gained promotion at court by his distant kinship to Charles Brandon, Duke of Suffolk. Like Cornwallis, he had a reputation as a soldier, having been in the service of Ferdinand of Aragon and at the Battle of Flodden, commanding the right wing of the English army, against the Scots. Their exploits on the battlefield, as well as long service at the Tudor court, made them ideal for their roles in the household of the Prince of Wales.

Sidney's trusted position as privy councillor and Lieutenant of the Tower meant that Edward's early years were almost entirely in the hands of the Sidney family. Lady Anne Sidney, William's wife, took over from Lady Bryan as the prince's lady governess. William's eldest son, Henry, was 10 years old when he was appointed as the 2-year-old's henchman.[9] The Sidney family's proximity to the Crown meant that Sir William was able to acquire several large grants of land. In 1539, he acquired Robertsbridge in Sussex and, in 1552, acquired Penshurst Place when it's previous owner, Sir Ralph Fane, was executed for treason.[10]

Sybil Penn, another Sidney relation, took over from Edward's wetnurse, Mother Jack, in October 1538, as the boy's dry nurse caring for his everyday needs. The prince adored Sybil, who was his *de facto* mother, and she was often with him when he made court appearances. When he met some German ambassadors, he was so overcome by shyness that he was reported as burying his face into his nurse's shoulder. Recognising that her position was a significant one she petitioned Thomas Cromwell for the advancement of her extended family, in the hope that they also might be placed in Edward's household. Once he became king, there is a legend that Sybil was given a permanent apartment at Greenwich. In 1553, Edward VI rewarded his nurse and her husband with the gift of property at Little Missenden as well as property near Amersham in Buckinghamshire. Although the Penns were able to build a new house on the proceeds of their newfound wealth, Sybil remained at court even when the king was too old for the care of women.

Mary, who chose to live, on occasion, with her younger half-siblings rather than at court, is recorded presenting the women who cared for her half-brother with various gifts from lengths of cloth and other apparel to gilt spoons and cash. She gave Mary Penn, the daughter of Edward's nurse, Sybil, a gold brooch.[11] During the New Year celebrations of 1537–1538, Mary gave her brother an embroidered crimson coat and a yellow satin kirtle to Elizabeth. There is no indication that she stitched them herself, her accounts demonstrate a greater enjoyment of gambling at cards than embroidery.[12] However, it is apparent that Mary, who loved children, was warming to her half-sister. Her accounts show that she gave Elizabeth numerous thoughtful gifts and on occasion paid Edward's musicians to play for them both. The royal nurseries took on an unexpectedly harmonious hue with the arrival of a legitimate prince.

Richard Cox was appointed to the post of Edward's almoner as well as becoming the prince's tutor. He was a graduate of King's College, Cambridge and was a convinced supporter of Protestantism. Forced from the university because of his Lutheran beliefs, he became the headmaster of Eton in 1529 before utilising his skills on the king's behalf, including the annulment of Henry's marriage to Anne of Cleves in 1540. His theology had become useful to the State and he rose swiftly, although his brand of Protestantism was too extreme for the king's more conservative personal preferences. He would continue in Edward's service as the boy's tutor when Edward became king and took an active role guiding him towards the establishment of a Protestant state. Cox was on the Windsor Commission which helped to compile Edward's prayer book in 1549.

Edward learned his prayers, manners and his letters from the women who cared for him and from Cox, who began to introduce him to Latin and the same books that his father, uncle and sisters studied. Roger Ascham described him as 'the greatest schoolmaster of our time'[13] having introduced an innovative syllabus at Eton based on humanist teaching methods. Cox also had a reputation as a disciplinarian which raises the question of whether or not Henry's son was the regular subject of corporal punishment. When he refused to memorise a long passage from Proverbs, Cox beat him to remind the prince that, in the classroom, authority belonged with the schoolmaster and to spur the boy forward in his studies.[14] If the prince avoided the rod after that, it is unlikely that his classroom companions were so fortunate.

As well as Latin, Cato, Aesop and Solomon's proverbs[15] Edward was taught court etiquette, how to ride and to dance and how to behave like a prince. His lady governesses may have consulted *Civilitie of Childhood* by Erasmus which was published in 1530 and addressed to Henry of Burgundy, the son of the Lord of Veere. It contained seventeen sections covering everything from belching to yawning. It provided advice about posture, including the correct way to sit and to stand as well as directions about the etiquette of bowing and curtseying. Edward was discouraged from folding his arms, wiping his nose on his sleeve or looking sad. When he learned to walk, he was trained to walk with a swagger and be assertive.

Elizabeth was never taught alongside her younger brother. He was being trained for kingship. Even so, her household began to change and more attention was paid to her lessons; she would be useful as a marital bargaining chip for Tudor foreign policy. Blanche Herbert, Lady Troy who was present at Edward's baptism with Elizabeth and Mary to bear the prince's train at the end of the service, replaced Lady Bryan as Elizabeth's lady governess when the latter was re-deployed. Although Lady Troy, born Blanche Milborne, was English there is a strong possibility, given her own upbringing in the Marches, that she spoke Welsh. Her marriage into the Herbert family and their long service to the Tudors may explain her appointment. She was also the mother of eleven of her own children and she served Elizabeth Somerset, Countess of Worcester, who was one of Anne Boleyn's ladies-in-waiting as well as being kin to Charles Brandon, Duke of Suffolk, the brother-in-law of the king. The connection took her into the business of caring for Henry VIII's younger children when the Countess of Worcester offered Lady Troy's services to Anne Boleyn in the matter of finding a potential wetnurse prior to the birth of Princess Elizabeth. As it happened, Lady Troy's suggested candidate was not selected. A Welsh wetnurse, Mrs Pendred, looked after Anne Boleyn's daughter when she was a baby.

Lady Troy, who was clearly part of Elizabeth's household from her earliest days, was to be assisted by four gentlewomen, three gentlemen, two chamberers and a chaplain. Lady Troy's granddaughter, Anne Morgan, who was about four years older than the princess, grew up with Elizabeth both as a companion and a servant to the king's daughter.[16] Among the women caring for the king's younger daughter were Lady Troy's niece, Blanche Parry and Katherine, or Kat, Champernowne who joined the household in 1536. She married John Astley, although Kat preferred Ashley, in about 1545. Astley was a kinsman of Elizabeth and a member of Prince Edward's household. It was his task to teach the prince to play the virginals as well as to fulfil the function of gentleman waiter. Kat Ashley and Blanche Parry would remain with Elizabeth for the rest of their lives.

Lady Troy cared for Elizabeth until 1546 and on occasion supervised Edward's education. It was Lady Troy who walked the tightrope that had become religious education. Henry may have broken with the Pope but he favoured a form of worship that was Catholic in all but name. And it was Blanche who oversaw the practical skills that Elizabeth was required to know as a virtuous woman, including sewing and embroidery. In 1539 the 6-year-old presented her brother with a linen shirt that she stitched herself.

The Sheltons were replaced by Sir Edward and Lady Baynton in April 1539. At the same time that the Bayntons were appointed to the households of Mary and Elizabeth, Mary Kingston was dismissed from her position. Baynton served in Anne Boleyn's household and his wife, Isabel, who was Catherine Howard's half-sister, was one of her ladies-in-waiting. Isabel was also one of the ladies who was at Jane Seymour's funeral to represent each year of the dead queen's life. It is not clear how long the Bayntons were responsible for Elizabeth but when the king took his fourth wife, Anne of Cleves, in 1540, the couple were restored to their previous roles of vice chamberlain and lady-in-waiting within the queen's household. Isabel retained her position when Catherine Howard became Henry's fifth queen but retired from court after her sister's execution having remained by her side throughout her imprisonment and trial.

King Henry finally had a legitimate male heir but the Tudor dynasty was far from secure. In 1539, Lady Margaret Bryan's son-in-law, Sir Nicholas Carew, was imprisoned, accused of involvement with the Exeter Conspiracy to depose Henry VIII and replace him with the Countess of Salisbury's eldest son, Reginald Pole. Nicholas Carew was executed on 3 March and his wife Elizabeth was evicted from their home at Beddington. Lady Bryan, a determined letter writer, pleaded with Cromwell once again, this time to intercede on her daughter's behalf.

During the same time that Lady Bryan's family faced the consequences of the king's anger, Mary's beloved long serving lady governess, Margaret Pole, Countess of Salisbury also fell under suspicion of involvement with the conspiracy. She was a conservative Catholic and, perhaps more important, was the daughter of George, Duke of Clarence the brother of King Edward IV. The countess was sent to the Tower, with her grandson Henry, where she remained until her execution on 27 May 1541. Margaret, who did not go gently to her death, declared that she was innocent of treachery, and asked witnesses at her execution to pray for Mary and sent her blessing to her luckless goddaughter. No one knows what happened to Henry Pole, who disappeared into the Tower never to be seen again.

While Edward learned how to behave as a prince and Elizabeth learned all she could from Kat Ashley, at court stepmothers came and went. Anne of Cleves became Henry's fourth queen on 6 January 1540 but was gone by the end of the summer having successfully managed the transformation from unwanted wife to respected sister. Katherine Carey, Mary Boleyn's daughter who was 15 years old in 1539, left Elizabeth's household where she was raised when the king married his fourth wife and took up a court position as a maid of honour. The queen's household was akin to both a finishing school for young ladies and a matchmaking agency. Families hoped that their daughters would acquire polish, position and a suitable spouse when they sent them to court. Katherine, who served both Anne of Cleves and Catherine Howard, married Francis Knollys in 1540, completing her transition from childhood to adult life. During the next five years she would give birth to four children and set up her own nursery at her home at Greys Court, in Oxfordshire.

The king's minister, Thomas Cromwell, the newly minted Earl of Essex, was executed on 28 July 1540. Royal favour, as ever, depended on giving Henry VIII exactly what he wanted, and he blamed Cromwell for the fiasco of his fourth marriage. Edward's father took for his fifth bride, on the same day that his chief minister was executed, Anne Boleyn's young cousin, Catherine Howard, who was another of Anne of Cleve's ladies. The besotted king is famously said to have described her as a rose without a thorn but she proved both ineffective as a stepmother and unfaithful to her aging spouse. She was beheaded, having practised laying her head upon the block the previous evening, on the morning of 13 February 1542.

During June 1543, Mary and Elizabeth met with Katherine Parr for the first time as a potential stepmother. On 12 July 1543 King Henry married Katherine at Hampton Court. The king's daughters were both present for the occasion. Katherine was twice widowed and the published author of *Psalms or Prayers* when she became Henry's sixth queen. Elizabeth returned to her household soon afterwards and the day-to-day care of Kat Champernowne who, thanks to her own education, had the responsibility for teaching her charge embroidery, dancing, reading, maths, history, languages and astronomy as well as desirable feminine characteristics including modesty, good manners and virtue; all under the supervision of Lady Troy.

Lady Troy continued as part of Elizabeth's household until her retirement in either 1545 or 1546. It is not clear when Blanche retired. A letter from Ascham to Kat in 1545 asking her to recommend him to Lady Troy shows that she was still responsible for Elizabeth but a household list dating to 1546 does not mention her. It has been suggested that she was edged out from her employment by Kat who became increasingly close to Elizabeth and who may have become eligible for the role of lady governess upon her marriage.[17]

A letter written by Sir Robert Tyrwhitt to the Duke of Somerset in January 1549 recounted the manner by which Kat disposed of challengers to her mistress's affections. It seems, from what Tyrwhitt was informed when he questioned Elizabeth's staff, that Lady Troy who slept in Elizabeth's room, was removed by Kat's machinations. Sleeping alone was unusual in the sixteenth century. It was usual for servants to sleep either in the same bed or a truckle bed alongside their masters or mistresses. Elizabeth's lady governess was responsible for her wellbeing, virtue and safety. Furthermore, Tyrwhitt discovered, Lady Troy intended that her niece, Blanche Parry, would replace her as Elizabeth's lady mistress when she retired. Kat, who made herself indispensable and who was jealous of Blanche Parry managed to have her removed from her place in Elizabeth's bedchamber as well. Tyrwhitt, who had his own agenda to discredit Mistress Ashley, painted a picture of acrimony but there is no indication other than his letter that anything was amiss in Elizabeth's household. Blanche Parry, who had rocked Elizabeth's cradle when she was a baby, remained part of the household, even if it was Kat, now lady governess, who shared the former princess's bedchamber to the exclusion of Elizabeth's other ladies.[18] In many respects Kat was the mother that Elizabeth never had and, besides which, she was a married woman, whereas Blanche Parry remained single.

Unlike Elizabeth, no element of Edward's care or education was left to chance. When he was 6 years of age the women who looked after him were dismissed, his household enlarged, and his education as his father's heir intensified. The prince's apartments were made to more closely resemble the king's own private chambers with tapestries depicting biblical and classical scenes. Like his father and uncle before him he was being groomed to look and think like a king. Nor was his military education ignored. Henry ensured that Edward, who history tends to think of as a sickly child, was prepared for both the tiltyard and the battlefield.

The prince's chamberlain, Sir John Cornwallis, died early in the summer of 1544. He left four sons and three daughters by his wife, Mary. The terms of his will provided for their future as well as ensuring a fine marble tomb in his parish church at Brome.[19] At around the same time, Sidney was replaced by Sir Richard Page, a gentleman of the privy chamber and the stepfather of Anne Stanhope, the wife of the prince's uncle, Edward Seymour.[20] His role as vice chamberlain of Henry FitzRoy's household provided him with the necessary experience for managing the Prince of Wales's establishment.[21] He was also one of the seven men initially arrested for adultery and treason with Anne Boleyn. Only he and the poet, Thomas Wyatt, escaped the headman's axe. It is unclear why he was entangled in the events around Anne's downfall or how his name was cleared. It perhaps helped that Page's stepdaughter, Anne Stanhope, was married to Edward Seymour, the Prince of Wales's uncle.

The prince was to receive as thorough a humanist education as his father. Cox remained Edward's director of studies but he was to be assisted by John Cheke, on the recommendation of Sir Anthony Denny, a highly favoured groom of the stool who was related through his mother to both the Stanley and the Howard families and whose connection to the Tudors was a long standing one.[22] Like Cox, Cheke was a reformer and even more importantly he became the first Regius Professor of Greek at the University of Oxford where he had worked since 1540 having attained both his first degree and his master's from St John's College, Cambridge in 1533. Cheke initially came to the king's attention through the royal physician, Dr Butts, who described his young friend's new improved study methods to Henry as well as his proficiency. Cheke differed in one key aspect. He did not adopt the biblical adage, 'Spare the rod and spoil the child' to which most schoolmasters and parents of the period adhered. He preferred to instil respect by enthusing his pupils rather than beating them.

Richard Cox, who was also one of the king's chaplains, remained to teach the prince grammar until 1546 as well as fulfilling duties as Dean of Christ Church College, Oxford. In January 1546, Cox was able to tell Cranmer that Edward had learned four books of Cato, Vives' *Satellitium* which had been written for Princess Mary as well as some texts from the Bible.[23] The texts studied by the prince were ones his father and Uncle Arthur read during their years in the schoolroom, including Aesop's fables in Latin. In 1547, Cox became Chancellor of Oxford University. His new duties meant that he directed the prince's education from afar while John Cheke worked alongside Edward in the schoolroom as well as continuing to write and to publish his translations. Other tutors were appointed for the prince as required. John Belmain(e), a Huguenot, became his French tutor in 1546,[24] on the advice of Cheke. Edward's grasp of the language was sufficiently advanced to write a letter to Elizabeth in French by the end of the year. When he met the French ambassador, de Selve, in February 1547, the pair conversed in Latin demonstrating that he was not yet fluent in the language. When Edward ascended the throne, Belmain became a gentleman of the chamber and continued to tutor the king. By 1550, Edward was speaking good French with his visitors.[25]

Like his siblings, the prince was also taught to play the lute. Musical accomplishment, one of Henry VIII's passions, was the mark of a Renaissance prince. It is likely this office fell to Philip van de Wilder, from Flanders, and one of Henry VIII's favoured musicians. The lutenist was resident at Henry's court from about 1520 and, on occasion, taught the instrument to Mary who shared her father's love of music.[26] Giles D'Ewes remained the best paid of Henry's musicians[27] but following the dissolution of the monasteries, de Wilder, who was also a wine merchant, profited from his links to the Crown with grants of property in Dorset once he became an English citizen. By the time of the king's death in 1547, de Wilder was the chief musician at court, known as the keeper of the instruments as well as being a composer and Edward's music teacher. De Wilder continued in his employments once Edward became king but was also given charge of the choir at the Chapel Royal.[28]

The prince was joined in his lessons by selected boys of his own age who, it was envisioned, would one day form a part of his court and council. Among their number was his cousin Henry Brandon, the eldest son of the Duke of Suffolk, Henry Hastings, the great-grandson of Lady Margaret Pole, and Barnaby FitzPatrick the son of the Baron of Upper Ossory, a hostage for his father's loyalty to the king. The group studied together and learned the other prerequisite skills of the nobility including riding, jousting and sword fighting. In 1545, Roger Ascham, one of Cheke's former students, presented the prince with a treatise in English entitled *Toxophilus*, on the subject of archery.[29] The law still required every male over the age of 7 to practise the longbow on Sunday after attending church. Ascham, himself a keen archer, wrote the book to show that the sport was a noble pastime suitable for a scholar. It was an instructional text and the dedication to Henry VIII drew both reward and the king's attention.

Elizabeth whose formal education was neglected by Henry during the years after her mother's execution, continued her own learning in the hands of Kat Ashley. It is thought that Sir Anthony Denny, who was a relation of Kat's through marriage, sent John Picton, about whom little is known, to Hatfield to help her teach the king's younger daughter.[30] It is likely that it was either Picton who first taught Elizabeth to write in an Italic style and to speak Italian or, if not him, John Belmain. Italic calligraphy was developed during the Renaissance in Italy and all of Elizabeth's tutors are known to have used the lettering. The slight changes in font formation across the course of her childhood provides some insight to the influence of the men who taught her to write clearly and with elegance.[31]

At court, Katherine Parr agitated on her younger stepdaughter's behalf. She sent another of her stepdaughters, Margaret Neville the daughter of Baron Latimer, to Ashridge where Elizabeth was then housed to maintain contact with the child who seemed to be in exile from her father's presence. Katherine eventually persuaded the king to allow Elizabeth to join her at Hampton Court in July 1544. The queen recognised the fierce intelligence of her youngest stepdaughter and was determined to provide Elizabeth with the best education she could. In November 1544 an Italian master, thought to have been Giovanni Battista Castiglione, was appointed for the girl. He may also have tutored Edward. Belmain was called in to provide Elizabeth with French lessons when he was not tutoring Edward. At about the same time that Castiglione took up his role, Cheke summoned William Grindal from Cambridge to take up an appointment as Elizabeth's permanent tutor. The young academic had been recommended to him by Ascham to teach Elizabeth Greek.

Katherine Parr, who loved books, was well educated by her own mother, Maud Green, and was possibly the best educated of all of Henry VIII's wives. Lady Parr, who was related to Lady Guildford by marriage, was a friend of Katherine of Aragon as well as one of her ladies-in-waiting. Maud provided a schoolroom not only for her own children but for her wider kinship network in the years after she was widowed. She was able to apply the model used for the education of Mary Tudor as well as the system advocated by Sir Thomas More. More's four daughters learned Latin and Greek as well as theology, arithmetic, astronomy and philosophy. His eldest daughter, Margaret Roper, was regarded as one of the most learned women in England and exchanged letters with Erasmus. It is not perhaps surprising then, that Katherine Parr encouraged her stepchildren with their studies at the same time as making a friend of Lady Mary. Elizabeth studied not only Latin but also Greek and, unlike Mary, there were no caveats placed on the kinds of books that she might read. More's system placed importance on the developing piety of girls and preparation for their adult lives as wives and mothers but did not censor them in the same way that Vives felt necessary.

During the New Year of 1545, Elizabeth presented her stepmother with a translation of Margaret of Navarre's *The Mirror or Glass of the Sinful Soul* with an embroidered cover, depicting the monogram KP and heartsease flowers, also worked by Elizabeth. An original copy of the text, first published in 1531, is thought to have been owned by Anne Boleyn. The work contained some radical religious ideas that the papacy declared heretical. An accompanying letter sent by Elizabeth from Ashridge excused the translation as 'unperfect and uncorrect'[32] and asked that Katherine 'rub out, polish and mend'[33] the words where they were ordered wrongly or used poorly. Henry's youngest daughter had found a woman whose intellect she could respect; who would provide her with the means to improve her own education and would bring her back from the margins of the court into the royal family. The book and embroidery helped to cement the relationship between Katherine and Anne Boleyn's precocious daughter.

Elizabeth's interests were not confined to the classics. She was also fascinated by astronomy and mathematics. In 1545 she asked William Buckley, her brother's mathematics tutor, to make her an astronomical ring dial. He presented it together with an instruction book for its use the following year.[34] Elizabeth maintained her interest in arithmetic, astronomy, geometry and navigation throughout her life. She understood both the financial and political importance of map making in an era of exploration and expansion. John Dee who became her court astronomer, charted many of the routes which Elizabethan trading companies relied upon. Her interest, and that of her brother Edward, may have sprung in the first instance from the collection of maps, globes and scientific instruments that could be found in all of Henry VIII's residences.

In 1545, Anne Morgan, the granddaughter of Blanche, Lady Troy, married Elizabeth's cousin, Henry Carey, who together with his sister, Katherine, had been placed in Anne Boleyn's care following their mother Mary Boleyn's disgrace in 1534. Widowed by the death of William Carey in 1528, she married for a second time to William Stafford, her social inferior and fell from royal favour. Henry Carey was made a ward of court and sent by his aunt to Syon Abbey to be educated[35] but Katherine Carey, born in about 1524, was one of the young women who attended her cousin Elizabeth and who was raised alongside her. Katherine witnessed Mary's humiliation when Anne Boleyn was queen and the way in which Elizabeth was ignored after the queen's execution. The cousins' friendship endured until Katherine's death in 1569. While it is unclear whether Henry Carey, born in 1526, was Elizabeth's half-brother, as a result of the king's affair with Mary Boleyn prior to his infatuation with Anne, it is almost certain that Katherine Carey was Elizabeth's unacknowledged half-sister.[36]

In 1546, Elizabeth, then aged 12 years, translated the queen's own book of *Prayers or Meditations*, dedicated to King Henry, into Latin, Italian and French as a New Year's gift. The book, written on vellum, is now at the British Museum.[37] As well as the Classics, French and Italian, Elizabeth would go on to learn German, Hebrew and Spanish. Like the earlier handwritten book, she also embroidered the canvas cover that bound the work. The princess's education ensured that the accomplishment of needlework was not overlooked and Elizabeth was demonstrating her various skills and asking her stepmother to improve upon them all. By the time Elizabeth I died in 1603, aged 70, she would have written more than two hundred texts that laid out her political and religious position from poems and prayers to speeches given to Parliament and letters sent to foreign princes.

Brass rubbing of Edmond Tudor's tomb at St David's Cathedral, Wales. (*CC0, via Wikimedia Commons*)

tained glass window of Lady Margaret Beaufort, ountess of Richmond and Derby, in St Mary's e Virgin Church, Petworth, Sussex. (*Photograph: yle Hewgill*)

Stained glass window of Jasper Tudor, Earl of Richmond and Duke of Bedford, with his wife, Catherine Woodville, Cardiff Castle, Wales. (*Wolfgang Sauber, CC BY-SA 3.0, via Wikimedia Commons*)

Raglan Castle. (*Photograph: Julia Hickey*)

Stained glass window in the Cordeliers of Nantes: Francis II, Duke of Brittany praying, 17th century. (*Gallica Digital Library, Public domain via Wikimedia Commons*)

Henry VII, after an original by Pietro Torrigiano. (*Public domain via Metropolitan Museum of Art, New York, accession no 09.200.2*)

The Marriage of Henry VII and Elizabeth of York: print, H. Cook after Jan Gossaert (also known as Jan Mabuse). (*Metropolitan Museum of Art, CC0, via Wikimedia Commons*)

Elizabeth of York, Queen of England. (*Cultural Heritage Agency of the Netherlands Art Collection, Public domain via Wikimedia Commons*)

Three Children of Henry VII and Elizabeth His Queen: Prince Arthur, Prince Henry and Princess Margaret 1748. George Vertue, 1684–1756. (*Yale Center for British Art, Paul Mellon Collection, B1977.14.10333 Public domain*)

Stained glass window of Prince Arthur in St Lawrence Church, Ludlow. (*Photograph: Kyle Hewgill*)

Ludlow Castle. (*Photograph: Kyle Hewgill*)

Effigy of Sir Richard Croft at Croft Church, Herefordshire. (*Photograph: Kyle Hewgill*)

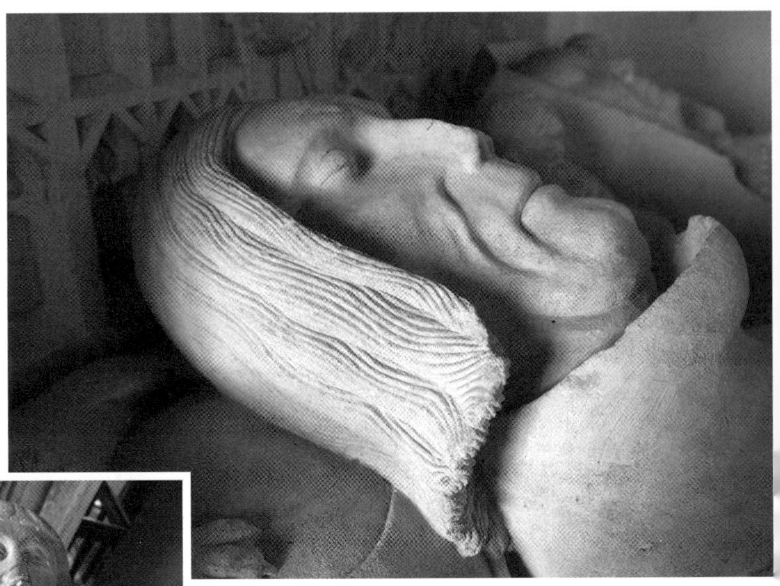

Effigy of Sir Henry Vernon, St Bartholemew's Church, Tong. (*Photograph: Kyle Hewgill*)

Hadden Hall, Derbyshire. (*Photograph: Julia Hickey*)

The tomb of Arthur, Prince of Wales at Worcester Cathedral. (*Photograph: Kyle Hewgill*)

Eltham Palace. (*Photograph: Adam Hewgill*)

King James IV of Scotland and Queen Margaret. Print published by John Thane, 1796. (*lisby1, CC BY 2.0 via Wikimedia Commons*)

Portrait of Henry VIII. Hans Liefrinck after Corenelis Anthonisz, 1539–1547. (*Creative commons, Rijksmuseum*)

Henry's reconciliation with Anne Boleyn. George Cruikshank, 1842. (*Library of Congress, Public domain via Wikimedia Commons*)

Jane Seymour. Wenceslaus Hollar, 1607–1677. (*Metropolitan Museum of Art ,The Elisha Whittelsey Collection, The Elisha Whittelsey Fund 1951, Public domain*)

Portrait of Edward VI, the future king of England, as a child. Anonymous, 1600–1699. (*Creative commons, Rijksmuseum*)

King Edward VI as an infant. Wenceslaus Hollar, 1607–1677 after Hans Holbein. (*Metropolitan Museum of Art, The Elisha Whittelsey Collection, The Elisha Whittelsey Fund 1951, Public domain*)

Portrait of 'Mother Jak'. Francesco Bartolozzi after Hans Holbein the Younger, 1797. Now known to be Margaret Giggs (1508–1570), the adopted daughter of Sir Thomas More. (*Creative commons, Rijksmuseum*)

Portrait of Edward VI. Anonymous. (Creative commons, Rijksmuseum)

King Henry VIII with Will Sommers, Edward VI, Mary I and Elizabeth I. Francesco Bartolozzi, 1728–1815, after Hans Holbein the Younger. (*Yale Center for British Art, Paul Mellon Collection, Public domain*)

Sir Thomas More. Jacob Houbraken after Hans Holbein the Younger, 1760. (*Creative commons, Rijksmuseum*)

Portrait of Desiderius Erasmus. Quinten Massijs (a copy after) after c.1535. (*Creative ommons, Rijksmuseum*)

Portrait of John Colet. (*Wellcome, CC BY 4.0 via Wikimedia Commons*)

A man designated as Thomas Linacre. Oil Painting, c.1900 (?). (*Wellcome Collection, cc by 4.0*)

Katherine Knollys (née Carey), Lady Knollys, 1562. (*Yale Center for British Art, Paul Mellon Collection*)

Plaque dedicated to Elizabeth Calthorpe, Church of St Martin at Palace, Norwich. (*Evelyn Simak, CC BY-SA 2.0 via Wikimedia Commons*)

Stained glass window of Lady Anne Shelton and Sir John Shelton in St Mary's Church, Shelton, Norfolk. (*John Salmon, Creative commons via Wikimedia Commons*)

Blickling Hall, Norfolk. (*Photograph: Kyle Hewgill*)

Ightham Mote, Kent. (*Photograph: Julia Hickey*)

Blanch Parry, Bacton Church. (*Photograph: Kyle Hewgill*)

Sir Anthony Denny. (*Wenceslaus Hollar, CC0, via Wikimedia Commons*)

Hampton Court Palace. (*DiscoA340, CC BY-SA 4.0 via Wikimedia Commons*)

The Execution of Lady Jane Grey. Paolo Mercurinaar after Paul Delaroche. (*Rijksmuseum, CC0, via Wikimedia Commons*)

An Allegory of the Tudor Succession: The family of Henry VIII. After Lucas de Heere, 1534–1584. (*Yale Center for British Art, Paul Mellon Collection*)

King Henry VIII, Edward VI, Queens Mary and Elizabeth. Hendrick Goltzius, 1584. (*Creative commons, Rijksmuseum*)

Chapter 10

Hard Lessons

On 30 December 1546, Henry VIII gave orders for his will to be rewritten. His son would succeed him as king of England but real power would have to rest in hands other than Edward's until he was old enough to take up the reins of government. Henry identified sixteen executors who were to form part of King Edward VI's Privy Council during his minority. Most of the men listed already served King Henry VIII but he shifted the balance of power within the council from the conservative faction who favoured Catholicism to a group who were inclined towards reform. Among the twenty-eight men named to rule on Edward's behalf were Edward Seymour, 1st Earl of Hertford and John Dudley who was created Earl of Warwick in 1547. Less famous for his inclusion in their number was Sir Anthony Denny, who by then was Henry VIII's chief gentleman of the privy chamber.

When Henry died on 28 January 1547, his 9-year-old son became King Edward VI. According to the terms of his father's will, the minority would last for nine years under the supervision of the Regency Council identified within the will. Three days later, the council elected Edward's uncle, Edward Seymour, as Lord Protector. The decision set aside Henry's wishes to keep power from the hands of any one individual, as it granted Seymour sovereign rights until Edward came of age. It would be Seymour's responsibility to rule as well as to teach his nephew how to govern. The king's other uncle, Thomas Seymour, was not pleased by the turn of events, believing that he also ought to have been named Edward's governor.

Edward learned that he was king on 29 January before going to Enfield Palace where he remained for a few days with the younger of his two half-sisters. Anne Boleyn's daughter was left behind when the new king returned to London but Elizabeth, at 13 years, was no longer on her own. She went to join her stepmother, Katherine Parr, at Greenwich. On 25 February she received a wedding proposal from Edward's over ambitious younger uncle, Lord Thomas Seymour, who was appointed Lord Admiral and became a privy councillor at the beginning of the month. The attempt by the Protector to mollify him for his lack of role in the regency government failed and Thomas was now determined to secure a royal bride. Elizabeth rejected the admiral, and having already been turned down by Mary, Seymour asked Henry VIII's widow to marry him. The pair, who began courting before the king took an interest in Katherine, were wed in secret on 3 March 1547 flouting all the mourning conventions of the period. Henry's widow was not immune from Seymour's good looks or charm. Having married three times from duty, Katherine married for a fourth time from love.

King Edward VI's uncle, who became Duke of Somerset on 16 February, behaved like a king in all but name and was quick to place men who owed their loyalty to him in positions of power. Historians are divided about the so-called Good Duke's religious beliefs, his motives and effectiveness. For the time being, though, Edward Seymour was the king's guardian. Edward's tutors were stricter than ever and he was expected to learn how to run his father's kingdom which meant attending council meetings. Edward's diary, which he called his chronicle, kept as part of Cheke's design to encourage the young king to write down his thoughts in an orderly manner, reflects his growing understanding of state matters. On a more personal level, Somerset was severe and, the king believed, kept him short of cash. Edward turned to his other uncle, Thomas Seymour, who supplied him with pocket money[1] so that he could reward his servants, including Kat Ashley's husband, John, who taught the king to play the virginals, a keyboard instrument similar to a harpsichord. Money was passed through the hands of a groom of the privy chamber, John Fowler, who found himself helping the admiral to try to influence the king in his favour. Seymour also made a point of making friends with other of the king's servants and on was on good terms with John Cheke, who remained by Edward's side. Most alarming of all, he even managed to gain possession of duplicate keys for the palace of Whitehall's doors.[2]

Somerset remained ignorant of his brother's activities. After Henry VIII's death, the duke continued to prosecute Henry's campaign, begun in December 1543, against the Scots known as the Rough Wooing to bring about the marriage of Edward to his cousin, Mary Queen of Scots. The first few pages of Edward VI's chronicle are full of news of the campaign which was led by the Protector.[3] Sir Richard Page, Edward's chamberlain, was appointed as one of the young king's temporary governors while the Protector, who was Page's step-son-in-law, was on campaign in Scotland. This appointment led to further resentment from the Lord Admiral who thought he should have been given the task. Thomas described Page as a 'drunken soul'.[4] There is no other evidence supporting Seymour's claim and it seems unlikely that Edward's care would have been entrusted to him if he was a drunkard. Page's continued service was cut short by his death in February 1548 while Seymour became more and more troublesome to his elder brother and the stability of the regime.

In 1547, Katherine's household, and Elizabeth with it, moved to Chelsea where Thomas Seymour made illicit visits. It was June before the dowager queen's marriage became public knowledge when Thomas confessed the truth to King Edward, having gained the boy's approval for the union by making him believe that it was he who first suggested it. He even persuaded the king to write a letter, which Seymour dictated, to Katherine, promoting the match. Now, Edward recorded that 'the Lord Protector was much offended'.[5] The king's sister, Mary, was horrified that her stepmother had broken social protocol for mourning the late king. She was immediately concerned for Elizabeth's reputation which might suffer simply because she was part of the household at Chelsea under her stepmother's protection. Mary, now aged 32 years and spending most of her time at Kenninghall, wrote directly to her half-sister inviting her to live with her. In addition to Katherine's scandalous behaviour, Mary could not forget that Elizabeth's mother was Anne Boleyn and she feared that her half-sister might be morally damaged by the events she witnessed. Perhaps she remembered Vives' injunction that young virgins should be kept from the company of men. But Elizabeth preferred to remain at Chelsea, confirming her elder sister's worst fears. Elizabeth had a warm relationship with Katherine Parr, as their letters to one another attest. The dowager queen had given Elizabeth's life stability, and a relationship with her father. Katherine encouraged her studies and took an interest in her wellbeing. Henry's sixth wife was the closest thing to an aristocratic mother that Elizabeth knew and daughters remained under their mother's supervision until they wed.[6] Besides which, the dowager queen loved music and dancing, just as much as Elizabeth. Life at Chelsea was likely to be much more enjoyable than in Mary's household.

Mary was right to be worried though. Thomas Seymour was Elizabeth's stepfather and effectively her guardian. It was his duty to protect her but he flirted with the girl even before his marriage to Katherine was made public. Kat Ashley, Elizabeth's lady mistress knew about Thomas Seymour's affection for her young charge. And Kat, who had a soft spot for the handsome admiral, was quick to reflect that Elizabeth would have married the man if the council permitted it. John Ashley was less sanguine. He noted that Elizabeth blushed if Seymour's name was mentioned and warned his wife of the dangers of the situation. But there was little that they could do. While Edward learned to rule a kingdom, his sister learned the dangers of being a vulnerable female in the care of a predatory guardian.

Within days of his residence becoming permanent, Seymour arranged to have copies of keys to all the rooms in Chelsea, including Elizabeth's chamber. Now that she was married, everything Katherine owned belonged to her husband who the law regarded as holding natural supremacy over her. To make matters even worse, Kat no longer slept in Elizabeth's chamber claiming that the room was too little for a truckle bed.[7] The girl, unusually for the time, was on her own during the night. Even though her maids were close at hand in an adjoining room, there was no one to protect her. Seymour took to arriving in Elizabeth's room, in his night shirt with his legs bare, early in the morning while his stepdaughter was still in bed. Elizabeth, recognising that such behaviour was improper, tried to be dressed and at her studies by the time Seymour appeared, in which case he bid her good day and left. If she was still in bed or only partly clothed, the admiral would try to get into bed with the girl, tickling her or slapping her across the buttocks in an entirely unfitting manner but which he passed off as horseplay. To modern eyes, the admiral's behaviour, scandalous at the time, was abusive whether or not Elizabeth was alarmed, excited or a mixture of both.

Kat Ashley was initially complacent about the admiral's behaviour but became sufficiently alarmed to report it to Katherine Parr. Elizabeth's stepmother, rather than confronting Seymour, initially chose to regard the whole matter as innocent fun. She even joined her husband in the morning romps to diminish their significance and, on one occasion, at Hanworth in Middlesex which had been one of Anne Boleyn's homes, she held Elizabeth while her husband cut her gown to ribbons leaving the girl clutching them to herself in order to maintain some degree of modesty. Kat failed to protect her charge and was unable to deter Seymour or the house gossip that muttered about the admiral's interest in Henry VIII's younger daughter. More importantly Kat did not insist that either she or another of Elizabeth's women move back into her bedchamber to act as a chaperone.

Throughout it all, Elizabeth continued to study during the day and spend the evening with her ladies but, even then, Seymour began to toy with her. While they were at Hanworth, Seymour, perhaps to deflect his wife's suspicions, claimed to have seen his stepdaughter in the embrace of another man when he happened to look out the window.[8] Kat challenged her and Elizabeth, in tears, denied the allegation. Mistress Ashley, who knew that the only man that the girl came into contact with was her tutor Grindal, assumed that the dowager was growing jealous of her stepdaughter's friendship with Seymour. Nonetheless, she decided to keep a closer watch on Elizabeth in the future.[9]

Katherine, Seymour and Elizabeth went to court for the Christmas festivities of 1547–1548. The crowded court gave the king's sister some respite from the admiral's advances. Besides, Seymour was otherwise occupied. He tried to persuade the king to sign a letter to Parliament in favour of his own suit as the king's governor but Edward sought the advice of Cheke before putting his name to the document. The tutor advised the 10-year-old not to agree despite the fact that Seymour thought the tutor was in his own pocket.[10] Cheke would later warn Edward against writing to anyone since he was the king and his words carried authority.

Elizabeth's new year got off to a poor start. Her likable young tutor, William Grindal, sickened and died from the plague during her absence that winter. Katherine wished to replace him with her lawyer, Francis Goldsmith, but Elizabeth preferred Roger Ascham from Cambridge who recommended Grindal and who was also a colleague of Edward's tutors, John Cheke and William Buckley. Ascham, who needed the funds that came with the post, petitioned Elizabeth and Kat for advancement while Goldsmith, who was already part of Katherine's household, flattered his mistress rather than his prospective pupil. It proved to be a mistake on Goldsmith's part when Elizabeth was permitted to make her own choice in the matter. It helped that the scholar had the support of the king's tutor, John Cheke. Even so, Ascham expressed the view when he first learned of the competition for the role of tutor that he was 'uneasy at being the cause of disagreement' on such an important matter and told Cheke that he advised Elizabeth to accept Katherine's choice.[11]

Ascham, who soon established a daily routine in the classroom, based his curriculum for Elizabeth on the Bible and on the classics, with particular emphasis on Greek.[12] It was his view that the best way to learn a language was through imitating the best authors.[13] By the spring of 1550 he acknowledged that his pupil surpassed the learning even of Thomas More's daughters. 'The brightest star' he wrote, 'is my illustrious Lady Elizabeth.'[14] Ascham considered there to be six ways to learn a language and become more eloquent at the same time. Imitation, by copying words, phrases and style, was but one and it served a dual purpose. He wanted his pupil to make comparisons and extract general principles of grammar and rhetoric from her understanding of the passages she read. The other methods for learning a language included: paraphrasing a passage; turning a piece of literature into another form, for example turning a poem into a piece of prose, which he called 'metaphrasis'; summarising or abridgement; recitation[15] and; finally, 'translatio linguarum' or the challenge of double translation which Ascham stated was by far the most common method of teaching a language.[16] Texts were translated from Latin or Greek to English before being changed back into their original tongue. Ascham was intent on developing a purity of style within his charge. Elizabeth read Cicero and Titus Livius to enhance her knowledge of Latin and the New Testament, as well as the works of Isocrates and Sophicles, to hone her Greek. He wrote with some pride of Elizabeth's precise and pared back style that rejected more convoluted modern writers. Known for his ability to inspire his students, it is scarcely surprising that Elizabeth flourished under his supervision.

In the afternoons Ascham believed that 'learning should be mingled with honest mirth and comely exercises'.[17] The view that pupils learned through pleasure and through games as well as traditional study methods meant that he encouraged Elizabeth to ride, to hunt, to dance and to practise music, for which he himself had something of a passion but feared it 'over-sharpened' men's wits if studied too much, as did the sciences.[18] Elizabeth's programme for exercise, with the exclusion of knightly pursuits, was very similar to the education provided for the male Tudors even though no one anticipated that Henry's younger daughter would ever become queen. She turned into a superb horsewoman who loved to ride long distances, often at speeds which terrified the men who were responsible for her safety. When she became queen, Elizabeth's stables housed as many as 300 horses, bred for their looks and their speed.[19] Like her cousin, Frances Brandon, she enjoyed hunting and is recorded as killing deer with a cross bow as well as liking hawking. Elizabeth was turning into a young woman who might best serve her brother through the making of a diplomatic marriage that would benefit the realm as a whole.

Unfortunately, the presence of Ascham in Elizabeth's life did nothing to deter Thomas Seymour from his pursuit. The admiral continued to flirt both with his stepdaughter, her lady mistress and her maids. Power did not lay in Katherine Parr's hands either at home or on the political stage. She was denied access to Edward VI so had no influence, and Somerset's wife, Anne Stanhope, was quick to diminish her. Elizabeth, on the other hand, was second in line to the throne after her sister Mary and, besides, Seymour was a man who was used to getting what he wanted. No one was able to advise Elizabeth on the predicament in which she found herself or her complicated feelings for the admiral. Her cousin, Lady Jane Grey, who was Seymour's ward, and part of the Chelsea household, was too young. The two cousins respected one another but Elizabeth, who was three years older, was on the cusp of womanhood. Although they studied together on occasion and shared a love of music, they were not of an age to confide in another. And Kat Ashley still harboured the view that the admiral would make an excellent match. Matters came to a head during the spring of 1548 when Katherine, who was pregnant with her first child, discovered Elizabeth in her husband's arms.[20] Rather than blame Seymour for either the betrayal of trust or the potentially disastrous scandal, the queen tore into Elizabeth and Kat Ashley for her failure to protect the girl.

Once she had time to think about it, Katherine decided that the best thing to do was to remove her stepdaughter from Thomas's company, which would also eliminate the temptations to which the Lord Admiral succumbed. Elizabeth would not accompany the Seymours to Sudeley Castle where Katherine intended to have her child. The king's younger daughter was to go into exile once more while Jane Grey accompanied the queen to the Gloucestershire home of Seymour, who had been created Baron Seymour of Sudeley in 1547.

Jane was a fortnight younger than her cousin, King Edward, having been born on 31 October 1537. She and her sisters, Katherine and Mary, grew up at Bradgate Park in Leicestershire. Like their royal cousins, the Grey girls were used to a routine, supervised by Jane's nurse, Mrs Ellen, which revolved around attending chapel to hear divine service and to the classroom under the supervision of staff employed to care for them and to educate them. Jane learned her letters and the prayers deemed essential in a pious household.

Their parents, Frances Brandon, the daughter of Henry VIII's sister Mary, and her husband, Henry Grey, 3rd Marquess of Dorset, were reformers who shared their religious viewpoints with the men they employed to educate their daughters. Their tutor, until Jane was 4 years old, was Dr Thomas Harding, who was also Henry Grey's chaplain. The Grey sisters were also taught etiquette, how to dance and to play musical instruments, including the lute, and how to sew as befitted well educated Tudor girls.

The Duke and Countess of Suffolk were ambitious for their daughters, who were of royal blood. They wanted Jane, Katherine and Mary to have a humanist education of the kind enjoyed by their royal cousins. In about 1541, Harding was joined at Bradgate by John Aylmer, who owed his education at Cambridge to Jane's father. As well as reading and writing, the Grey sisters studied languages and history. Jane excelled at both Latin and Greek. She also learned French, Spanish, Hebrew and some Arabic. It was later recorded that Jane spoke eight languages including Italian which she learned from Michelangelo Florio who dedicated a grammar book to her.[21] Like her cousin, Elizabeth, she was tutored in handwriting, the Bible, dancing, music and deportment. And all three of the sisters were required to be proficient needlewomen. Their parents, who were keen hunters, insisted that Jane learn how to ride, to hunt and to go hawking, because that was what was expected of a noblewoman.

The Greys were also extremely ambitious, so when Thomas Seymour promised Henry Grey that he could facilitate a marriage between the king and Jane, the couple were captivated, even though Edward was supposed to marry his 5-year-old cousin, Mary Queen of Scots. Under the terms of Henry VIII's will, Mary and Elizabeth who had been returned to the succession in 1546, stood between Jane and the throne. Jane's mother, Frances, should have come before her daughters but was omitted by the king. A marriage between the king and Jane would trump Henry's will and bypass the order for inheritance dictated by the Act of Succession.

It was not unusual for aristocratic children to be educated in the houses of people other than their parents and it helped that Seymour offered Grey £2000 for the guardianship of his eldest daughter in return for the guarantee that Jane would marry the king.[22] Placing children and young adults in households of higher-ranking members of the nobility was seen by Tudor parents as a sensible way of attaining patronage and a method for tightening political and social ties as well as sound strategy for making a good marriage, or being introduced to life at court. Often education and service were intertwined as a way of gaining a chance at upwards social mobility. Bess of Hardwick was the daughter of a Derbyshire squire but her service as one of Francis Brandon's ladies-in-waiting bought her into contact with her second husband, Sir William Cavendish, who had amassed a fortune through his work for the Tudors. For the Greys, Seymour's guardianship presented access to power and the possibility of political gain of the kind they dreamed about. Practically, Jane found that Seymour was kinder than her own parents, who punished her with 'pinches, nips and bobs'[23] when she failed to meet their exacting standards. Little else changed for Jane in the short term during her residence at Seymour Place or in the household of Katherine Parr. Unlike Elizabeth, she was not subject to the admiral's advances.

It was Katherine Parr's responsibility to instil feminine graces in Jane and Elizabeth. She was well used to training noble girls who entered the queen's household to complete their courtly education and to improve their marriage prospects. The royal cousins may have studied together on occasion, Aylmer and Ascham were glad of one another's company and compared the curriculums that they were using to teach the two girls. Jane may also have heard some of the shocking rumours that were circulating within the household about the admiral and her cousin. If her parents were privy to any of the gossip after Elizabeth's departure from Katherine's residence for the home of Sir Anthony Denny at Cheshunt, they should have removed Jane from Seymour's custody. But they did not. Either Katherine acted quickly to squash any talk that was harmful to Elizabeth's reputation, or the Greys had their eye on a crown rather than their daughter's wellbeing.

In May 1548, Elizabeth was sent to Cheshunt in Hertfordshire. Her hasty departure from Chelsea bought home the danger that the admiral represented. In future she would be more circumspect. History can only speculate on the extent to which the whole experience of Seymour's pursuit, and its subsequent consequences shaped Elizabeth's personality and views about marriage. Katherine's choice of new guardian was an interesting one. She admired Sir Anthony Denny who was a moderate reformer and a humanist. He was also the only man with sufficient courage to tell Henry VIII that he was on his deathbed. Denny was not someone who could easily be intimidated. He was also known to be a serious-minded scholar, encouraged learning and took an interest in Elizabeth's development when she was a young child under the tutelage of Kat Ashley. Denny was a student of William Lily, the first master of St Paul's Cathedral School before attending St John's College, Cambridge. Ascham, Cheke and Henry Howard, Earl of Surrey were among the men who admired him. His home contained part of the library from Waltham Abbey[24] and one of his former roles involved maintaining the king's extensive collection of clocks. He had also been appointed as keeper of the royal mansion at Hatfield in 1542, so was known to Elizabeth who often resided there before Henry VIII's death.[25] Elizabeth's new governor was both powerful and discrete. He could safeguard her from the admiral's ambitions and provide her with intellectual stimuli. Ascham, who knew Denny and had sought his patronage in 1549,[26] must have been pleased at the thought of closer contact with his pupil's new guardian and the prospect of future patronage.[27]

Even more importantly, unlike Kat, who may have been Lady Denny's sister or aunt, Lady Denny was both pious and practical;[28] and Elizabeth's stepmother trusted her with her life. Lady Denny was known to be an ardent reformer, with the reputation for being something of a scholar[29] when she became one of Katherine's ladies-in-waiting in 1543, having served before her marriage as a maid of honour to Henry's first queen. She risked her own liberty to send Anne Askew 8 shillings after she was arrested on charges of heresy in 1546 for denying that the actual body and blood of Christ were present in the Eucharist. The woman's association with Katherine and a circle of reformers meant that she was targeted by Bishop Stephen Gardiner and the conservative court faction who wished to bring Henry VIII's last queen down.[30] Anne Askew and Joan Denny proved unswerving in their loyalty to both Katherine Parr and to their faith. As well as having the necessary court background, Lady Denny and her husband had raised twelve children. Despite this, Elizabeth refused to be separated from Kat Ashley and continued to refer to Kat rather than Lady Denny in the role of mistress. By July, Elizabeth who was troubled with ill health throughout the summer, had settled into the household at Cheshunt, appointed Thomas Parry as her cofferer, and was exchanging friendly letters with her stepmother who lamented that Elizabeth could not be with her.[31]

Admiral Seymour's plans to gain power for himself through Henry VIII's widow and younger children were beginning to unravel. Edward's tutor, John Cheke, became alarmed by the amount of money that the king had in his possession and discovered that Seymour was sending his nephew huge sums of cash. At the same time, the tutor learned of the plan to marry the king to his cousin Jane Grey. Edward VI fully intended to fulfil his father's wishes for him to marry Mary, Queen of Scots or else he intended to find a wealthy bride of his own choice. Jane did not feature in his calculations, even if he did enjoy her company when they played cards together. When Somerset discovered what his brother had been doing, he was furious and told Thomas that his meddling must stop. But all it did was foster the admiral's continued jealousy of his brother and stoke his desire to supplant Somerset.

Meanwhile, for Jane Grey at Sudeley Castle it was an opportunity to become close to the dowager queen who encouraged the girl with her studies and with her developing fervour for reform. Katherine's book *The Lamentation of a Sinner* published in January 1547 was a personal attestation of her shift from Catholicism to a stand point of justification by faith of the kind Luther preached. She is also likely to have owned prescribed texts that were regarded as heretical during the reign of Henry VIII. It was religious dissent that placed her in the shadow of the block during the summer of 1546 when Bishop Gardiner, and the conservative faction, began their campaign against the queen beginning with the torture and trial of Anne Askew. At that time Katherine's household included Joan Denny and Elizabeth Tyrwhitt who were both committed Protestants, as was Katherine's friend and Jane's step-grandmother, Katherine Willoughby, who married Mary Tudor's widower, Charles Brandon, Duke of Suffolk, in 1533. In short, Jane was well provided with exemplary role models of well-educated evangelising women in addition to having grown up under the roof of Henry Grey who was known for his anti-Catholic views.

Katherine Parr and Elizabeth continued to exchange letters during the final months of the dowager's pregnancy but they were not destined to meet again. On 30 August, Katherine gave birth to a girl called Mary but succumbed to puerperal fever and died on 5 September. Jane Grey was her chief mourner and expected to comport herself with royal dignity at the funeral which took place in Sudeley's own chapel. Seymour wrote to Jane's parents telling them the news, explaining that he intended to disband the queen's household and that it would be best if their daughter returned home. It was unfitting for Jane to remain in his custody given her age. People would have concluded that he intended to take his ward as his second wife when she was old enough to wed. Despite his stated intentions, Seymour did not dismiss his wife's household after Jane's departure for Bradgate. It was an expensive extravagance and there was no justification for retaining it without the presence of the dowager queen, Elizabeth or Jane Grey who were, respectively, second and third in line for the throne.

Seymour did grieve for the loss of his wife but it did not take him long to send a messenger to Elizabeth who was still at Cheshunt with Lord and Lady Denny mourning for Katherine. In private, Kat was enthusiastic about the admiral's renewed suit. Elizabeth, who turned 15 in September, had learned much from the humiliating experience of the spring and refused to send him a letter or to encourage him. She recognised that her stepfather's flirtation had nearly ruined her. And, if Elizabeth were to marry without the consent of the council, it would be treason. Whenever Kat raised the subject, her royal mistress would remind her that she would agree to nothing unless the council 'were content'.[31] Early in 1549, the admiral joined the army in Scotland at Musselburgh but rumours were spreading in London about his intentions towards Anne Boleyn's daughter.

In October 1548, Elizabeth moved her household to Hatfield, still in Sir Anthony Denny's care. Ascham also remained with her although her studies were so far advanced that she no longer needed a tutor. However, her stepfather was also kept informed about what was happening in Elizabeth's household. On the morning that she left Cheshunt for Hatfield, Kat Ashley spoke with one of Seymour's servants and John Seymour, Somerset's eldest son from his first marriage also arrived. His uncle had sent a message to Kat, 'whether her great buttocks were grown any less or more'?[32] It was a jest in poor taste as well as a reminder that the admiral had unfinished business with Elizabeth. Mistress Ashley remained enthusiastic about a match with Thomas Seymour but Kat's husband was angry with her meddling in a topic that bordered upon treason.[33] He was right to be worried. It was not long before the Regency Council heard the rumours linking Seymour to Edward's sister.

Events took a turn for the worse when Elizabeth, who wished to attend court that Christmas, sent Thomas Parry to ask the admiral if there was any house where she might stay during her visit since Durham House, left to her by her father, was being used by the Duke of Somerset as a mint. Parry swiftly became convinced by Seymour's smooth tongue and began to reveal information about his mistress and the household at Hatfield. The death of Katherine Parr effectively made Elizabeth the head of her own household but Parry was not used to balancing the accounts of so large a retinue and his mistress did not live within her means. On his return to Hatfield, the cofferer commended the admiral to Elizabeth and passed on Seymour's suggestion that she swap her lands for ones that adjoined his own. Elizabeth had no intention of allowing Thomas Seymour to meddle with her affairs even if Kat, fully updated by Parry, was all in favour of the admiral's plans.

Mistress Ashley was given a scare when she was summoned by the Protector's wife and informed of the rumours that were now awash in London and that she 'was not worthy to have governance of a king's daughter'.[34] It was said that Seymour had not disbanded Katherine Parr's household because he intended to pay court to Elizabeth. Furthermore, the countess added, Kat had not chaperoned Elizabeth as she should have been when the girl was resident in the dowager queen's household. Anne Stanhope had never liked Katherine Parr and had no time for her brother-in-law. Now she threatened Kat that she would replace her in Elizabeth's household with someone who was up to the job.

Having heard what Kat had to say when she returned from her errand, Elizabeth decided to remain in Hatfield for the Christmas of 1548. Parry, having reflected on events, thought that Seymour had not behaved well but Kat remained determined that the king's uncle would make an ideal husband. The lady mistress might have found Seymour handsome or even have been worried about how far things had gone at Chelsea. If Elizabeth did marry Seymour, then there could be no question of an assault upon her virtue. She confided in Parry that Katherine Parr was jealous of her stepdaughter. While Elizabeth had learned reticence, it appeared that her lady mistress was far too garrulous for comfort.

On 17 January 1549 Thomas Seymour was arrested after he forced his way into the king's bedchamber at Hampton Court. As he broke into the royal apartments, Edward's beloved spaniel began to bark and Seymour, who panicked, shot the dog. The effect of which was to alert the guards and ensure that Edward raised no voice on his uncle's behalf when he was accused of trying to kidnap the king and marry Elizabeth unlawfully. The Privy Council lost no time in gathering depositions from Seymour's household, from the king's servant, John Fowler,[35] and from the admiral's peers to find sufficient evidence to try him for treason. The affair was chronicled by the Imperial ambassador, François van der Delft, who added that the admiral was hoping to marry the Lady Elizabeth, who was now also under suspicion, and put her on the throne in her brother's stead.[36]

Kat Ashley and Thomas Parry were sent to the Tower on 20 January, while Elizabeth was placed in the custody of Sir Robert Tyrwhitt, whose wife was at Katherine Parr's bedside when she died. In February 1549, Elizabeth Tyrwhitt, who had been one of the dowager's ladies-in-waiting and was a close friend, gave her deposition about the queen's final days including her words that she was 'not well handled' by her husband and had been subject to 'many shrewd taunts'.[37] Tyrwhitt, who was appointed Katherine Parr's master of horse when she became queen,[38] subjected Elizabeth to a serious of unpleasant interrogations in an attempt to prove she consented to Seymour's plans. He even forged a letter which he placed in the hands of Blanche Parry knowing she would take it to her mistress. At first Elizabeth admitted nothing. It was only when she read the statements bearing the confessions and signatures of Kat and Parry that she became disconcerted, but only briefly. Elizabeth understood that she was fighting for her reputation and if she was implicated in Seymour's wild scheme to seize the king, then she was in danger of her life. All she would agree was that marriage was discussed as a possibility but only with the agreement of the council. In the end there was not enough evidence to arrest her and she remained stubbornly silent. Tyrwhitt thought extracting a confession from a teenage girl was going to be easy but he was forced, in the end, to concede that Elizabeth was a worthy opponent.

Henry VIII's daughter did not take kindly to Mistress Ashley languishing in the Tower or to her being dismissed from her post. She was even less amused by the damage that rumour and gossip might do to her reputation. Elizabeth was very aware of whose daughter she was. Anne Boleyn was condemned for adultery with five men as well as incest with her brother. People would readily believe that her daughter was tainted by the same bad blood. Elizabeth wrote to the Protector on 28 January 1549, relating what had taken place between her and Lord Seymour but added nothing more than the Tyrwhitts already knew. In addition to seeking to exonerate Kat, she noted that the change in governess gave the rumours that she was pregnant by Seymour some credence. These she declared were against her 'honour and honesty which above all other things I esteem'.[39] The Protector was in no mood to be sympathetic. He would shortly sign his brother's death warrant.

When Kat Ashley and Thomas Parry were finally released from the Tower they were not permitted to return to Elizabeth's household. Tyrwhitt's examination of Parry's accounts revealed their failings and Kat's deposition was damning. Lady Tyrwhitt, Katherine Parr's cousin by marriage, was to replace Mistress Ashley as lady governess. The council sent Elizabeth a letter instructing her to receive Lady Tyrwhitt's service's 'thankfully, and also hear and follow her good advice'.[40] No one told the men who served the king that the 15-year-old had a mind of her own, and a royal one at that. The Tyrwhitts were not so sanguine. They expected the storm that broke over their heads when they shared the news with Henry VIII's daughter.

Seymour was beheaded on 20 March 1549. Until Thomas Seymour killed the king's pet dog, Edward was fond of him in a way that Somerset never managed. Now he recorded the event without emotion in his journal. Elizabeth kept her own counsel. She is reported to have said, 'this day died a man of much wit and very little judgement'. Her own interrogation and that of her household, as well as Seymour's death, was another lesson, if one was needed, following on from the executions of her own mother and of Catherine Howard, of the dangers of marriage. The assets of wariness and silence would stand her in good stead when her sister Mary ascended the throne after Edward's death and tried to return the kingdom to Catholicism. Elizabeth's childhood was over. She would reinvent herself as a virtuous Protestant princess while England, torn by religious differences and economic difficulties, tumbled into widespread unrest.

Chapter 11

Final Lessons

In May 1549, once the furore over Seymour subsided, Elizabeth wrote, in English, to Edward sending him her portrait. It was the first time that she used a portrait of herself as a tool to make a statement about how she wished to be perceived.[1] Elizabeth knew that she had to appear in public in order to restore her reputation rather than languishing in the country.[2] Thanks to her education at the hands of Grindal and Ascham, the king's sister was a talented writer who knew how to present herself, but she also understood the power of images to communicate in the same way that Henry Tudor, Margaret Beaufort and her own father had done. Within a few months, she was restored to favour and Elizabeth, now 16 years old, went to court to celebrate Christmas.

By the end of 1549 the Duke of Somerset was unpopular with both his royal nephew and with the rest of the country. His religious reforms and debasement of the coinage coincided with enclosure of common land and harvest failure which culminated in widespread unrest. John Dudley, Earl of Warwick, who put down Kett's Rebellion in Norfolk in the summer of 1549 and who had an established reputation as a successful soldier, was the safe pair of hands who forced Somerset from office and emerged as the council's new leader in early 1550. Edward recorded that his uncle was guilty of 'ambition' and 'vainglory' as well as 'enriching himself' at the expense of the king, which was perhaps what angered the boy, who had been kept short of cash, most.[3] The duke was initially imprisoned in the Tower but soon released and reconciled with Warwick who was now the Duke of Northumberland. But the following year Somerset was returned to the Tower on charges of treason and put on trial. The king wrote a lengthy entry in his journal identifying the judges as well as summarising the content of his uncle's defence[4] which did not prevent his execution on 22 January 1552.

The new Protector reorganised the king's household to ensure that his own men were in positions of influence. Sir John Gates, a gentleman of the king's privy chamber, assumed the position of vice chamberlain. Gates, a lawyer, was married to Sir Anthony Denny's sister and had been trusted along with Denny to hold Henry VIII's 'dry stamp' which could be used instead of the king's signature to approve privy purse finances. In the spring of 1551, he became a privy councillor and was appointed Chancellor of the Duchy of Lancaster. Sir Thomas Darcy, a cousin of the king's, who had risen to the position of vice chamberlain under Somerset was now promoted to the post of chamberlain and created Baron Darcy of Chiche. Like Gates, his service to the Tudors was long standing, having first been appointed as carver of the king's table in 1540. Now he was captain of a strengthened Yeoman of the Guard and instructed to lead a commission to reform the revenue courts. Among the other men appointed to serve the king were Northumberland's brother, Andrew Dudley, and his son, Robert Dudley, who spent time being schooled alongside the king. Henry Sidney, the husband of Northumberland's daughter Mary, was also appointed. He was raised alongside the king as one of his companions during his father's term of office as Edward's chamberlain from 1538. Edward made a note of all the changes in his journal[5] which included the appointment of Sir Henry Neville as a gentleman of the privy chamber. He had also served Henry VIII, was his godson and a witness to the king's will. He was also a convinced Protestant. None of the king's entries made any analysis of the political reasons behind the new appointments or the manner by which access to him was even more restricted than it was while Somerset was in charge.

Northumberland's success with the king lay in recognising that Edward resented his uncle Somerset's dictatorial approach to governorship and that the king wanted to be involved in the government of his realm. From 1550 onwards Edward's journal contains more information about matters of state, including a grasp of the effects of debasing the coinage on Crown income. In 1551, William Thomas, the clerk for the privy council, presented the king with a manuscript translation of Giosafat Barbaro's *Travels to Tana and Persia*.[6] It was just one of a series of master classes designed to provide the king with the information he needed about his country and its successful management. By 1551 Edward VI was regularly attending council meetings, writing memoranda for its attention[7] and contributing to the discussions there as well as to the decisions being made. He may have been coached beforehand but Edward's own perception of his growing power was an important factor in his goodwill towards Northumberland.

For Elizabeth, the change in regime meant the removal of the Tyrwhitts who were still in control of her household in February 1549. It is unknown whether her relationship with Lady Tyrwhitt improved in the interim since even her husband declared that she was 'not sane' when it came to religion being 'half a Scripture woman'.[8] More positively the lady governess was a scholar in her own right. A book of her poems and prayers entitled *Morning and Evening Praiers, with Divers Psalmes Himnes and Meditations* was published in 1574. The original, a tiny girdle book covered in gold, today held by the British Museum,[9] was given to Elizabeth when she was queen. The volume also contains a partial version of *The Queen's Prayers* by Katherine Parr, so perhaps the two Elizabeths did find some common ground during their time together at Hatfield.

Sir Henry Parker was appointed as Elizabeth's chamberlain by Northumberland's Privy Council. He was the son of the 10th Baron Morley, who was raised in the household of Lady Margaret Beaufort, and Alice St John who was Margaret's niece. Parker's father, a courtier, served Henry VIII throughout his reign, condemning his son-in-law, George Boleyn, to death and in 1542 he was present in the House of Lords when the Bill of Attainder was read out against his own daughter, Jane Viscountess Rochford, for her part in Catherine Howard's adultery. Elizabeth's new chamberlain had been present at Anne Boleyn's wedding and coronation[10] but was more prominent in an administrative capacity in both Hertfordshire and Essex than at court. His appointment had much to do with his religious beliefs, his service on local commissions[11] and the death of Sir Anthony Denny in September 1549 which left a void in the region's local government. Parker's own end, before his father, in 1552, resulted in the appointment of Sir Walter Buckler, Katherine Parr's former secretary, as Elizabeth's chamberlain. Buckler was already part of Elizabeth's household when he was selected. Like many of the other appointments made by Northumberland and the council at that time he was a supporter of the Protestant reformation and a former colleague of Sir Anthony Denny. He would eventually be removed on the orders of the Privy Council in March 1553 but the exact reason for his dismissal is unclear.

The beginning of 1550 marked the end of Roger Ascham's first tenure as Elizabeth's tutor. Her relationship with the scholar had cooled as the result of an argument between him and Parry. Nor did Ascham much like court life which he regarded as superficial and frivolous. He also missed Cambridge and visiting it was difficult. He complained that Elizabeth would never let him go anywhere.[12] In January 1550 he returned briefly to his college before accepting the post of secretary to Sir Richard Moryson, the English ambassador at the court of the Holy Roman Emperor. Before Ascham left England to take up his new post, he visited Bradgate Park where he encountered Jane Grey who was reading Plato's *Paedo* in Greek while the rest of the household were out hunting. In 1570, Ascham published *The Schoolmaster* which contained an account of their conversation that winter's day.[13] He contrasted Jane's love of learning with the cruelty of her parents and her fear of them. The treatise would ensure Jane's reputation as a gentle scholar and make her a role model for the education of girls during the Victorian period. It meant that Frances Brandon would be cast as an ambitious and tyrannical mother while Jane's father, Henry Grey, Duke of Suffolk, was painted as a weak and greedy man.

Jane and Ascham continued their correspondence but, by April 1552, Ascham was back in Elizabeth's service, not as a tutor, but as a friend and mentor sharing her studies. Some of the reason for his return lay in his ongoing financial difficulties, bought about in part because of his love of gambling and cockfighting.[14] In a letter from Ascham to Cheke, sent on 11 November 1550, he described his visit to Antwerp, Louvain and Cologne with the embassy but also revealed that he asked Elizabeth for funds because of his lack of money.[15] In 1552, as his embassy came to an end, he wrote to William Cecil hoping to gain a post at Cambridge teaching Greek, or failing that some employment that would pay either at court or abroad.[16.] Ascham would eventually become Queen Mary's Latin secretary. It was a position he would hold until his death in 1568.

Edward VI's school lessons continued in parallel to his education for kingship but they took on a more practical hue. Cheke arranged for Thomas Gemini, the Flemish engraver and instrument maker who settled in London and found favour with King Henry VIII as well as his son, to make a brass astronomical quadrant for the king and an astrolabe used to calculate time and the position of the planets. He also purchased a copy of Robert Record's *First Principles of Geometrie.* Edward wrote an exercise entitled *In Defence of Astronomy* in the same year.[17] It took the form of an oration in Latin but is more theological than scientific in content. The quadrant and the manuscript taken together reflect the growing importance of exploration and foreign trade to the management of the Tudor economy. John Dee, the mathematician and astronomer, was among the men who gained patronage from the king during his brief reign while the Milanese physician, Cardano, who stayed with John Cheke in 1550 described a 'boy of wondrous promise'[18] who was able to talk to his visitor about the nature of comets.

In August, the king's tutors were dismissed and his formal education came to an end. Ambassadors visiting court were impressed by Edward's grasp of Latin, French and Greek. He also excelled at horsemanship, weaponry and tennis. He was not the ailing boy of modern popular imagination. In March 1551, he and sixteen of his companions were challenged to 'run at base, shoot and run at ring' against any seventeen of his servants and courtiers.[19] The competition required the king to be able to run, shoot arrows at a target, and place a lance through a ring while galloping towards it on horseback. It was all followed by a tournament.[20] The previous year he was present at a bear hunt and during a progress of 1552 was occupied by 'killing wild beasts'.[21] Skidmore suggests that Edward evolved from a promising scholar into a brilliant young man.[22] Afterall, he was trained for kingship from the moment he drew breath. Holbein painted him as a baby, waving a gilded rattle as through it was a sceptre.

Northumberland promised that the king would focus on statecraft. Edward's power remained limited despite his desire to rule for himself but the duke's religious reforms and Cranmer's prayerbook were changes of which the king approved. The king's interest in religion found a focus in his sister Mary who refused to conform to her brother's prayer book. Edward challenged his sister Mary's Catholicism and tried to force her to conform to his beliefs. The pair argued in March 1551 about her right to hear Mass. In the middle of it all, Mary burst into tears and Edward, who loved his sister, also cried.[23] When their tears were dry, the king promised he would not harm Mary whose defiance of the Privy Council began when she was just a child. When it became clear that the king would not say what had been rehearsed prior to Mary's arrival, the meeting was drawn to a close and the council sent a letter instead. The last paragraph was written by the king and it made plain that he intended to have his laws obeyed by everyone who lived within his realm, including Mary.[24]

By contrast Elizabeth, whose education lay in the care of the same group of humanist reformers as her brother, thanks to Katherine Parr's influence, was made very welcome at court. Her religious education continued at the hands of her new chaplain, Edmund Allen, who was another of the Cambridge circle of scholars. Allen, who was skilled in Latin and Greek, wrote a short text on bringing up children in the knowledge and commandments of God. Since 1547 it was a legal requirement for clerics to have a licence to preach. Elizabeth sought one in 1547 for her chaplain, Hugh Goodacre, and did so again in 1550.[25] She was still not legally of age but there were no more attempts to appoint governors or another lady governess to monitor Elizabeth. Instead, the Privy Council retained oversight of her estates and at some time in 1552 Sir William Cecil, who began his career in Somerset's household, was appointed as her surveyor. Loades suggests that her estates were managed by the Court of Augmentations during her minority but there is no evidence of it in any accounts.[26] Legally girls might marry when they were 12 years old but they remained minors until they were 16 years old if they did not marry. Wardship for male heirs ended when they reached 21 years and their age was verified by a jury of witnesses. At a minimum, Elizabeth remained a ward of the Crown until she celebrated her 16th birthday, but there is no conclusive record of the manner in which she or her estates were managed or the age at which the Privy Council determined she was an adult. In general, society and the law determined that women were naturally inferior to their male counterparts. Aristocratic girls were supervised and protected by their guardians until they married and then they became subordinate to their husbands. Most of them were wed before they were 21 years of age.[27] Her formal education was coming to an end and the Privy Council was eager to arrange Elizabeth's marriage for the benefit of the State as well as avoiding the possibility of another ambitious man seeking to use a union with Edward's younger sister to make a play for power.

In February 1553, Edward developed a chest infection that he was unable to shake off. By April physicians began to fear that the king would not regain his health. Edward VI did not wish to be succeeded by either of his sisters and Northumberland was determined not to see the country return to Catholicism, or to lose his own position. The duke wrote to the Duke of Suffolk setting out the proposition that Mary's beliefs were 'sufficient reason for setting aside her claim'.[28] Elizabeth could not be included if her half-sister was excluded. Mary, Queen of Scots, the granddaughter of Margaret Tudor, was likewise discounted because, under a law of 1351, she was a foreigner so could not succeed to the throne. Northumberland urged either the Duchess of Suffolk or her eldest daughter to accept the crown if it was offered to them. Besides placing Jane on the throne, the duke also suggested that she wed Guildford, his youngest and only unmarried son.

Grey initially protested that Elizabeth was a 'worthy lady, and a Protestant'[29] but it did not take long to overcome Suffolk's reservations.

Fearing that his sisters might take foreign husbands and that his religious forms revoked, Edward wrote down his preferences, entitled a 'Devise for the Succession'. He hoped that he might live long enough for his cousins Frances Brandon or Jane Grey to have a son to wear the crown. He also listed potential male heirs of Jane's sisters Katherine and Mary as well as those of 12-year-old Margaret Clifford, the daughter of his cousin Eleanor Brandon, Countess of Cumberland. In May, when Edward knew that he was dying, the 'Devise', which was still only a draft, was changed to name only Lady Jane Grey and her heirs. None of Edward's wishes carried any legal weight. Even though the 'Devise' was issued under terms of Letters Patent there was no amendment made to the 1546 Act of Succession. Letters Patent could not turn over an Act of Parliament on their own.

Northumberland, the *de facto* ruler of the realm, behaved as though nothing was wrong with the king but continued, behind the scenes, to secure an alternate succession that would leave him in control of the realm. Jane Grey's marriage to Guildford Dudley was celebrated on 21 May 1553 but the king was too ill to attend the event. Jane's sister, Katherine, was wedded at the same time to William, Lord Herbert, the heir of the Earl of Pembroke; Mary Grey found herself betrothed to Lord Grey of Wilton and Margaret Clifford was engaged to Northumberland's brother, Andrew Dudley. Once the celebrations were over Jane returned with her parents to Suffolk Place while Katherine went to live at Baynard's Castle with her new husband, although they were allotted separate bedchambers. The Lord Protector believed that the unions strengthened his hold on the Tudor regime.

By August, Edward was sickly enough for it to be commented upon and at the end of October he developed a rash which the king described as measles and smallpox. He celebrated his 15th birthday at Hampton Court but it was becoming apparent to those closest to him that the king was suffering from consumption, as tuberculosis was then known, and that his reign would not be a long one. All of Henry VIII's plans and marriages had availed him nothing. The succession pointed in the direction of Mary who refused to comply with the Privy Council in any matter other than her marriage as directed by the terms of Henry's will and then of Elizabeth, who had proved remarkably adroit at outwitting the men sent to trap her over the matter of Thomas Seymour.

On 4 July 1553, Mary and Elizabeth were summoned to appear at Greenwich to comfort the sick king. Both of them had learned the lessons of their difficult and often dangerous early years. Mary, who was at Hunsdon in Hertfordshire, proved herself to be her mother's daughter when she rode out into the darkness on the same evening. She covered 40 miles of her journey on the first night to reach Sawston Manor in Cambridgeshire. She continued to Framlingham Castle in Norfolk where she planned to raise troops to defend her rightful claim to the throne. When Jane Grey was declared queen on 10 July, four days after Edward's death, Mary sent a letter to the Privy Council demanding their allegiance. Although no queen had ever sat on England's throne before, Mary had no intention of being denied what was rightfully hers.

Elizabeth, who was at Hatfield, having learned the value of prevarication, sent a message that she was unwell and took to her bed. She gave no indication of supporting Mary or otherwise. Nor did she voice any thoughts about Edward's attempts to cut her out of the succession. Only when it was certain that Mary was triumphant did Elizabeth put pen to paper to congratulate Queen Mary I and enquire whether or not she should wear mourning for their brother. When she arrived in London, on 29 July, before her sister, she came dressed in Tudor green and white accompanied by 2000 men to take up residence in Somerset House.[30] Mary's little sister, who was now heir to the throne, had, it transpired, learned about the importance of appearance and symbolism, just as the earlier Tudors had done. Like her grandfather, Elizabeth was never educated to sit upon the throne and like him she faced an uncertain future before the crown was set upon her head in 1558 but the men and women who were responsible for raising her had prepared her well.

A Who's Who of Lady Mistresses and Governesses Who Raised the Tudors

Those trusted to raise Tudor princes and princesses were required to be experienced married women, of gentle birth and impeccable reputation, with proven credentials. These were either acquired through sustained service to the monarchy, in all its hues, or through familial ties to the Crown itself, preferably both.

Financial accounts record the names of lady mistresses, governesses and tutors with an exactness of address not always evident in ambassadorial reports or other correspondence. Any gently born woman, whether they were wives, widows or daughters, was entitled to be addressed as mistress, while only the wives of knights might be called 'Dame'. This form of address became increasingly old-fashioned as the sixteenth century progressed, and was replaced by the word 'Lady' but still appeared in legal documents including wills. Women who held titles in their own right or whose father possessed a title, from the rank of baron upwards, retained their rank even if they married beneath them. Daughters of dukes were all permitted to use 'Lady' before their given names and family name.

Anne Herbert, who cared for Henry Tudor during his childhood, for instance, might have been addressed as Mistress Devereux before her marriage; Dame Herbert after her wedding to Sir William; and Lady Herbert when her husband was elevated to the rank of baron in 1461. The hierarchical system was complicated by the fact that the term 'Lady' was used as a form of respectful address by social inferiors to their betters. Cromwell consistently refers to the daughters of wives and knights in this form, especially if they held an integral role in the royal nursery. A mistress of the royal nursery might be addressed as an honorific 'Lady' whatever her place in society.

Jane Guildford was also known as 'Mother Guildford' in correspondence from her former charge, Henry VII's daughter, in the same way that Edward

VI called his childhood nurse 'Mother Jack', demonstrating that women employed to look after and to supervise the day-to-day care of the royal family could become more like foster mothers than governesses. This was particularly true if their service was of long standing, spanned generations or involved a number of royal siblings. However, not all Tudor monarchs wanted their children to be nurtured in a loving environment. Governesses were also responsible for instilling discipline and on occasion seemed, to their charges at least, more like tormentors and goalers.

Katherine Ashley (Astley) née Champernowne (d.1565)
Katherine, or Kat, was the daughter of Sir Philip Champernowne of Modbury, Devon and his wife, Katherine Carew. The Champernownes were an extensive gentry family who were related to the Bonvilles, Courtenays and Hungerfords as well as the Carews and Raleighs.[1] Large numbers of children and the use of common forenames across different branches mean that it is not always possible to identify the exact nature of familial relationships. Kat was either a sister or aunt of Lady Joan Denny. The pair of them were kin to Katherine Raleigh, the mother of Sir Walter, but some texts describe Katherine as Kat and Joan's sister while others identify her as a sister-in-law.[2]

What is certain is that both Kat and Joan were well educated for women of their social rank by the time that they came to court. Katherine gained a position, which was initially unpaid, in Elizabeth's nursery by the autumn of 1536 due to the influence of Thomas Cromwell. At that time Henry VIII was little interested in appointing a tutor for his younger daughter or devising a programme of study. It fell to Kat, under Lady Bryan's watchful gaze, to teach Elizabeth to read, write and to sew. The position gained greater formality in 1537 when Lady Margaret Bryan was called upon to care for Prince Edward. In later years the queen gave Kat credit, 'for great labour and pain in bringing me up in learning and honesty'.[3] It was not long before Kat recognised that Elizabeth's learning was outpacing her own and sought assistance from other, more learned, tutors.

In 1545, Kat married John Astley, or Ashley, who was distantly related to Elizabeth through the Boleyns. Kat Ashley's married status was perhaps one of the reasons that she replaced Blanche Herbert, Lady Troy as Elizabeth's governess at around the same time that her charge's household joined Katherine Parr's at Chelsea in 1547. By then, Kat was Elizabeth's close confidante.

Mistress Ashley foolishly encouraged Elizabeth to look warmly upon the courtship of Thomas Seymour both before and after his marriage to the dowager queen, Katherine Parr rather than protecting her from the admiral's attentions in 1547 and 1548. Following Seymour's arrest for treason, in January 1549, Kat was sent to the Tower of London and questioned until she confessed all she knew about Seymour's designs and her own part in it. Her husband, John, was imprisoned in the Fleet at the same time. It was only in 1551 that Kat was reinstated to her former position. Elizabeth refused to recognise the appointment of any other governess beside her beloved Kat.

It would not be the last time that Elizabeth was deprived of Kat's company. In 1556 she was suspected of involvement in the Dudley Conspiracy, which aimed to remove Queen Mary and place Elizabeth on the throne in her place. The plotters' plan was for Elizabeth to marry Edward Courtenay, the grandson of Catherine of York. Evidence showed that members of Elizabeth's household knew about the plan. Kat was imprisoned and dismissed from her post once again.

When Elizabeth became queen in 1558, she appointed Kat to the influential post of chief gentlewoman of the privy chamber. She was unable to resist encouraging various suitors for Elizabeth's hand in marriage; it was, after all, unthinkable that her former charge would not marry. In 1562 she encouraged the suit of Erik XIV of Sweden in an attempt to break off Elizabeth's scandalous relationship with Robert Dudley.

Kat died in 1565 at Richmond, in her early sixties, much to the queen's evident distress. She had been ill some months previously but seemed recovered. In June, her condition suddenly deteriorated. The woman who had been a mother to Elizabeth, knew her secrets and nursed her when she was unwell was gone. Blanche Parry, who had rocked the queen's cradle and read to Elizabeth when she was a little girl, was appointed to Kat's position.

Isabel Baynton, (d.16 February 1573)

Isabel was the daughter of Sir Ralph Leigh and his first wife Joyce Culpeper. Sir Ralph was a lawyer and rose to become Treasurer of the Inner Temple while Joyce reared a family of five children. Sir Ralph died at about the same time as Henry VIII became king, but it was four years before Joyce, a wealthy widow with property, remarried to Edmund Howard. Her new husband preferred jousting with the king and his friends to the legal career that his father planned for him and was struggling with debt when he married Joyce.[1]

He was the third of Thomas Howard, 2nd Duke of Norfolk and Elizabeth Tilney's sons, and one of ten children in addition to their half-siblings from Elizabeth's first marriage to Sir Humphrey Bourchier. Isabel's new relations included the Boleyns, the Howards and the Bourchiers, of whom Lady Margaret Bryan was one. Joyce and Edmund had six more children, including Isabel's half-sister, Catherine Howard.

Little is known about Isabel's early life other than it was spent at Edmund Howard's home at Lambeth where Edmund made limited progress as a local justice, lost the king's favour and got himself deeper into debt with each passing year. Joyce's assets were soon mortgaged to meet the family's needs and Edmund's gambling debts. It is uncertain when Isabel's half-sister, Catherine Howard, was born. It could have been at any time between 1518 and 1527. It was not unusual in Tudor society for the birth of daughters, especially younger ones, not to be noted. For Edmund, the arrival of another daughter meant the need to find another dowry if the girl was to make a reasonable marriage. By the time of Isabel's wedding to Sir Edward Baynton at the beginning of 1531, her stepfather was on the verge of prison and Joyce Culpeper was dead. Sir Edward Baynton was a widower with seven children but she was more fortunate than her little sister Catherine, who was sent to live and be educated by the dowager Duchess of Norfolk, at Chesworth House in Horsham, Sussex.

Isabel was a good match despite the fecklessness of her stepfather. One of her cousin's, through Joyce's marriage into the Howard family, was Anne Boleyn. Although the king was not yet married to her, the Howards were becoming ever more influential at court. The connection to Anne Boleyn ensured that Baynton, who was a soldier, administrator, courtier and a supporter of reform,[2] enjoyed royal favour. In 1533, he was appointed vice chamberlain of the new queen's household. For the next three years Isabel resided either at court where she served Anne or at one of her husband's homes in Wiltshire. In July 1535, Isabel even played hostess to the king and queen at Bromham Hall, while they were on their summer progress.

Henry soon fell out of love with Anne. In 1536, the king determined to rid himself of his second queen who failed to give him a son. On 2 May Anne was arrested at Greenwich Palace on charges of adultery and treason along with six courtiers and her lutenist Mark Smeaton. Sir Edward was given the task of interrogating the men. Smeaton confessed to the crime of adultery. But even then, it was only after he was racked and his evidence was inconsistent with the known facts of the queen's diary. For Anne to sleep with a commoner was almost as unthinkable as being convicted of committing incest with her own brother, George Boleyn, Viscount Rochford. The woman for whom Henry VIII renounced the authority of the papacy was executed on 19 May, four days after George Boleyn, Francis Weston, Henry Norris and William Brereton. Of the seven who were originally arrested, all but Smeaton maintained their innocence. The poet Thomas Wyatt and Sir Richard Page were permitted to escape with their lives.

When Henry VIII married Jane Seymour on 30 May at the Palace of Whitehall, the Bayntons were invited to the wedding and Sir Edward was given the job of the queen's master of horse in addition to his responsibilities as vice chamberlain. The couple attended the baptism of Prince Edward at Hampton Court a year later, by which time Isabel was a mother herself. In 1537, Isabel was one of the twenty-nine women who walked behind Jane's coffin to mark each year of her life. The queen's household was broken up soon afterwards.

In 1538, Sir Edward and Isabel were appointed as vice chamberlain and lady mistress of the king's daughters, where they remained for the next two years. Although Mary and Elizabeth were both provided with their own households, they lived in the same residence. Cromwell revoked Mary Kingston's employment at the same time as notifying the Bayntons of their new status. The service of Lady Kingston, a granddaughter of Henry Scrope 4th Baron Scrope of Bolton, extended back to the funeral of King Henry VII. As wife of the Constable of the Tower, she was another of the women given the task of watching over Anne Boleyn before her execution. In October 1536 she helped carry Mary Tudor's train at the baptism of Prince Edward and was at Jane Seymour's funeral the following month. Afterwards she joined Princess Mary's newly re-established household but it is unclear why she was removed from the position.

In 1540, when the king married for a fourth time, Sir Edward resumed his position as vice chamberlain to the queen's household while Isabel returned to her employment as one of the queen's ladies. Like many of the other women who cared for the Tudors, Isabel Baynton remained as part of the extended network in correspondence with them. During the New Year's celebrations of 1544 she gave Mary, who was known for her love of clothing, a kirtle made from carnation coloured satin valued at 10s.[3]

Among the women appointed to serve Anne of Cleves, at the instigation of Thomas Howard, 3rd Duke of Norfolk, was Isabel's own half-sister, Catherine Howard. By July 1540, Anne of Cleves was queen no longer and the king had his gaze on a new bride — Catherine Howard. As Henry became more besotted, the influence of Catherine's uncle, Norfolk, grew. Catherine's extended family began to reap the rewards of royal favour as well as shifting the balance of power in the direction of conservative Catholicism. Isabel may have wondered for how long her little sister would be a pawn in the deadly game of faction politics at Henry's court.

By the summer of 1541 Queen Catherine was meeting Thomas Culpeper in secret and Thomas Cranmer, Archbishop of Canterbury had also discovered that Catherine was not as virtuous before her marriage, while she was in the care of Agnes Tilney, the dowager Duchess of Norfolk, as the king supposed. On 23 November 1541, Catherine Howard was taken from Hampton Court to Syon Abbey with only four ladies to care for her having been accused of immoral behaviour before she married, and sleeping with Thomas Culpeper subsequent to her union with the king. One of the women that accompanied the distraught queen was her half-sister. It is not known whether Isabel remained with Catherine through the trial that followed or stayed with her right up until her execution.

After 13 February 1542, Isabel does not appear on any further lists of ladies-in-waiting, although she was present at Hampton Court with her husband to see Henry VIII married for a sixth time to Katherine Parr. Sir Edward was appointed as the queen's vice chamberlain for the fifth time; it is unknown whether Isabel remained at court or chose to live with her children at their country home. Baynton's household duties did not prevent him from serving in the king's French campaign of 1543–1544. He died in November 1544, having bequeathed his estates to his sons. Isabel received the dower promised under the terms of their marriage contract, made in 1531. She wed for a second time to Sir James Stumpe, the widower of her stepdaughter Bridget, after 1545. When Stumpe, a wealthy Wiltshire clothier, died in 1563, she was married for a third time to Thomas Stafford.

Lady Margaret Bryan, 1st Baroness Bryan (c.1468–1552)
A descendent of King Edward III, Margaret Bourchier was born in about 1468. Her father, Sir Humphrey, a Yorkist, was killed during the Wars of the Roses at the Battle of Barnet in 1471. Margaret's brother, John, who

was not yet 5 years of age became a ward of Sir John Howard. Their mother, Elizabeth Tilney, an heiress in her own right, married John's son, Thomas Howard. Even though the Howards were a wealthy Norfolk family, related to the Mowbray dukes of Norfolk, at first glance it was not such a good marriage for Elizabeth, even if the Howards could claim descent from King Edward I.

Elizabeth Howard juggled the responsibilities of motherhood to a brood of nine children,[1] with employment as a lady-in-waiting to Edward IV's queen, Elizabeth Woodville. She had served the queen since her marriage to Edward became public knowledge in 1464, accompanied her and her children, including Elizabeth of York, into sanctuary in October 1470 and was present at the birth of Edward IV's son on 2 November.

Edward IV's death in 1483 changed the fortunes of the Howards. Margaret's stepfather was a personal friend of Richard, Duke of Gloucester and the family supported him when he became King Richard III. With the disappearance of Richard of York, Elizabeth Woodville's youngest son, who held the Duchy of Norfolk by right of his deceased bride, Anne Mowbray, Sir John Howard was elevated to a dukedom and Elizabeth's husband became the Earl of Surrey. Thomas carried the sword of state at Richard III's coronation and Margaret's mother was one of Anne Neville's attendants as well as becoming a lady of the bedchamber to the new queen.

Surrey was badly injured at Bosworth in 1485, attainted of treason and imprisoned in the Tower but Elizabeth Howard was permitted to keep her own estates and made the changeover to the Tudor court. For a time she and her children, not including Margaret who was married by then, found themselves under the guardianship of John de Vere, 14th Earl of Oxford. Surrey was pardoned in 1489 and restored to his title and some of his estates. His countess became one of Elizabeth of York's ladies and in 1489, as the Duchess of Norfolk, was one of Margaret Tudor's godmothers, reflecting not only Henry VII's desire to unite his kingdom under the Tudor rose but perhaps an enduring friendship forged between Margaret Beaufort and the Countess of Surrey during their time together in Elizabeth Woodville and Anne Neville's households.

Lady Bryan, who was raised with her half-brothers and sisters, was married three times. Her first marriage was arranged in 1478, under the auspices of the Howard family, when she was 11 years old, to John Sandys of the Vine who was about 14 years old.[2] Following his death she married for a second time before 1495, to Sir Thomas Bryan, the son of the Chief Justice of the Common Pleas. When Henry VIII ascended to the throne in 1509, Bryan was promoted to vice chamberlain in the household of Katherine of Aragon. Margaret accompanied her husband to court as one of the queen's ladies of the privy chamber. It was her job to attend to the queen's day-to-day requirements and to sit with her. It was during this time that Katherine's ladies embroidered, read books, or played musical instruments, danced and sang for the queen, as well as running any errands that the queen required. Margaret was attended by her two daughters, Elizabeth and Margaret, as well as by Lettice Peniston who was her ward. Like her mother before her, Margaret managed her role as Katherine's attendant as well as raising her own family. It was expected that anyone employed by the royal household would put the needs of their own families after those of the princes and princesses they served.

Lady Bryan's son, Francis, was a close friend of King Henry, having been raised with the king as one of his companions. The presence of the Bryans in both the king and the queen's households meant that as well as acquiring a courtly polish, Margaret's daughters were both eligible brides. In May 1512, Margaret the younger, married Sir Henry Guildford, another of the king's childhood companions and the son of Joan Vaux, a former lady mistress of the royal nursery at Eltham and a much-loved maternal figure.

At around the same time, it was rumoured that Margaret's younger daughter, Elizabeth Bryan, who was still only 12 years old, came to the notice of the king. The girl had been educated at court and was known to have performed in court masques and other entertainments. She is credited with persuading her Oxford educated uncle, John Bourchier, 2nd Baron Berners, to translate romantic tales into English including a Spanish story called *The Castle of Love*. Henry VIII gave her a diamond necklace and a fur coat and it was rumoured that in return she presented the king with a child before she turned 13-years.[3] Speculation aside, it was true that he granted Lady Margaret Bryan £500 at the time of Elizabeth's wedding, in 1514, to Sir Nicholas Carew, one of Henry's favourites. It is almost certain that the king arranged the match, given his attendance at the wedding and the accompanying large gift of land to Elizabeth's new husband worth 50 marks.[4] The newlyweds were at the heart of court life, hosting members of the royal family at their homes at Beddington and Bletchingly. They were part of the retinue that went to France for the meeting in 1520 between the kings of England and France, known as the Field of the Cloth of Gold. The king even gave Margaret's son-in-law his own tilting yard.

In 1516, upon the birth of Princess Mary, Margaret Bryan, who might perhaps be described as having a pedigree as a professional-lady-in-waiting as well as a proven track record as a parent, became a baroness in her own right, and was appointed as lady governess of the royal nursery to replace the king's own governess, Elizabeth Denton. Katherine of Aragon remained with her daughter, so far as her responsibilities permitted, and was much concerned with the manner in which her daughter was raised. The new baroness, who had the rank to control the princess's nursery without interference, was part of the extended Tudor family and client network as well as being familiar with the customs of court and Lady Margaret Beaufort's *Royal Book* of ordinances.

In 1519, when Mary was 3 years old, Lady Margaret was transferred to the nursery of Henry FitzRoy. His mother, Bessie Blount, was one of her daughter, Elizabeth Carew's, friends. The birth of the king's illegitimate son was a private matter, supervised by Cardinal Wolsey, and there is little record of the boy's upbringing until 1525 when he was elevated to the peerage. However, given the reorganisation of Mary's household in 1519, and the replacement of Lady Bryan with Margaret Pole, Countess of Salisbury, it is probable that Lady Bryan was placed in charge of a new nursery. The alternative is that Henry's acknowledged son was permitted to spend his earliest years in the care of his mother, Bessie, now married to Gilbert Tailboys, 1st Baron of Kyme.

In 1525, Princess Mary was sent to Ludlow and Henry FitzRoy took his place upon the public stage. At the age of 6 he was too old to be in the care of a woman. Lady Margaret's services as a foster mother were no longer required. The Bryans' fortunes were not tied with those of Katherine of Aragon or to Lady Margaret's former charge, even though they continued to maintain a show of friendship with Henry's first wife and his elder daughter.

Scandal was never far from the surface of Henry VIII's court. There were rumours that the king wanted to set Katherine aside. He had always taken his pick of mistresses from among the queen's ladies. In 1522, the king was in love with Lady Bryan's niece, Mary, a daughter of Elizabeth Howard and Thomas Boleyn. That Easter she played the part of Kindness in a pageant entitled *The Assault on the Castle of Virtue*. She was already married to William Carey, a gentleman of the privy chamber, so there was no scandal when her kindness led her into Henry's bed. After Mary became pregnant and gave birth there was no need for the king to acknowledge the child, named Katherine. It is less certain whether or not Mary's second child, Henry Carey, born in 1526 was the king's offspring or not. He had demonstrated that he was capable of fathering sons and was already more interested in Mary's sister. How much choice any woman was allowed when it came to the king's affections is a matter of speculation but in 1527, he was openly infatuated with Anne Boleyn — a woman who famously knew how to say no, until Henry offered her a kingdom.

When Anne Boleyn was crowned in June 1533, she was six months pregnant. In September, Margaret Bryan became governess to Anne's daughter, her own great-niece, Princess Elizabeth, and went with the child to Hatfield. It did not take long for the king's relationship with his new queen to sour. Anne's failure to produce a male heir was followed by her downfall and execution in May 1536. An Act of Parliament transformed Princess Elizabeth into a bastard like her sister, Mary. Lady Bryan complained bitterly, in a letter sent in August 1536 to Thomas Cromwell, about the chaos in her charge's household because it's staff no longer knew how to treat the toddler and there were insufficient funds for Mary and Elizabeth to each have a household of their own, even if they did reside under the same roof. The result was a power struggle between Lady Bryan and the household's steward, Sir John Shelton, about how the household should be ordered. Lady Bryan's letter reminded Cromwell that the king made her a baroness in her own right precisely so she should have charge of the way the nursery was run.

Margaret may also have been worried about her own future. Sir Thomas Bryan died in about 1517. She married for a third time to David Zouche, a younger son of John Zouche and Eleanor St John, who was part of Lady Margaret Beaufort's extended kinship network through her own mother Margaret Beauchamp but, by 1536, Zouche was dead. Besides which, being a part of the extended Tudor family was no longer a guarantee of preferment. She and her children were part of the disgraced Howard family. Even worse, Sir Francis Bryan, who had a reputation as a rake, was questioned about his relationship with Anne soon after her arrest. Unlike George Boleyn, Margaret's nephew, he was neither arrested nor executed. It helped that Francis quarrelled with George Boleyn, in public, in late 1534. Instead, Francis emerged unscathed as the chief gentleman of the privy chamber, a post which was previously held by Sir Henry Norris who was executed on 17 May 1536 for alleged adultery with the queen. Lady Margaret may have felt that the destroying angel passed close by her immediate family that spring. Public life at the Tudor court required men and women to be consummate politicians as well as to have the right connections.

Following the birth of Jane Seymour's son, Edward, in October 1537, Margaret, still responsible for raising Elizabeth, became the prince's governess with day-to-day care of Henry's younger daughter falling to Katherine Champernowne, who was appointed to the nursery in 1536.

The court became a more dangerous place as the king aged. Henry was often in pain and it made him irascible. His health problems were the result of old jousting injuries; an ulcer on his leg was the product of a tournament wound in 1527 and when he tumbled from his horse during a competition, in 1536, he was unconscious for two hours as well as suffering from crushed legs. Now he experienced headaches and the ulceration in his legs was often difficult to manage. The king was fearful about the succession; his heir was still only 3 years old and Henry had no wish to see a return to the troubled times of the fifteenth century. He began to believe that anyone with sufficient Plantagenet blood in their veins might seek to usurp the Tudor throne. There was also the problem of religion. Henry might have ensured that he was the Supreme Head of the Church of England but the Six Articles of 1539 confirmed that failure to conform to traditional religious beliefs would lead to charges of heresy, even if the Pope was no longer an authority. Reformers pressed for further change while other men agitated for a return to the papacy.

In 1539, Lady Bryan's son-in-law, Sir Nicholas Carew, who was not always successful in hiding his feelings relating to the king's divorce from Katherine of Aragon, was implicated in the Exeter Plot which aimed to remove Henry from the throne and replace him with his cousin, Reginald Pole, the son of Lady Margaret Pole, Countess of Salisbury and return England to Catholicism. Henry Courtenay, 1st Marquess of Exeter, the king's own cousin and childhood companion was also arrested in the purge that followed discovery of the plot. He was a political rival to Thomas Cromwell as well as being a conservative. The same could not be said of Carew who, despite remaining Catholic, allied himself with Cromwell to bring about Anne Boleyn's downfall, was present at Prince Edward's baptism and helped suppress the northern rebels of the Pilgrimage of Grace. Even so, Carew was out of favour with the king when he was arrested. He was tried for treason based on the alleged contents of a letter that implicated him in the plot. Francis Bryan sat on the jury that convicted his brother-in-law on 14 February 1539. After the execution, Margaret, still Prince Edward's lady mistress, and a regular correspondent concerning the prince's progress, wrote to Thomas Cromwell on a personal matter. She asked for help for her daughter, Elizabeth Carew, and her grandchildren who were left with nothing. Cromwell, who was likely to have been removing a potential threat to his own power base when he arranged Carew's arrest, addressed the matter with his customary efficiency.

After Edward became king in January 1547, Lady Margaret retired from court to her estate at Leyton in Essex with a generous annuity of £70 a year having raised all four of Henry VIII's acknowledged children. She died in 1552 and was buried with her second husband, Thomas Bryan, at Cheddington in Buckinghamshire. The baroness was predeceased by Francis who died in Ireland in 1550 and by both Margaret and Mary.

Jane (Amata, Amy or Anne) Calthorpe (c.1485–1543)

Jane, a daughter of Sir William Boleyn and Margaret Butler, the heiress of the 7th Earl of Ormond, was born at Blickling Hall in Norfolk. She was one of at least ten children, of whom several died young and are commemorated in Blickling Church. Their father William, a wealthy mercer, died in October 1505 and was buried in Norwich Cathedral.

The family, which grew in prominence from the start of the fifteenth century onwards, were successful merchants who made strategic marriages for their children. Purchase of land and kinship connections turned the Boleyns into a prominent part of the local gentry. County gentries, built around tight-knit family connections and land ownership, administered Crown offices and formed their own local network of patronage. Access to the right contacts in the gentry's client-based hierarchy could lead to preferment at court, although its manner was not always so dramatic as the Boleyn family's climb to the throne during the second half of the 1520s.

Blickling Hall was inherited by Jane's brother, Thomas Boleyn, but it was Thomas's wife, Lady Elizabeth Howard, a daughter of the Duke of Norfolk, who inherited William's property in Kent, Hever Castle. The couple used the latter as their main seat. Thomas, as the head of the family, became responsible for the future of his unmarried sisters, Alice and Margaret who remained at Blickling. There is no mention of Jane in their father's will, or of her husband. Lack of clarity and the duplication of the same name across several generations in the Boleyn and Calthorpe pedigrees also clouds historical accounts. However, Alice Boleyn's will confirms that she had a niece called Elizabeth Calthorpe. It was not that Jane did not exist, simply that she was not mentioned in her father's will for one reason or another.

Jane married Sir Philip Calthorpe of Erwarton in Suffolk on 4 November 1518. He was a widower with a family. Jane had only one child of her own, Elizabeth, who received a bequest from Alice, born in 1521. During that same year Lady Margaret Pole, Princess Mary's lady governess, was temporarily dismissed from her post and the Calthorpes were appointed in her stead. Elizabeth Calthorpe may have grown up in the same household as her parent's royal charge, Princess Mary, who was 5 years old when Lady Calthorpe was given the responsibility of raising the king's daughter. Jane had no extant record of prior experience of royal childcare. She did have an extended family connection to Margaret, Lady Bryan[1] but there is no evidence of any recommendation being made. Yet, a letter from the king to Wolsey on 13 October 1521 indicated that he wished the Calthorpes to 'attend upon my lady princess' and set their shared annual salary at £40.[2] Earlier correspondence announced their arrival at court and their wish to 'offer themselves according to his Graces desire, to serve my Lady Princess'.[3] In 1525, after four years as lady mistress, Jane accompanied Mary to Ludlow as one of her gentlewomen while Lady Margaret Pole, Countess of Salisbury, re-appointed to her former position, took responsibility for the supervision of Mary's household and education there.

Sir Philip made his will in 1532. He died in 1535 but Jane's stepson, another Philip rather confusingly also married to a wife named Jane, disagreed about her dower rights. The legal entitlement for a widow was one third of her husband's estates for their lifetime. On 8 May 1537, Cromwell and Sir Thomas Audley, who was the Lord Chancellor, were called upon to decide which of them held the manors of Smallburgh and Sprowston in Norfolk.[4] Jane's daughter was provided with the manor of Riddlesworth in Norfolk as a dowry.

Jane, living in Norfolk, is recorded as giving her former charge, the Lady Mary, a New Year's gift of a pair of sleeves with lace in 1543–1544. Her sister, Lady Shelton's gift was also clothing.[5] There is no record of how either sister felt about Mary's demotion from princess to base born daughter of the king, or the part that their niece, Anne Boleyn, played in it. Lady Calthorpe died in 1544 and was buried in St Andrew's Church, Norwich.

Alice Clere (d.1538)

Alice Boleyn, sister of Jane and Thomas, was the third of William Boleyn and Margaret Ormond's daughters to survive to adulthood. She was married, in 1506, to the recently widowed Sir Robert Clere of Ormseby. The Cleres, like the Calthorpes, were an integral part of Norfolk's gentry and bound to one another through a web of marriages down the generations. Already a stepmother to four children, Alice gave her husband four more sons.

In 1533 she and her sister, Anne Shelton, were sent to join Princess Elizabeth's household where they were subsequently placed in charge of the king's elder daughter Mary, whose title was stripped from her. Alice's niece, Anne Boleyn, issued instructions that Katherine of Aragon's daughter was to be humiliated. Alice is often recorded as being kinder to Mary than her sister who gained a reputation for callousness during the difficult years when Henry's eldest daughter refused to accept the Supremacy or the new order for the succession. Alice's nephew, George Boleyn, wrote to both Alice and to Anne warning them against showing too much consideration for Mary.[1]

Following Anne Boleyn's downfall in 1536, Alice, a wealthy widow with manors on the Norfolk coast as well as a house in Norwich, may have continued to be a part of Elizabeth's household. Alternatively, she retired to her home at Ormesby where she remained until her death on 1 November 1538. Her will, dated 28 October 1535, in addition to a number of bequests, left a 'pomander of gold to my niece Elizabeth Calthorpe'.[2] She arranged that the younger of her sons receive the manor of Fretenham while the remainder of the twenty manors left to her by her husband,[3] passed into the keeping of her eldest son John Clere, as might be expected. She was buried with her husband at Ormseby St Margaret, near Caister in Norfolk. Robert Clere died in 1529 and left money to the church there for masses to be said for his soul.

Anne Cromer (c.1470–after 1520)

The Cromers, or Crowmers, were a gentry family associated with Tunstall, near Sittingbourne in Kent. The family had a tradition of holding the county shrievalty and one of the Cromers was executed by Jack Cade's rebels in 1450. Nothing is known for certain about Anne apart from her name and that she was Princess Mary, later Queen of France's, lady mistress at Eltham in 1496, prior to the appointment of Joan Guildford.

In 1503, Anne is listed as one of Elizabeth of York's gentlewomen and was paid a salary of £10.[1] Weir speculates that she may have been the daughter of Sir James Cromer, who was in the Yorkist lines at the Battle of Tewkesbury and knighted afterwards. If this supposition is correct, Alice Haute, who was a part of the Woodville family, was Anne Cromer's sister-in-law.[2] The Hautes, another gentry family from Kent, were first cousins of Elizabeth Woodville and were invited to court when she married Edward IV. Alice served as the queen's lady-in-waiting during the 1460s, and would have been well known by Elizabeth of York. A recommendation by Alice could go some way to explaining Anne's presence in the queen's own household. It might also account for why Mistress Anne Cromer, a woman of gentle birth, might have been identified by her maiden name rather than her married one. Anne married William Whetenhall, or Whetnall, of Hexstall's Court in 1489[3] which complicates any certain identification of Anne as Mary's lady mistress.

Elizabeth Darcy (c.1436–1507)

Elizabeth was the first of the lady mistresses appointed to raise Tudor princes and princesses. She was initially based at Farnham, with Prince Arthur's household, where she ensured that Margaret Beaufort's ordinances for the management of the nursery were followed. Not that she needed them, she was familiar with their terms from her time caring for the children of Edward IV and Elizabeth Woodville. She was a familiar face from Elizabeth of York's own childhood at Eltham, returned to the palace to care for the Tudor royal family with the arrival of Arthur's younger siblings.

Lady Darcy, to give her the honorific title associated with her employment, married twice and originated from an East Anglian family with a long association with the House of Lancaster. Her grandfather, Sir John Tyrell of Heron in East Horndon, Essex was 'treasurer to the house'[1] of King Henry VI as well as being the Duchy of Lancaster's chief steward north of the Trent and Speaker for the House of Commons. Her uncle, William Tyrell, was executed in February 1462 for his part in a plot against Edward IV led by John de Vere, 12th Earl of Oxford.

Afterward, the family changed its allegiance to the House of York. William's son, James, was placed under the guardianship of the king's mother, Cecily, Duchess of York but she returned the boy to his mother to be cared for and he eventually entered the service of Richard, Duke of Gloucester. He was recorded as present in the lines at the Battle of Tewkesbury[2] and was knighted afterwards by King Edward IV. Sir James Tyrell is best known for his confession, in 1502, to the murder of Edward V and his brother, Richard, Duke of York, and the ensuing debate as to whether he told the truth of the matter or not. If nothing else, his services to the House of York demonstrate another thread by which his cousin Elizabeth may first have fitted into life at court.

Elizabeth was not mentioned in her father's will when he died in 1477. She was already wedded to Sir Robert Darcy of Maldon, who was both sheriff of Essex and Hertfordshire and would not have expected to inherit much. Any dowry that a girl took with her to a marriage was viewed as her share of any inheritance. The marriage took place before 1456 and Elizabeth gave her husband two sons and a daughter before he died in 1469.[3]

Elizabeth's next marriage, after November 1469, was to Richard Haute of Ightham Mote in Kent. Richard's stepmother was Joan Woodville, an aunt of Elizabeth Woodville. It meant that Lady Darcy's new husband was a prominent member of Kent's gentry as well as being welcome at court. In 1472 he was appointed to tutor Edward, Prince of Wales while his father, who also accompanied the boy to Ludlow, was made comptroller of the household there.[4] By January 1480, Elizabeth was lady mistress of the nursery at Eltham, caring for Elizabeth Woodville's younger children and received a grant for life, thanks to her good service, of a tun of wine yearly in the port of London.[5]

According to Sir Thomas More's account of the events surrounding the disappearance of the Princes in the Tower in 1483, Richard Haute was with Edward V's retinue making its way to London from Ludlow when it was intercepted at Stony Stratford by the Dukes of Gloucester and Buckingham. Lady Darcy's husband was arrested with Anthony Woodville. While Woodville was awaiting his execution at Pontefract Castle, he wrote his will and made Haute his executor. *Hall's Chronicle* claimed that Richard was executed on 25 June though this was incorrect.[6] Elizabeth's home at Ightham Mote had already been confiscated by Sir Thomas Wortley on the orders of the Duke of Gloucester on 14 May 1483.

Elizabeth, having made a prudent marriage into the Woodville family, now suffered under Richard's regime because she was identified with the queen's faction. There is no indication where she or her children were in the spring and summer of 1483. It was only when Henry Tudor became king, in 1485, that Haute's property, including Ightham Mote, was restored to him. He died in 1487, when Edward Haute, Elizabeth's son, was still only 11 years old. Twenty years later, when Lady Darcy died, in 1507, she requested that she should be buried beside her first husband in Maldon.

Joan Denny (d.1553)
Joan was the daughter of Sir Philip Champernowne of Modbury in Devon and his wife, Katherine Carew. She was married to Sir Anthony Denny, a favourite of the king, in 1538 and had at least nine children. She was Sir Walter Raleigh's aunt and is thought to have been either the sister or the niece of Katherine Champernowne, the lady mistress of Henry VIII's daughter Elizabeth. Both Katherine and Joan were well educated and Joan, no doubt influenced by humanism, gained a reputation as a fervent reformer.

Joan served in the households of both Anne of Cleves and Katherine Parr where she joined a circle of studious women who supported Protestantism. She was linked with Anne Askew and was one of the ladies that the conservative faction tried to use to bring down Henry VIII's sixth queen.

In 1548, when Katherine Parr was finally forced to acknowledge the developing relationship between her own husband, Thomas Seymour, and her stepdaughter, Elizabeth, it was to Joan that the dowager sent the girl so that she would be safe from any scandal.

Elizabeth Denton (d.1519)
Elizabeth was born into the Jerningham family which was a part of the Suffolk gentry. She was the daughter of Sir John Jerningham, of Somerleyton Hall near Lowestoft in Suffolk, and his second wife, Agnes Darell. Her half-brother, Edward[1], inherited the bulk of their father's estate when he died in 1474 but under the terms of Sir John's will, upon the death of her brother Osberne, Elizabeth was to inherit the manor of 'Little Worlingham with all the commodities etc. within the towns of Little Worlingham, Cove, Ellough and Great Worlingham … and in default to Elizabeth Denton, my daughter, for life, and after to Walter Denton, her son for life, and after to be sold'.[2]

Even after Elizabeth's skills were no longer required in Henry VIII's household, the Jerninghams continued to work for the king. One of her brothers, Richard, was a gentleman of the chamber and is recorded as being sent to Germany in 1511 to buy armour on Henry's behalf. The family's service to the Tudors saw them climb the social ladder during Elizabeth's lifetime, marrying into both the Dacre and Stanhope families. The former brought with it kinship to East Anglia's pre-eminent magnates: the Earls of Oxford and Suffolk. Elizabeth was married, as was expected, when she gained her employment as lady mistress. Little is known about her family except that her husband was called John Denton and the couple had at least one son, Walter, mentioned in his grandfather's will.

The former lady mistress was one of three governesses to be found in the retinue that accompanied Princess Margaret to Scotland in 1503. Elizabeth returned home when James IV reduced the size of his new wife's household. King Henry VIII made her 'keeper for life' of Lady Margaret Beaufort's home at Coldharbour and the following year gave her a tun of Gascon wine every year.[3] Henry was signalling the deep affection in which he held his governess, and also a duty of care to the woman who was an important part of his childhood.

She returned to royal service in 1510 when Katherine of Aragon gave birth to her first child. Sadly, Prince Henry died soon afterward and none of the queen's infants survived more than a few weeks, except for Princess Mary who was briefly cared for by Elizabeth Denton. By 1515 she was a widow and was granted a further annuity of £50 by the king for services to Henry VII and Elizabeth of York, in whose household she remained when she was no longer needed at Eltham. From 1517, it was Lady Margaret Bryan who was the recognised lady mistress of the royal nursery.

Elizabeth became a tenant at Blackfriars' Priory, London and in 1518 she erected a tomb for herself there. Her will, dated April 26 1518, stipulated that she was to be buried near the stained-glass window which featured St Thomas Aquinas.[4] She ensured her last resting place with gifts to the monastic community beginning with the prior who received 20 shillings and concluding with 12 pence for each of the novices at Blackfriars. In return the prior, priests, friars and novices were to pray for the souls of Elizabeth and her husband.[5] The content of the will is conventional. It cannot be unexpected that Elizabeth Denton was a pious woman given that Lady Margaret Beaufort, who took a close interest in the royal household, was one of the advisors who had a hand in the selection of nursery staff. The family of Elizabeth's eldest half-brother chose to remain Catholic and to emigrate to America when Queen Elizabeth I sat upon the throne. It was, perhaps, not a surprise. The Jerninghams were also among the first of the Suffolk gentry to declare their loyalty, in 1553, to Queen Mary and Elizabeth's nephew, Henry, was one of the executors of the queen's will.

Joan Guildford (d.4 September 1538)
'Mother Guildford' cared for both Margaret and Mary Tudor during their childhoods but her career in the service of the Tudors began in the household of Lady Margaret Beaufort. She and her husband both came from a family with solid Lancastrian credentials. Her father, Sir William Vaux, died at Tewkesbury in 1471. Her mother, Katherine Penyston, or Penyson, was one of Margaret of Anjou's ladies-in-waiting.[1] Katherine was captured shortly after the battle at Tewkesbury along with Margaret, the Countess of Devon and Anne Neville who was married to Margaret's son, Edward of Lancaster.

Katherine originated from Piedmont in Italy, although it is likely that her father was English. She came with Henry VI's bride to England in 1445 and became an English citizen in 1456 at about the same time that she married Joan's father. Five years later, after the Battle of Towton, Katherine and William lost their home at Great Harrowden, in Northamptonshire, and were forced to flee. Nicholas was an infant but Joan was probably born in about 1463 while the family was in exile. Joan grew up speaking Italian and French before returning to England at the Readaption of King Henry VI in 1470.

After the collapse of Lancastrian rule in 1471, Joan and her brother, Nicholas Vaux, were raised in the household of Lady Margaret Beaufort. Katherine Vaux chose to share her mistress's imprisonment in the Tower of London and accompanied her back to France in 1476 following the Treaty of Picquigny between England and France. She witnessed Margaret's will in 1482 before returning to England after the queen's death. She was in receipt of the income from the manors of Stanton and Markham which she originally held as a jointure with her husband. Edward IV granted the income to Katherine in February 1478 in response to her petition that she and her children had 'nothing earthly to live upon'.[2]

When King Henry VII ascended the throne, the attainder against William Vaux was reversed and Joan's brother, Nicholas, inherited his father's estates. At about the same time, he married Elizabeth FitzHugh, a cousin of both Richard III and his queen Anne Neville. The union ensured that Elizabeth, who had previously served her cousin Anne at Middleham and when she became queen, was protected as was the inheritance of her children from her first marriage to Sir William Parr who died in 1483.

Katherine Vaux and, in all likelihood, Joan entered the service of Elizabeth of York soon after Henry became king. Katherine was at Prince Arthur's baptism and both mother and daughter attended the queen's coronation in 1487. By 1489, Joan was married to Sir Richard Guildford who was an associate of Lady Margaret Beaufort's man of business, Sir Reginald Bray, and whose second marriage it was.

Guildford and his father had taken part in Buckingham's Rebellion of 1483 and sought refuge in Brittany with Henry before returning to England in 1485. On 29 September he was appointed as the master of the royal ordinance and armoury. He was also a chamberlain of the exchequer, sat on the Privy Council and was rewarded with various land grants and wardships as well as holding key administrative roles in his home county of Kent. In 1496 he was one of the commissioners who negotiated the marriage alliance between Prince Arthur and Katherine of Aragon.

In addition to a family of stepchildren, Joan had one son, Henry Guildford who was an established favourite of Henry VIII. The king was only three years younger than Joan's son and Guildford was one of his childhood companions. In May 1512 Henry Guildford married Lady Margaret Byron's daughter, Margaret. Princess Mary gave the couple 6s 8d and the king granted the couple estates in Warwickshire, Northumberland and Lincolnshire as well as making Henry the Constable of Leeds Castle in Kent where most of his family's estates lay. In 1525 Henry was appointed comptroller of the king's household. So great was the king's fondness for Guildford that he even remained in favour despite a deep-seated dislike of Anne Boleyn, recorded by Chapuys, and opposition to a divorce from Katherine of Aragon without papal consent. The king's generosity stemmed not only from his friendship with Henry Guildford but from his childhood memories of Joan. In 1499, she was appointed lady governess to the princesses Margaret and Mary. She went on to be one of Katherine of Aragon's ladies when she first came to England.

Lady Guildford's husband died while he was on a pilgrimage to Jerusalem in 1506. Her second husband, Anthony Poyntz, was a cousin of Elizabeth of York. Poyntz's mother, Margaret, was the illegitimate daughter of Anthony Woodville. The Poyntz family recorded various messages in Joan's *Book of Hours*, using the devotional text in a similar fashion to an autograph book to express their friendship and love for her. Similar sentiments were expressed by Henry VII and Elizabeth of York as well as all her former royal charges including Henry VIII and his queen, Katherine of Aragon, who wrote a verse before the section of the Book of Hours containing prayers:

> I thinke the prayers of a frend the most acceptable unto God and because I take you for one of myn assured I pray you remembre me in yours.[3]

In 1514 Mary Tudor, who had been betrothed to the Prince of Castile in her childhood, found herself enmeshed in a marriage to King Louis XII of France. No one, least of all her brother, King Henry VIII, took any notice of the fact that Louis was three times Mary's age or that she was in love with one of the king's own companions, Charles Brandon the Duke of Suffolk. Mother Guildford accompanied Princess Mary to France to marry King Louis XII. She was dismissed after the wedding celebrations and sent home, along with the rest of Mary's ladies. The princess wrote furious letters to her brother and to Cardinal Wolsey demanding that Joan be allowed to return to her service, demonstrating the depth of her feeling for the woman who cared for her from about the age of 10 years onwards.

Joan returned to England where Henry VIII granted her an annual pension totalling £60. She returned to Tudor service to care for the king's own daughter, Princess Mary. At the very back of Lady Guildford's Book of Hours, translated from Latin to English, is a hand-written version of Thomas Aquinas's prayer made by Mary in about 1527 when she was 11 years old.[4] Like the rest of her family the princess added her own message asking Joan to remember her when she prayed. When the king sought a divorce from his first queen, Joan testified that Katherine and Arthur had been in bed together, unattended, for either five or six nights. Henry Guildford, who had only been 12 years of age at the time, was also required to testify. Whether it was Joan or someone else who inked over the references to Queen Katherine and Princess Mary is another matter but it reflected the changing world in which Mother Guildford ended her days.

Joan outlived her son, who died in 1532. When Sir Anthony died in 1533, Joan retired to accommodation in the precincts of Blackfriars. After Joan's death in 1538, she was buried in the church at Blackfriars and left £20 to the monks there so that they would pray for the souls of her and her family.[5] Hers would be one of the last interments to take place under the auspices of its monastic inhabitants as it was dissolved in the same year. The friary precinct was granted to Sir Thomas Carwarden in 1550. He converted the church into a tennis court.[6] If Lady Guildford's grave was not lost before, it was finally destroyed in 1666 during the Great Fire of London.

Lady Anne Herbert, Countess of Pembroke (c.1433– d. after June 1486) Anne, born at Bodenham in Herefordshire, was a daughter of Sir Walter Devereux who served as Lord Chancellor of Ireland under Richard, 3rd Duke of York between 1449 and 1451. It was Devereux who imprisoned Edmund Tudor at Carmarthen, in 1456, shortly before Henry Tudor's birth. Anne's Yorkist credentials included the part played by her brother, Walter, who was with the duke's force at Ludford in 1459 and who was knighted after Edward IV's victory at Towton in 1461.

Sir Walter arranged for Anne to marry William Herbert of Raglan in about 1445, although some sources provide a later date.[1] It was a union that fostered and strengthened kinship networks within the Yorkist affinity of South Wales and the Marches. At the time the union was a strategically advantageous one for Herbert, whose family controlled the lordship of Usk, because it extended his network of allies into Herefordshire. It is not known whether the wishes of the bride were considered but, family and political interests aside, interaction between the families in the service of the dukes of York meant that the couple were at least acquainted with one another before they wed. They went on to have at least ten, or more, children, including Maud, who it was planned would marry Henry Tudor while he was Herbert's ward. Anne's second son, Walter, was born in around 1461 and raised alongside Henry Tudor who was only a few years older.

After 1461 when Anne's husband was the most influential magnate in the region she became the leading noblewoman in Wales. In 1467, Margaret Beaufort and her husband, Sir Henry Stafford, stayed at Raglan Castle for a week where they were entertained by Anne and her family while Margaret spent some time with her son. In September 1468 she became a countess when her husband was given the earldom of Pembroke. It must have seemed to Anne during those years when she entertained guests and the local gentry at Raglan Castle, which was not only an impressive fortification but also a luxurious residence, as though she was blessed by good fortune. Anne is pictured in John Lydgate's *Troy Book* and *Siege of Thebes*,[2] along with her husband, kneeling at the feet of a king, reflecting the fact that they owed their rise from the gentry to the monarch. The book was originally commissioned by King Henry V but the manuscript held by the British Library was probably transcribed on the orders of the Herberts to present to either King Henry VI at the end of the 1450s or to Edward IV before 1462.[3]

When Richard Neville, Earl of Warwick rose in rebellion against King Edward IV in 1469, he was determined to cut down the men who he saw as taking away the authority that he believed to be rightfully his own. Among their number was Anne's husband. He gave orders for Herbert to be executed following his defeat and capture at the Battle of Edgecote. The countess was at her brother's castle at Weobley in Herefordshire, or arrived soon after, when news of the defeat and her loss was brought to her by Sir Richard Corbet who led Henry Tudor to safety from the battlefield. For Anne there was now the uncertainty of widowhood, fears for her young family, and concerns about what would happen to her husband's wards.

Anne was one of her husband's executors according to the terms of the will which he wrote in 1468 and to which he added a codicil immediately prior to his death. In it, William asked his widow to become a vowess which required taking an oath of perpetual chastity before a priest, 'to take the mantle and the ring and live a widow'.[4] The ring, given to her at the time of her vow, turned the countess into a bride of Christ but was not accompanied by vows of obedience or poverty. Nor was she required to live an enclosed life. It was not uncommon in the fifteenth century for aristocratic women to take such vows — Richard of York's widow, Cecily Neville was one such and Lady Margaret Beaufort would take a similar vow with the agreement of her then husband, Thomas Stanley, after their marriage in 1472. Both Cecily and Margaret are known to have lived their lives around monastic routines of prayer. There is no record of whether or not Anne was especially pious before Pembroke's death. The vow would enable Anne, or so her husband believed, to help their children financially since it ensured that even if the dowager countess wore a nun's hood for the rest of her life that she was a wealthy woman in her own right. A widow's dower was composed of one third of everything that her husband owned at the time of their wedding. Herbert's will identified the strategically important lordship of Chepstow,[5] whether he was an attainted traitor or not. In addition, a couple often held jointure rights over some property, meaning that it was inherited by the surviving partner upon the other's death. The earl intended that the estates that he had been granted should remain under the control of his wife and children rather than a portion of them falling into the hands of any second husband that Anne might consider. The earl may also have believed that

Anne's profession would help speed his wife's soul through purgatory after her death.[6]

The countess's life continued to be disrupted by the ups and downs of the Wars of the Roses. In 1470, when the Earl of Warwick succeeded in putting Henry VI on the throne for a brief time, the earldom of Pembroke and the Herbert estates including Raglan were granted to Jasper Tudor. Holinshed suggests that Henry Tudor was with the countess at Pembroke when the Lancastrian regime was re-established while the writer of Chepstow's annals[7] argues that it was just as likely that Herbert's widow made her home there as the lordship was part of her dower.

Even after the battles of Barnet and Tewkesbury in 1471 that secured Edward's throne, intermittent violence continued to play its part in the lives of the Welsh Marchers. In 1479, Edward IV became so tired of a quarrel between Anne's sons, William and Walter Herbert and their Vaughan kinsmen that he forbade the Herberts from crossing the Severn into Wales for an entire year. Failure to abide by the restrictions imposed on them incurred a fine of £1000 per man. Anne and her brother Walter Devereux, Lord Ferrers of Chartley faced a similar fine as guarantors for Walter's good behaviour.[8] It was something of a disaster for the 2nd Earl of Pembroke who was unable to access Raglan, Pembroke or even Chepstow where his main power base lay, although there was no caveat preventing the dowager from doing so. Despite the fact that Anne's eldest son, another William, was Edward IV's brother-in-law and that his father had died in the king's service, the earl had fallen out of favour with the Yorkist king. A few months later he was deprived of his earldom and dispossessed of his lands. In exchange he was provided with the earldom of Huntingdon and half a dozen or so manors.[9]

In 1485, the Herbert family and their adherents did not move to intercept Henry Tudor as he and his army advanced through Wales to Bosworth. By then William, Anne's eldest son, was married to Richard III's illegitimate daughter Katherine Plantagenet but it appears that pragmatism, or perhaps memories of a boy who had once been his companion, stayed William's hand. Walter Herbert joined his foster brother's army and fought for him at Bosworth.[10] His branch of the Herbert family thrived under Henry's rule and Anne's son can be found serving Jasper Tudor in South Wales as well as attacking the French in Brittany in 1489.[11] When William died without a male heir, it was Walter who inherited Raglan Castle.

Anne must have been a caring guardian of Lady Margaret Beaufort's son. When Henry became king, he asked for Anne, who he remembered kindly, to come to London where he granted her his protection and gave her an annuity. He confirmed the rights of her son, William Herbert as Earl of Huntingdon on 17 May 1488. The exchange of Huntingdon for Pembroke having initially been established by King Edward IV in 1479. Henry and Margaret Beaufort's gratitude to Anne for the care she gave to the king in his childhood was reflected in the friendship that the pair extended to the countess's daughter, Anne who married John Grey, 1st Baron Grey of Powis,[12] another of Anne's wards from 1466 onwards.

It is thought that when Anne died, in about 1486, she was buried at Tintern Abbey with her husband. Herbert asked to be buried near his father in the Herbert Chapel at the priory church of Abergavenny but for some reason his wishes were not carried out. Instead, he and Anne were buried in a chest tomb near the high altar. Henry VIII's dissolution of the monasteries saw its destruction, along with the tombs of Anne's son William Herbert, Earl of Huntington and his first wife, Mary Woodville.[13]

Blanche Herbert, Lady Troy (d.c.1557)

Blanche was one of the eleven co-heiresses of Simon Milborne and his wife, Jane Baskerville, who were an established part of Herefordshire's hierarchy. When Blanche married she took with her as a dowry the manor of Icomb in Gloucestershire. Her first husband, James Witney, died in 1500 by which time she was the mother of a family of young children. She married for a second time, shortly after her bereavement, to William Herbert of Troy Parva. He was the son of William Herbert, 1st Earl of Pembroke by one of his mistresses. Soon after her marriage, Blanche was called upon to entertain Henry VII who knew Herbert from his own childhood, and Elizabeth of York at her new home near Monmouth.

Herbert died in 1525, having requested that his wife would not marry again. His will planned for his effigy to lay between his two wives. Blanche, a wealthy widow thanks to her dower rights, joined the household of Elizabeth Somerset, Countess of Worcester whose husband, Charles Somerset, was the heir of the Herbert earls of Pembroke. Some historians believe that Blanche acted as a governess to the countess's nine children. An alternative view is that Blanche returned with Princess Mary's household from Ludlow.

The association of Lady Herbert with the Countess of Worcester ensured that Blanche's childcare skills were recognised once Anne Boleyn became queen. The countess was one of Anne Boleyn's ladies and served her during the feast that followed the coronation. The queen and her lady were close friends, the latter borrowing £100 from the queen which was never repaid. When Princess Elizabeth was born in September 1533, Blanche was involved in selecting a potential wetnurse for the child. Three years later, after Anne's arrest and imprisonment, the countess was said to be one of the queen's accusers, although other accounts describe her as being distressed by Anne Boleyn's situation. Lady Troy, who was no longer part of Elizabeth Somerset's household, subsequentially appears in an account of Prince Edward's baptism in October 1536. She helped Elizabeth to carry her half-brother's train, suggesting that Blanche was part of the nursery household.

Lewys Morgannwg's elegy, composed in Blanche's memory shortly after her death, described her as being a governess in her youth, that she was responsible for teaching ladies at court their various accomplishments and that she gave service to Queen Mary and to King Henry VIII's children:

> She was [a] Lady [in charge] of Queens, A governess she was in her youth. She knew in a fitting manner The accomplishments of the ladies of the court, [And she was the] guardian, before she passed away, Of Henry VIII's household and his children yonder. To King Edward she was a true [And] wise lady of dignity, In charge of his fosterage [she was pre-eminent], [And] she waited upon his Grace.[1]

The work, dating from 1557, gives an indication that Elizabeth and her half-brother's households, which often shared the same accommodation, also shared staff. Lady Troy could potentially have taught both Elizabeth and Edward their letters as well as having oversight of who was appointed to Elizabeth's household and how it was managed. Among the women who lived at Hatfield and the other residences associated with the royal nursery were Blanche's granddaughter, Anne Morgan, and her niece, Blanche Parry.

Lady Troy retained the post until her retirement in 1546 or 1547. Elizabeth's Household Accounts for 1551–1552 show that she sent a regular pension, of 70s, to her former governess, which was delivered by the Knights Marshall's servant for the additional sum of 5s.[2] Lady Troy trained her niece, Blanche Parry, to succeed her as Elizabeth's lady mistress. The daughter of Alice

Milborne grew up at Newcourt, at Bacton in Herefordshire, with her siblings. Her mother taught her the essential skills that girls needed before they married. She also became a skilled horsewoman and developed a passion for books. In 1522, her father, Henry Myles, died and it is likely that Blanche was sent to join her aunt, Lady Herbert, who was at that time in the household of the Countess of Worcester. By the time she entered Elizabeth's household she was about 25 years old and was fully trained in childcare and possessed the basic skills necessary to teach a young child. She was not, however, as well educated as Kat Champernowne. She and Kat would be listed next to one another in Elizabeth's household accounts throughout Kat's life. Although Kat deprived Blanche Parry of employment as lady mistress, it was with Blanche that the princess went riding. The accounts show that Lady Troy's niece was the only one of Elizabeth's ladies to receive payment for keeping a horse.[3] She would serve her mistress for 56 years.

Margaret Pole, Countess of Salisbury (1473–1541)
Margaret Plantagenet was born the daughter of George, Duke of Clarence and his wife Isabel Neville. Her uncle was Edward IV and her grandfathers were Richard, 3rd Duke of York and Richard Neville, 16th Earl of Warwick.

When she was born her father was third in line to the throne but after Henry VII's accession in 1485 she and her brother Edward Plantagenet, 17th Earl of Warwick, were considered dangerous reminders of the Yorkist past. The king who arranged for the younger members of his wife's family to be placed under the guardianship of Lady Margaret Beaufort, welcomed her to court but arranged a marriage with Sir Richard Pole, a kinsman of his own, in 1487.

Margaret joined her husband in Wales and the Marches, at Stourton Castle in Staffordshire, where she began to raise a family of four sons and one daughter, Ursula, who was born in 1504. In 1501, she became a member of Katherine of Aragon's household at Ludlow. The women remained friends for the rest of the Spanish princess's life. Sir Richard died in 1505 and with very little income available to her, she was forced to give her talented second son, Reginald, born in 1500, to the Church to raise. With nowhere else to turn, she and her children lived at Syon Abbey for the next four years, until Henry VIII became king in 1509. Katherine of Aragon reinstated Margaret as a lady-in-waiting and in 1512, her kinsman, Henry VIII, returned some of the estates associated with the earldom of Warwick as well as creating

Margaret Countess of Salisbury in her own right. The title was one which belonged to her great-grandfather, Richard Neville, 5th Earl of Salisbury by right of his wife Alice Montacute. She went from poverty to being one of the wealthiest women in the country.

Like Katherine of Aragon, the countess was a supporter of humanist learning, and as one of the queen's oldest friends, it is perhaps not surprising that in 1520, she was appointed as Princess Mary's lady mistress. Unfortunately, the following year, her sons were implicated in a conspiracy that focused on the suspicion that Edward Stafford, 3rd Duke of Buckingham saw his own claim to the crown as being better than the king's. His treason included listening to prophecies relating to Henry's death and saying that the Tudor line was cursed. To make matters worse, Margaret's daughter, descended from Edward IV's brother, was married to Buckingham's heir, Henry Stafford. Margaret Pole was dismissed from her post as lady governess and replaced by the Calthorpes.

When Princess Mary was sent to Ludlow in 1525, the Countess of Salisbury, restored to her position, accompanied Katherine's daughter. When, in 1533, the princess was illegitimised, the countess refused to return the princess's plate and jewels to the king. She even suggested, in December, that she should fund Mary's household. The countess did not return to court until 1536 but her son, Reginald, now Cardinal Pole, sent a letter opposing the royal supremacy.

In 1538, Margaret's son, Geoffrey, was arrested for his part in the Exeter Conspiracy. The countess was arrested and questioned. Although Geoffrey was pardoned and his mother protested her innocence, by November 1539 the Countess of Salisbury was incarcerated in the Tower. Her eldest son, Henry Pole, had been executed there at the beginning of the year. She remained there for the next two and a half years until the morning of 27 May 1541 when the countess was executed, still protesting her innocence.

Geoffrey Pole, whose admissions led to the arrests of his elder brother and his mother and were instrumental in their executions, tried to commit suicide and in 1548 went into exile. His son, Arthur Pole, who was arrested at the same time as other members of the family was released before 1552 and went into the service of the Duke of Northumberland for the remainder of Edward VI's reign. His lineage and conservative religious beliefs would return, like a curse, to haunt him and his two brothers during the reign of Elizabeth I, when in 1563, their support for Mary Queen of Scots saw them arrested for treason and imprisoned in the Tower, like their grandmother before them.

Anne Shelton (c.1483?–1555)

Anne was born at the Boleyn family home of Blickling in Norfolk. She married Sir John Shelton, of the Norfolk village of Shelton near Norwich, in about 1503. The following year she gave birth to Shelton's heir, named John after his father. Stained glass windows at Shelton Church depict the couple at three different stages of their life and it would appear from the images that a typical union between two gentry families to further the bonds of kinship resulted in an enduring love between the couple.

Anne's home was at Shelton Hall just outside Norwich. She raised three sons and seven daughters there. However, Anne and her sister, Alice's, lives were about to change. At some time during the first half of 1528, the Shelton family sat for the court painter Hans Holbein, at a time when the artist was closely connected with the family of Sir Thomas More and with the king's building works at Greenwich. Among the men who wanted their portraits was Anne Shelton's brother, Sir Thomas, who had advanced steadily through the ranks of courtiers and whose daughter, Anne Boleyn, was being ardently pursued by the king. The Boleyns and their extended family, were in the ascendant.

The Sheltons began to play a more prominent role at court after their niece became queen in 1533. Anne Shelton's daughters, Margaret and Mary, became two of Anne's ladies-in-waiting. Mary Shelton formed a friendship with Lady Margaret Douglas, the king's niece, and with Lady Mary Howard, the bride of Henry FitzRoy. The three girls studied together and wrote courtly love poetry which survives as the *Devonshire Manuscript*.[1] Mary Shelton is often credited with being responsible for most of its transcription, suggesting that her mother, Anne Shelton, had notable skills as a teacher that were worthy of comment. After Princess Elizabeth's birth in 1533, the queen arranged that Anne Shelton was employed as Elizabeth's chief gentlewoman of the privy chamber. She was accompanied by her sister Alice Clere. Lady Margaret Bryan assumed the role of lady mistress with responsibility for overseeing the princess's care and education.

King Henry's elder daughter, Mary, stripped of her rank and her own household, was sent to Hatfield to serve her half-sister in 1534. Rumour, and the Imperial ambassador, Eustace Chapuys, believed that Anne Boleyn wished for Katherine of Aragon's daughter to be humiliated. Henry VIII was determined that the daughter he once cherished should accept her new status as the Lady Mary rather than a legitimate princess. It fell to Anne Shelton to govern Mary's behaviour. She could show no sympathy for the young woman whose arrival disrupted the smooth running of the royal nursery. The queen, it was said, instructed Anne to be as spiteful as possible and even to slap her face if she persisted on using her royal title.[2] Chapuys also wrote that Mary was refused permission to attend Catholic Mass and that she had very few clothes. It was Anne Shelton who delivered Henry VIII's message that Mary was encouraging conspiracies against him, and it was she who refused Chapuys and his servants access to the former princess for fear that they might carry her off. She threatened to beat the princess, and added that she might even be beheaded if she continued to defy her father by refusing to take the oath relating the Act of Succession. Despite it all Mary refused to submit to her father's will. Chapuys reported that the princess feared she would be poisoned.[3] He laid his accusations at the feet of Anne Boleyn but the queen's agent at Hatfield was her aunt. Anne Shelton was described as both impertinent and rude.[4] Rather than blaming her, perhaps culpability for Mary's treatment belonged with the Duke of Norfolk and Anne Boleyn's brother, George, who accused both his aunts of treating Mary too kindly. Anne Shelton retorted that even if she was a poor man's daughter, Mary ought to be respected and treated with kindness for her good character. Anne Shelton spent two years as Mary's governess. It was an invidious position which was about to get worse and Mary remained as defiant as ever.

One of the Shelton sisters, either Margaret, known as Madge, or Mary, is believed to have become Henry VIII's mistress at the beginning of 1535. And the tide was turning against the Boleyn faction at court. Anne Boleyn had not presented her husband with a male heir as she promised but was once again with child. By that time the king was in his mid-forties and Mary Shelton might have been as young as 15 years old but it is possible that the king sought the girl's company to distract him during the queen's pregnancy or even that Anne Boleyn placed one of her cousins in his path as a strategy to prevent him from becoming infatuated with another of her ladies. Chapuys wrote that the king was in love with one of the Sheltons' daughters[5] but failed to identify which one. Scholars are divided as to whether it was Margaret or Mary who caught the king's eye.

In 1536, Margaret Shelton was betrothed to Henry Norris, a widower, who was one of the king's favourites but her name was also linked with Francis Weston. Both men were arrested on charges of adultery with the queen and executed on 17 May. Margaret and Mary's hopes of advancement at their cousin's court came to nothing. The rumours about the Shelton sisters, the misery associated with Norris's execution as well as years of unpleasantness governing Mary took its toll on the relationship between Anne Shelton and her niece. Sir John's wife was one of the women, known for their lack of sympathy to the queen, selected by Thomas Cromwell to wait on the disgraced queen in the Tower before her execution.

In July 1536, Anne Shelton and her husband were officially designated Elizabeth's governor and governess. It was no longer necessary to subject Mary to any harshness, especially after she submitted to the king's wishes. She and Lady Shelton must have arrived at an accommodation with one another. There were New Year's gifts in 1537, and again in 1540, for Elizabeth and Mary Shelton, two of Lady Shelton's daughters. In January 1544 Mary gave the former lady mistress two cushions, worth 7 shillings and Anne sent gifts to her former charge.

Anne Sidney (d.1543)

Anne Pakenham was married first to Thomas FitzWilliam, who was killed at the Battle of Flodden in 1513. She married for a second time in 1514 to Sir William Sidney who was such a favourite with the king by 1536 that he was placed in charge of Prince Edward's household at Hampton Court.

By then Anne was mother to four daughters as well as a son born in 1529 and named after Henry VIII. She taught her daughters, Mary, Lucy, Anne and Frances, the skills that they would need as wives as well as good manners, modesty and needlework. Like all gentlewomen, Anne Sidney had an understanding of dairy work, spinning, weaving, and housework, not because she was required to do it but so that she could oversee the way in which her household officers and domestic servants did theirs. It is also likely, given the Sidneys proximity to the royal family, that Anne's daughters received a more extensive humanist education than basic reading, writing and arithmetic. Her youngest daughter, Frances, born in 1531 and a lady of the bedchamber to Elizabeth I, left £5000 in her will to found a new college at Cambridge University. At court she was a patron of literature and music. Anne's granddaughter, Lady Mary Sidney, was viewed as one of the most notable scholars of her day, along with her brother, Philip Sidney. As courtiers, all of Anne Sidney's children needed to be able to play musical instruments, sing, dance and to have a mastery of Latin, as well as other languages and subjects, similar to the model laid down by Sir Thomas More for his own daughters.

Anne was initially appointed as Edward's governess, her granddaughter, Jane Dormer, also became part of the household. She was raised with Edward as a companion for him during his youngest years. Mary Sidney, Anne's daughter, died in February 1542. Jane would go on to become one of Mary I's ladies, as well as one of her closest friends. She married the Duke of Feria in 1558 after the queen's death and in 1559 left England with her husband.

Elizabeth Tyrwhitt (d.1578)

Elizabeth Oxenbridge was the heiress of Sir Thomas Fiennes of Etchingham in Sussex. Her parents were Sir Goodard Oxenbridge and his wife, Anne Fiennes. She grew up in East Sussex at Brede, near Hastings. In 1536, Elizabeth was sent to court as one of Jane Seymour's ladies of the privy chamber. Before the end of the summer of 1539, she was married to Sir Robert Tyrwhitt, the son of a member of Lincolnshire's gentry, and gave birth to a daughter, Katherine.

The marriage brought her into contact with Katherine Parr who was part of her new husband's extended kinship network. Tyrwhitt would become Katherine's master of horse when she became queen in 1543 while Elizabeth, one of the queen's ladies, joined an inner circle of Protestant reformers. She gained a reputation as a zealous reformer early in her marriage. She was known to be sympathetic to Anne Askew who was arrested and executed for heresy in 1545 and was gifted a copy of the Wycliffe Bible, written in English at a time when such things were banned.[1] Robert Tyrwitt recognised that his wife was more fervent in her beliefs than was prudent.

Elizabeth was Katherine Parr's close friend and was with the dowager queen at Sudeley Castle when she died from childbed fever in September 1548. At the same time that the Privy Council interrogated Thomas Seymour's servants, following his arrest in January 1549, they also took a statement from the women who surrounded Katherine Parr on her deathbed. Among their number was Lady Tyrwhitt. Her testimony was damning. Even though she conceded that the queen's 'mind was far unquieted',[2] Lady Tyrwhitt repeated

Katherine's fevered accusations against her husband. It is unknown the extent to which she blamed the queen's stepdaughter for her friend's misery.

In 1549 when the scandal surrounding Thomas Seymour was at its height, Lady Tyrwhitt's husband was sent to Hatfield to question Elizabeth's servants as well as Elizabeth to find out the extent of her involvement in the admiral's plot to gain control of the king. The Privy Council appointed Lady Tyrwhitt as Elizabeth's governess, but King Edward's sister refused to acknowledge Kat Ashley's removal and continued to refer to her rather than Lady Tyrwhitt as her mistress. She even wrote to the Lord Protector to express her consternation at the appointment of Lady Tyrwhitt.

It is feasible that Lady Tyrwhitt's supervision of her charge was more thorough than Kat Ashely's organisation of Elizabeth's bedchamber had been. While long hours of study were nothing out of the ordinary it is probable that Elizabeth was kept more closely confined and directed towards tasks that encouraged virtuous Christianity rather than activities like dancing which brought with them the threat of immorality.

When Elizabeth became queen in 1558, Sir Robert Tyrwhitt and his wife retired to their Huntingdonshire home. Lady Tyrwhitt wrote poems and hymns attesting to her faith which were published in 1574: *Morning and Evening Praiers, with Divers Psalmes Himnes and Meditations.* Queen Elizabeth's unwanted former lady governess died at her home in Clerkenwell on 28 April 1578. Her will, dated 28 February 1577, contained professions of her faith. She was buried with her husband, who died in 1572, and their daughter, who died in 1567, at St Mary's Church, Leighton Bromswold, Cambridgeshire.

A Who's Who of Governors, Mentors and Household Officers Who Raised the Tudors

King Henry VII understood that the men he trusted to raise his heir, along with their families and clients, would be well placed to ensure their own advancement when the next generation of the Tudor dynasty sat upon the throne. The same men, who stood in *loco parentis* of Prince Arthur, would influence his thoughts, beliefs, and even loyalties as they raised him to the throne. The king may have even considered the propaganda surrounding the eventual fate of Anthony Woodville, 2nd Earl Rivers, who was Edward, Prince of Wales governor and guardian from 1473 while the prince's household was at Ludlow. Did the earl really intend to reinforce Woodville power under Edward V in order to persecute the faction's political enemies? Had there really been a plot to prevent Richard, Duke of Gloucester from assuming his rightful place as protector? Henry VII, known for his exercise of caution, had no desire that a powerful faction should return England to civil war after his demise or that his heir's rule should be weakened by an archetypal 'bad advisor'.

Henry was determined not to give so much power into the hands of a single guardian. Instead, Henry selected officers, mirroring those appointed to his own household to raise Arthur. It was the responsibility of the Council of Wales to teach him how to govern. They would all play their part but none of them would become dominant. Henry Tudor's eventual successor, Henry VIII, followed the same policy for the governance of the households of his children. Often, but not always, the spouse of a lady mistress might be chosen as a steward or comptroller. These household appointments created governors who were in charge of the fabric of the building and the provision of resources but, as Lady Bryan reminded Cromwell in 1536, they were not in charge of raising the sons and daughters of kings. For that, Henry VII and Henry VIII turned, when the need arose, to the appointment of a knightly mentor when a prince became too old to be in the care of lady mistresses.

William Blount, 4th Baron Mountjoy (d.1534)

Blount, born in Derbyshire, was the heir of John Blount. When his father died in 1485 his mother married twice more. Mountjoy received an excellent education and in 1498 went to Paris with Richard Whitford, a fellow of Queen's College, Cambridge, who later became his chaplain. While they were there, Erasmus became Mountjoy's tutor. The scholar baron was admitted to the circle of humanists that included John Colet and Thomas More.

He was appointed to mentor Henry VII's younger son. It has been suggested that his selection was based upon a recommendation by his stepfather, Thomas Butler, 7th Earl of Ormond, who was Elizabeth of York's chamberlain.[1] Although the evidence is circumstantial it offers another piece of evidence to shine a light on the role played by the queen in the raising of her children.

Mountjoy was established as one of Henry VIII's trusted courtiers and was appointed as commander of Hammes Castle, a post which his father held before him. In 1512, he succeeded his stepfather as Katherine of Aragon's chamberlain. He remained part of the queen's household but was placed in the invidious position, in 1533, of trying to persuade her to accept Henry's new marriage to Anne Boleyn and her new rank as dowager princess. In October he requested that he should be relieved of his responsibility as chamberlain.

He died on 8 November 1534 at his home near Barton Blount in Derbyshire and was buried there. Mountjoy's lasting legacy was his enthusiasm for learning and his belief in Henry VIII as a scholar that encouraged Erasmus to visit England briefly in 1499, before returning for a second visit in 1505, and a final stay lasting from 1510–1515 when he stayed with Sir Thomas More.

Sir Walter Buckler (d.1554 or 1558)

Buckler, a younger son from a Dorset family, studied at Merton College, Oxford and was a student in Paris during 1530. He was also known to have journeyed to Padua for a time. On his return to England he found employment with Thomas Cromwell as a diplomat and a messenger. By 1539 he was part of the English embassy in Venice, working for its ambassador, Edmund Harvel. His career carried him across Europe while his humanist credentials linked him with Sir Anthony Denny, Henry VIII's favourite.

When Katherine Parr became queen in 1543, Buckler was appointed as her secretary. His new employment did not prevent the king from sending him on a mission to Germany in 1544. Two years later he married the widow of Sir Edmund Tame. At the time of his marriage Buckler can be found conveying properties to his future brothers-in-law, Sir Walter and Maurice Denys.[1]

In 1549, after Thomas Seymour's arrest, Sir Robert Tyrwhitt and Sir Walter Buckler, both senior officials in Katherine Parr's household, were sent to take control of Elizabeth's establishment. They were described as her governors in official accounts of the period. Buckler was required to investigate the failures of Elizabeth's household accounts and then to remedy their discrepancies. He countersigned all of her accounts for the duration of his employment[2] and in January 1552 he was appointed as her chamberlain following the death of Sir Henry Parker. The following March he was replaced by Sir Nicholas Strange on the orders of the Privy Council, but the reasons for his dismissal are unclear. It may have had something to do with poor health as his widow, Katherine Buckler, was married for a third time by 1554.[3]

Sir Philip Calthorpe (c.1463–1535)

The Calthorpes were a long established East Anglian gentry family[1] serving as sheriffs for Norfolk and Suffolk during the fifteenth century[2] and earlier. Calthorpe, who was the MP for Norfolk during Henry VII's parliament of 1491–1492, inherited the family estates upon his grandfather's death in 1494.[3] Three years later, he demonstrated his loyalty to the Tudors when he joined the king's army to defend London from Cornish rebels at Blackheath. He was knighted soon afterwards and is recorded as being at Henry VII's funeral in 1509 as well as various court functions during the early years of Henry VIII's reign.[4] In 1520 Calthorpe was part of the retinue that accompanied King Henry VIII to meet King Francis I at the Field of Cloth of Gold between Guînes and Ardres in the north of France.[5] It was something of a family gathering. Calthorpe's brother-in-law, Sir Thomas Boleyn, helped to organise the event and his niece by marriage, Mary Boleyn, was present with her husband, William Carey, as well as several of their Howard relations.

In 1521, it was the king who suggested that Jane and Philip Calthorpe should be placed in charge of the care of his heir, Princess Mary. Rather than being named the princess's governor, Calthorpe became the chamberlain of her household. It was Calthorpe's responsibility to manage the household's funds. In 1525 Mary was provided with her own household at Ludlow. Calthorpe continued in the role of vice chamberlain while his wife was listed as one of Mary's gentlewomen.

Peter Courtenay, Bishop of Winchester (c.1432–1492)
Courtenay was descended from the Lancastrian earls of Devon who spent much of the early part of the fifteenth century feuding with the Bonville family for superiority in the West Country. However, Peter's father was Sir Philip Courtenay of Powderham, a cadet branch of the family, whose eldest son, William, married Elizabeth Bonville. This union resulted in the 5th Earl of Devon laying siege to Powderham Castle in 1455.[1] During the civil war that followed the Courtenays of Powderham sided, mostly, with the Yorkists rather than conforming with the Lancastrian affiliations of the earls of Devon or their own earlier family attachments. Philip was part of Walter, 1st Baron Hungerford's affinity during the reign of Henry V and Peter's mother was Elizabeth, Walter's daughter. Besides being a staunch Lancastrian, Hungerford also raised Owen Tudor in his own household as a page and then a squire. The baron's patronage of his son-in-law ensured that Philip Courtenay was granted various properties as well as guardianship of James Luttrell of Dunster, who was married to Philip's daughter, Elizabeth, in 1450 to ensure that Courtenay family retained his estates.[2] It was a complicated pedigree that meant that Peter and his siblings were tied by blood to the most important baronial families in the region. They wielded significant political power because of the affinity that formed around their father as the traditional role of the earls of Devonshire deteriorated and were accepted, at various times throughout the turbulent fifteenth century, by both the houses of York and Lancaster.

As a younger son Peter was destined for the Church, becoming an Archdeacon of Exeter in 1453. He attended the University of Oxford in 1457 before studying law at Cologne and Padua. In 1462 he returned from Italy to enter the service of King Edward IV as a diplomat and legal advisor by which time the senior line of the Courtenay family had lost the earldom of Devon with the execution, and subsequent attainder, of Thomas, 6th Earl of Devon following his capture after the Battle of Towton. Peter's branch of the family was happy to fill the vacuum.

During the early 1460s Peter's father and siblings played a more important part in the West Country's politics and government because of their adherence to George, Duke of Clarence whose authority in Devon expanded at around the same time. Peter became the duke's secretary while his father and brothers were a part of the duke's West Country affinity, owing their loyalty to him in return for preferment. One brother, John, was a merchant stapler and burgess in Calais. This connection was also likely to have originated with Clarence.[3] The association ensured that the family was caught up in the growing resentment felt by the duke and the Earl of Warwick towards the king at the end of the decade. On March 16, 1469 the Courtenays of Powderham and their cousin, Sir Hugh Courtenay of Boconnoc, were among the men for whom Edward IV issued arrest warrants and later confiscated their goods.

Peter proved that his loyalty was to his family rather than the monarchy when he turned his coat and joined them in rebellion against Edward. His adaptability ensured a place in Henry VI's Readeption government as King Henry VI's secretary. The family's adherence to Clarence meant that they followed the duke's lead and re-joined the Yorkist cause in 1471 before the Battle of Barnet. This fortunate switch meant that Peter was once again in service to the winning side when Edward IV resumed the throne. The king did not pursue a grudge against the Courtenays and Sir Hugh of Boconnoc's heir was even allowed to inherit his father's possessions after receiving royal pardon.

Peter continued in the role of secretary and by 1476 was Dean of Windsor. In 1477 he acquired the office of Dean at Exeter and was also made a member of the King's Council. In 1478, Peter was elected Bishop of Exeter. During his time as Exeter's bishop he oversaw, and paid for, the completion of Exeter Cathedral's north tower. The bell there is called the Peter Bell and it strikes on the hour. It is stated that the astronomical clock that governs the time at which the bell sounds was a gift from the bishop. The Earth is at the centre of the clock with the moon and the sun, represented by a fleur-de-lis, revolve around the planet.

In 1483, after the death of Edward IV, the bishop supported Richard III's ascent to the throne but in October, for reasons which remain unclear, he joined in Buckingham's rebellion as part of the Devon and Cornwall Rising even though the rest of his family, with the exception of a younger brother, Walter, remained loyal to Richard. The *Croyland Chronicle* stated that the bishop fled as Richard III's army approached Exeter. He was attainted of treason in 1484 and all his goods forfeited. He and Walter made their way to Vannes where they swore allegiance to Henry Tudor. During the summer of 1485, when Richard III issued a proclamation against Henry and his followers, Peter Courtenay's name was at the top of the list.

The brothers returned to England with Henry Tudor and were at Bosworth. Peter was one of the bishops who officiated at Henry's coronation. Peter's attainder was reversed, his goods returned and he was made Keeper of the Privy Seal. He was also entrusted with the care of Henry's son, Prince Arthur. On 29 January 1487 he translated from the bishopric of Exeter to Winchester following the death of Bishop Waynflete. During the same year he was succeeded by his colleague Richard Foxe, the new Bishop of Exeter, as Keeper of the Privy Seal, but despite his age continued to serve the Tudor administration and to be rewarded by Henry. In 1492 he became one of Prince Henry's godfather's when Arthur's brother was baptised at Greenwich.

Courtney was Prince Arthur's guardian throughout the boy's infancy until he left his nursery and was sent to Ludlow to learn how to govern. In 1490 he witnessed Arthur's creation as Prince of Wales and was present at the ratification of the marriage treaty between England and Spain He died on 23 September 1492 and was buried either at Winchester or at Powderham.

Sir Anthony Denny (1501–1549)

Anthony, the second son of Sir Edmund Denny, was sent to St Paul's Cathedral School in London to be educated. The school was founded by the cathedral's dean, John Colet, in 1509 to educate 153 children. Colet, a friend of Sir Thomas More and Erasmus, ensured that the curriculum included Greek as well as Latin. Erasmus even wrote text books for the scholars. Afterwards, Denny progressed to St John's College, Cambridge. The college had close associations with both Lady Margaret Beaufort, who was its founder, and with Erasmus. As Denny advanced in the king's esteem, he worked for the benefit of both educational foundations and maintained a library of books at his home in Cheshunt, some of which were rescued from Waltham Abbey Library at its dissolution.

By the 1520's Denny was in the service of Lady Margaret Bryan's son, Francis. By the time Anne Boleyn became queen, Denny had progressed to employment as part of the king's household and was able to marry Joan Champernowne, the daughter of Sir Philip Champernowne of Modbury in Devon. In 1539 he replaced his patron, Francis Bryan, as second gentleman of the privy chamber and deputy groom of the stool. It was his job to assist the king at his toilet. The very personal nature of the task meant that Denny was increasingly trusted by the king as well as having more influence at court. Denny's advancement owed something to both Bryan and to Thomas Cromwell.

Henry VIII confided in Denny about his dislike of Anne of Cleeves and in 1542, the king's favourite was named keeper of the privy purse. However, it was only after the king's French campaign of 1543–1544 that Denny was knighted. Joan Denny was part of the queen's household during the same time. In 1546, Lady Denny's association with Katherine Parr's circle of reforming ladies and her support for Protestants, including Anne Askew, led to suspicion being cast in Denny's direction by the court's conservative faction but Anne Askew would implicate no one.

By 1547 Denny was of central importance to a stable change of regime. It was he who told the king that he was dying and acted as one of the executors to Henry's will. On 31 January 1547 he was named as a privy councillor and was appointed as Edward VI's groom of the stool. In 1547, he and Sir Richard Page were nominated by the Duke of Somerset to remain in London to act as royal protectors while Somerset was on campaign in Scotland.

In May 1548, Denny and his wife were called upon to open their home to Elizabeth when it became clear that she could not stay in Katherine Parr's household. The following year he took part in the campaign to suppress Kett's Rebellion but was taken ill and died on 10 September 1549.

William Herbert, 1st Earl of Pembroke (c.1422?–d.1469)

William Herbert was part of the Welsh gentry, served in France and was knighted by King Henry VI. His father, William, was the younger son of a Welsh squire in service to the Beauchamp family before taking on the office of steward to the lordship of Usk which belonged to Richard, 3rd Duke of York. William, the father, proved to be a capable administrator and made two marriages that advanced the family's influence within the local area. He also acquired Raglan Castle and began to undertake building work there.

The Herberts' loyalty, like many other families in the region, was to its most powerful magnate, Richard, 3rd Duke of York, who they served as administrators and enforcers. They also served as soldiers in England's campaigns against the French in Normandy. In 1450, William Herbert, later Earl of Pembroke, was captured at the defeat at Formigny.[1] After his release he returned to York's service. He and his wife's Devereux kinsmen seized the castle at Carmarthen and imprisoned Edmund Tudor there. The Lancastrian council could only treat Herbert's infraction with leniency because of his service to both the Duke of York and the Earl of Warwick. By contrast, Anne Herbert's father and brothers were sent to London for trial and only released in February 1458.[2]

Herbert, who was perhaps hedging his bets, took no part in events at Ludford Bridge in 1459 when the Duke of York and the earls of Salisbury and Warwick, believing that they were being threatened, gathered an army. The arrival of an army led by the king led to the flight of the earls and the sack of Ludlow. The Lancastrian regime, who wished to win Herbert's allegiance for themselves, rewarded him with grants from the estates of both York and Warwick in the immediate aftermath of the episode to try and strengthen his ties to their cause.

In 1460, when Warwick returned to England from exile in Calais, Herbert decided that the time was right to support the Yorkist cause rather than going to the aid of Margaret of Anjou and her faction. After the Yorkist victory at the Battle of Northampton, Herbert was granted extensive authority in South Wales. In October, he represented Hereford when Parliament was summoned and presented with York's claim to the throne. Herbert's backing of the Yorkists at the Battle of Mortimer's Cross, in February 1461, and his acclamation of Edward as king at Baynard's Castle on 3 March, was rewarded when he was created Lord Herbert of Raglan at Edward IV's coronation. In return Herbert and his family were required to police the Marches and capture Wales for the Yorkists.

In 1462, the Yorkist victory at Twt Hill forced Jasper Tudor out of Wales and secured the region. Edward, a grateful king, granted Herbert the stewardship of Pembroke and its castle, made him a Knight of the Garter and welcomed him into his Privy Council. He was also awarded guardianship of Henry Tudor. The various grants and rewards gave Herbert the status he needed for his hegemony to dominate South Wales and the Marches. Henry's guardian continued to receive preferment from the Crown including custody of the 3rd Duke of Buckingham's Welsh estates during his minority. It was only after Herbert's capture of Harlech Castle, which was besieged from 1461 until August 1468, that he was elevated to the peerage with the grant of the earldom of Pembroke. By that time, Herbert had secured numerous offices including becoming Justiciar of both South and North Wales. Raglan was transformed from the seat of a squire to the power base of an important magnate.

William's ambition secured him enormous wealth and prestige but less than a year after he gained his earldom a quarrel between the king and Richard Neville, Earl of Warwick resulted in his death. Warwick, also known as the Kingmaker, felt that his own position in Edward's government was being weakened by the king's reliance of new men, Herbert included. The honours, estates and administrative responsibilities that the Earl of Pembroke accrued, irked Warwick. A marriage into the royal family and the creation of Herbert's eldest son as Lord Dunster irritated him still further, while the presence of Herbert at the scene when George Neville was forced to resign the Great Seal could best be described as incendiary. Warwick was determined to put an end to his upstart competitor's empire in the Marches and in Wales and replace it with a power base of his own.

In 1469, Neville was behind a rebellion against the king led by the shadowy captain, Robin of Redesdale. The so-called Kingmaker intended to remove the cousin he put on the throne in 1461 and replace him with Edward's own brother, George, Duke of Clarence who was now Warwick's son-in-law. When the king arrived in Nottingham on 9 July 1469, he realised he lacked troops, so summoned help. Pembroke led a force of men north but was beaten by the rebels at the Battle of Edgecote, near Banbury, on 27 July 1469. He and his brother, Sir Richard Herbert, were captured and executed at Northampton on 29 July, on Warwick's orders and without a proper trial. Another brother, Thomas Herbert, was executed at Bristol.

Prior to his execution, Pembroke added a codicil to his will requesting that his wife Anne Devereux, should become a vowess. It was his desire to be buried in the priory church at Abergavenny but he was interred in Tintern Abbey in front of the high altar there. Herbert, who was one of the abbey's patrons, as well as its steward, left the monks 100 tons of stone for the building of their cloisters.[3] Richard Herbert's body was also transported back to Wales and did find its way to St Mary's Priory where it was interred in the Herbert Chapel.

Henry Howard, Earl of Surrey (1516–1547)

Henry's father was Thomas Howard, 3rd Duke of Norfolk, who at that time was then Earl of Surrey. Howard was in the ascendent when his heir was born. His father ensured that he received an excellent education which included French and Italian in its curriculum.

In 1530, when Surrey was only 13 years old, he was sent to Windsor to join Henry FitzRoy, who much preferred sport to his studies. The tutors Cardinal Wolsey appointed to teach the boy, Palsgrave and Croke, proved ineffectual. It was hoped that Surrey's presence as one of FitzRoy's companions would inspire the boy to work harder. As it happened the two boys bonded over their shared passion for sport, as well as their growing interest in women.

In 1532 FitzRoy and Surrey accompanied the king and Anne Boleyn, who was Howard's cousin, to Calais to meet with Francis I of France and then remained in the household of the dauphin and his brothers. There were pledges of Henry VIII's good faith for the terms of the rapprochement that the two kings agreed. At Fontainbleau, Surrey was exposed to the art and literature of Europe's Renaissance. The summer of 1533 was spent travelling to Provence before Surrey returned to England.

He was already married to Lady Frances de Vere, the daughter of the Earl of Oxford but they would not live together until 1535. In 1536 Surrey was part of the group of men who tried the queen for treason and he accompanied his father north to suppress the Pilgrimage of Grace. Even so, in the summer of 1537, the Seymour faction at court tried to suggest that Surrey, who was a Catholic, was sympathetic to the cause of the rebels. He also got into a fight, lost a hand as a consequence and was placed under arrest at Windsor. It was not the first time that the earl found himself in trouble for brawling. He was once arrested for striking a courtier. On another occasion he walked through London late at night throwing stones and breaking windows.

While he was confined the earl concentrated on writing poetry. Surrey's reputation is a complex one. He is sometimes called the 'poet earl' because he, together with Thomas Wyatt, introduced a new style of poetry to England that originated in Italy. Rehabilitated by the end of 1537, he was Jane Seymour's chief mourner at her funeral and continued his career as a poet, soldier and Tudor administrator.

Known for his arrogance and recklessness, Surrey eventually fell from the king's favour. In 1546, his command in France was replaced by Edward Seymour. Facing disgrace and accusations of financial misconduct, Surrey became embroiled in an argument about who should have control of the regency following Henry's death. His description of the Privy Council and its members was far from complimentary. In June, the Duke of Norfolk suggested an alliance between the Seymours and the Howards cemented by marriage. Surrey's plan was that his sister, Lady Mary Howard, the widow of

Henry FitzRoy should become Henry VIII's mistress and use her influence to advance her family. It was a provocation too far, and together with the earl's lack of discretion, it was not long before he was arrested. On 12 December, Surrey was sent to the Tower as a prisoner.

Surrey was tried for treason on 7 January 1547 and found guilty to the charge of displaying his own coat of arms with the royal arms. In August 1545, the earl had adopted into his own arms the heraldic device of his maternal grandfather, Edward Stafford 3rd Duke of Buckingham as well as part of the Mowbray arms supposed to belong to Edward the Confessor. The elaborate quarterings were, the court agreed, an act both of pride and rebellion. On 13 January Surrey, together with his father who was charged with concealing treason, were sentenced to death. The earl went to his death on 19 January, becoming the last person to be executed during the reign of Henry VIII. Norfolk's execution was to take place on 28 January. Fortunately for him, the king died during the night and the Privy Council decided not to start Edward VI's reign with a beheading.

Sir Richard Page (d.1548)

Page began his career in the service of Cardinal Wolsey, whose chamberlain he was. It was his responsibility to manage the household and control who had access to the cardinal. He was advanced through Wolsey's patronage to the king's privy chamber. In 1525 he was sent with Henry FitzRoy to Sheriff Hutton in North Yorkshire. He was the household's vice chamberlain as well as being a member of the Council of the North.

In 1527 he became the Recorder of York but was back at court working for both Wolsey and the king at a time when Henry's divorce from Katherine, the so-called Great Matter, was beginning to dominate all that Cardinal Wolsey did. Wolsey trusted Page sufficiently to give him letters to Anne asking her to intercede with Henry on his behalf when he fell from royal favour.[1] Anne did not reply. Page's court connections resulted in a working relationship with Arthur Plantagenet, Lord Lisle, who was Captain of Calais. There are several letters from him among the Lisle correspondence and in return Page preferred suits to the king on Lisle's behalf.[2] By 1530 he had two annuities worth £100 each and after Wolsey's fall was granted the Essex manor of Throby which was previously in the hands of Cardinal College, Oxford.[3]

Sometime before 1534 he married Elizabeth Stanhope, who was Sir Edward Seymour's mother-in-law through his marriage to Anne Stanhope. Page was Elizabeth's fourth husband. The couple had one daughter, Elizabeth.

In 1536 Page was arrested and imprisoned on charges of treason and adultery with Anne Boleyn. He was released by 18 July, perhaps because of his association with Thomas Cromwell. Lord Lisle's man of business in London, John Husee, shared the news with Lord Lisle, although he added that Page was banished from the king's presence. This information was only rumour; in October Page was with the king at Welbeck and by November he was sheriff of Surrey and Sussex.

In June 1537 he entertained Mary Tudor, rehabilitated with her father since the fall of Anne Boleyn. The entertainment was provided by one of the king's musicians who played a sackbut, something akin to a trombone, and was rewarded by Mary.[4] Page's wife, Elizabeth, sent a servant with strawberries and cream to Mary the same month, as did Page later in June.[5]

Page benefitted from grants of several monastic manors in Hertfordshire and Buckinghamshire during the ensuing years. After Cromwell's fall from power and execution in 1540, Page became lieutenant of the king's gentlemen pensioners, a royal bodyguard armed with axes. He was increasingly linked with the Seymour faction, to whom he had ties of kinship. During 1542, he oversaw the fortification of Hull, which included cleaning the moat as well as rebuilding its walls. In 1544 he was appointed as chamberlain to Prince Edward's household and made the transition to Edward VI's court.

Sir John Shelton (c.1476–1539)

Sir John, whose mother was part of the Clere family, served as sheriff of Norfolk in 1504 and was knighted at the coronation of Henry VIII. Shelton's career was that of regional administrator. He was a justice of the peace and served a second term as sheriff in 1522. In 1533 Lady Shelton was appointed to the royal nursery at Hatfield and by July 1536, Sir John was its steward. He and Lady Margaret Bryan wrestled over the way that the household should be run. Shelton was adamant that he was 'master of this house' but Lady Bryan, who was a baroness in her own right, wrote to Thomas Cromwell. The following year, any lingering friction disappeared when Lady Margaret transferred, with the birth of Prince Edward, to a new household. As reward for his service, Shelton was granted the site of the dissolved nunnery of St Mary at Carrow, near Norwich, in 1538. Sir John and his wife turned the prioress's house into a family residence.

He died on 21 December 1539 and was succeeded by his namesake who was married to Margaret, the daughter of Sir Henry Parker. Sir John, senior, was a wealthy man but his will attempted to change the terms under which he possessed some of his estates. Property owned outright could freely be transferred to an heir but any land which was held by feudal right was subject to a tax and could not be willed to an heir. Shelton consulted with three different lawyers before drawing up his will to avoid John Shelton the Younger having to pay the feudal fees due to the Crown. In February 1540, his 'crafty conveyances' which were contrary to the Statute of Uses were annulled by an Act of Parliament.[1]

In 1553, John Shelton the Younger, who filled various local government roles during the rule of Edward VI, would be among the first of Norfolk's gentry to join Queen Mary at Kenninghall but died less than nine months before his cousin, Elizabeth, became queen of England. His son and other members of the family benefitted from Sir John and Lady Anne's ties to the new queen and made advantageous marriages as well as finding positions at court.

Jasper Tudor, Earl of Pembroke and Duke of Bedford (c.1431–1495)

In 1452 Jasper and his older brother, Edmund, were formally recognised as Henry VI's kinsmen and elevated to the peerage before being sent to South Wales to administer the region on the king's behalf. It was a time when difficulties between supporters of Richard Duke of York, Henry VI's cousin, and the faction led by Margaret of Anjou, the Duke of Somerset and Earl of Suffolk led to increased tensions at court. Jasper recognised that the stresses arising from the enmity between York and Somerset were dangerous not only for the stability of the kingdom but for his own future wellbeing. Unlike the Percy and the Neville families, the Tudors had no powerful family network or tradition of landownership backing their position in society. They were entirely reliant upon King Henry VI's regime and their half-brother's continued goodwill.

In May 1455, Jasper was present with the Lancastrian army at the First Battle of St Albans when England stood on the edge of civil war. At that time Yorkist leaders did not regard him as a rival, so he was not hunted down on the battlefield and killed in the same manner as the Earl of Northumberland

and Lord Clifford. It was only after Edmund Tudor's death in 1456 when Jasper became the king's lieutenant in South Wales that Yorkist attitudes towards him began to harden.

The Earl of Pembroke, always loyal to Henry VI, led the Lancastrian forces when open warfare broke out in Wales in 1459 and gave shelter to Margaret of Anjou and Prince Edward after the Lancastrian defeat at Northampton in 1460. In February 1461, the army he commanded was defeated at Mortimer's Cross by Edward, the eldest son of the Duke of York. He was not present at Towton, a few weeks later, when Edward defeated the main Lancastrian army and claimed the crown for himself. Instead, Jasper continued to hold Wales in the name of his half-brother until he was defeated by Sir William Herbert at the Battle of Twt Hill. Afterwards he fled to Brittany and left his nephew, Henry Tudor, at Pembroke.

The fugitive earl continued to agitate on Henry VI's behalf and was in Northumberland at Bamburgh Castle which held out for Henry VI until it was forced to surrender on Christmas Eve, 1462. Jasper was fortunate to escape to Scotland. Although he did become a member of Louis XI's household for a time, it is difficult to pin down the earl's exact location throughout 1463 and 1464. Edward IV exerted pressure on the French to have Jasper returned to England but it did not suit King Louis, sometimes known as the 'universal spider' because of the web of plots he spun, to betray his cousin. Instead, he gave Jasper 500 livres and sent him to Scotland. In 1468 Jasper returned to Wales and burned Denbigh but did not succeed in capturing the castle there and was eventually forced to flee once more, to Brittany.

In 1469, King Louis seeing the opportunity to cause Edward IV difficulties, and perhaps to supplant a regime hostile to himself with one who would ally itself to France, officiated in the negotiations between Margaret of Anjou and the disaffected Earl of Warwick and his son-in-law George, Duke of Clarence. Jasper had an important part to play in the discussions and, an agreement having been reached, accompanied Neville back to England to restore Henry VI to the throne. It was only a temporary reversal of Lancastrian fortunes. Following the deaths of Warwick and his brother at the Battle of Barnet on 14 April 1471 and of Prince Edward of Lancaster at Tewkesbury on 4 May, the Lancastrian Earl of Pembroke became a fugitive again.

It fell to Jasper Tudor, to keep his nephew safe. Events at Tewkesbury had changed the status of Henry Tudor, not because he was the nephew of Henry VI but because his mother was a Beaufort, descended from John of Gaunt. Roger Vaughan was dispatched by King Edward to seize Tudor and the young earl. Vaughan was swiftly killed, if Polydore Vergil is to be believed, when Jasper outmanoeuvred him and his men, surrounded them and executed his enemy. The ruthlessness with which Jasper acted preserved his and Henry's freedom. It may also have been an act of vengeance for the death of Jasper's father, Owen Tudor, in the immediate aftermath of Mortimer's Cross. Another man, Morgan Thomas, was sent to do what the king's first agent could not. Within eight days Pembroke Castle was completely cut off and the Tudors were trapped.

Fortunately for Jasper, Thomas's own brother, David, created a diversion so that he and Henry could escape to Tenby where they were hidden by Thomas White, Tenby's mayor,[1] until they were able to take a vessel to France. Their vessel, blown off course, landed in Brittany. Jasper would spend the next fourteen years as a fugitive protecting Henry and, from 1483 onwards, plotting with Lady Margaret Beaufort to establish his nephew as the rightful king of England.

On 7 August 1485, Jasper and Henry Tudor, who was aged 28 years by then, landed at Milford Haven in Pembrokeshire where Jasper was able to summon more men in the form of old allies, including Sir Rhys ap Thomas, whose father, Thomas, had fought alongside Jasper during the 1460s. Jasper was one of his nephew's commanders at the Battle of Bosworth, together with John de Vere, 13th Earl of Oxford who had escaped from his prison at Hammes Castle near Calais to join Henry.

Once Henry ascended the throne as Henry VII, he returned his uncle's title and estates as well as rewarding him with ennoblement to the royal Dukedom of Bedford. Jasper, who was one of the king's most trusted advisors, became a privy councillor, Henry's justiciar in South Wales, Captain of Calais and Lord Lieutenant of Ireland. In 1486 he received the lordships of Abergavenny and Sudeley in Gloucestershire. He was also granted the lordship of Glamorgan which was part of the Despenser inheritance that rightfully belonged to the Countess of Warwick but which she returned to the Crown when she arrived at an accommodation with the Tudors.

Bosworth was not the last time that Jasper and the Earl of Oxford rode into battle together. They commanded the king's army at the Battle of Stoke on 16 June 1487, which saw the defeat of supporters of Lambert Simnel. Yorkists, including Francis Lovell, one of Richard III's closest friends and John de la Pole, Earl of Lincoln, claimed that Simnel was either Edward V or Edward Plantagenet, 17th Earl of Warwick. Jasper, who was in his late fifties in 1487, had fought in the first and last battles of the Wars of the Roses.

Now that Henry was king, Jasper married Catherine Woodville, Elizabeth of York's aunt and the widow of Henry Stafford, 2nd Duke of Buckingham. Catherine had lost everything when her husband was attainted of treason by Richard III but she did not go to Jasper as a penniless bride. Henry VII restored Catherine's dower rights. Her newly acquired lands became Jasper's upon their marriage. However, he did not become responsible for Catherine's children. Lady Margaret Beaufort was named the guardian of Jasper's stepchildren, including Edward Stafford, 3rd Duke of Buckingham.

The Duke of Bedford would have no legitimate children of his own, although Catherine was only 27 years old when she married Jasper and they lived together for ten years. The marriage may have been a strategic one for both the partners. It is thought that he was father to Joan Tudor who was married to William ap Yevan of Llanishen. He was one of the men who answered Jasper's call to arms in 1485 before the Battle of Bosworth and remained in the duke's service afterwards.[2] It is also sometimes alleged that Joan was related to Henry VIII's minister, Thomas Cromwell, in some manner. A second daughter Elin, or Helen, married a man named William Gardiner in London and their son, Thomas, became a monk at Westminster. The earliest reference to Elin is in the Heraldic Visitation of the northern counties made in 1530. It contains a claim by Thomas, who was the prior of Tynmouth Abbey in Northumberland.[3]

For most of his life Jasper served either the needs of his half-brother or his nephew. It was only during the relatively stable years between the time when he was made Earl of Pembroke and the Battle of Mortimer's Cross that he had been able to spend any time making his mark on his earldom, including building a manor house at Pembroke Castle to make it more comfortable and improving Tenby's defences. Between 1485 and 1492, Jasper continued to work on his nephew's behalf but he used some of his new found wealth to begin some form of church building programme, including the tower at Llandaff Cathedral which is named after him.

At the end of 1495 Jasper, who was at his manor in Thornbury in Gloucestershire, wrote his will, dated 15 December. He died eleven days later, with his wife, nephew and Lady Margaret Beaufort by his side. The duke's entrails were removed and buried at Thornbury Church but his body was buried according to his instructions at Keynsham Abbey, Somerset, of which only ruins now remain. The king and queen were both present for the duke's funeral service. Jasper returned most of his possessions and estates to his nephew but provided a significant sum for several monasteries to pray for the souls of his parents and his brother, Edmund, as well as his own soul. At Keynsham, it was intended that four priests would sing masses for the Tudors and Henry VII arranged for a chantry to be built at Thornbury.

After Jasper's death, Catherine Woodville was now a wealthy widow, even if Jasper did not leave her much in his will, other than what his executors thought fit. She married for a third time to Sir Richard Wingfield without royal permission. She died on 18 May 1497. When Henry VIII dissolved the monasteries, the tomb of the man who did so much to ensure the success of the Tudor dynasty was lost.

Sir Robert Tyrwhitt (c.1504–1572)

Tyrwhitt was raised at court as an esquire of the body. He eventually became the master of horse for Katherine of Aragon and joined Henry VIII on his French Campaign of 1544. In 1545 he became the member of parliament for Lincolnshire. He retained the seat throughout the parliaments of Edward VI and Mary I.

In January 1549 Tyrwhitt was sent to question Elizabeth's involvement with Thomas Seymour. His wife, Elizabeth, was unsympathetic to Henry VIII's daughter because she was a close friend of Katherine Parr. Tyrwhitt believed that Elizabeth was guilty of colluding with the Lord Admiral but without a confession could not find any reason to arrest her as well as her servants, Kat Ashley and Thomas Parry. The Privy Council, for the avoidance of any further conspiracies centred on Elizabeth who was third in line to the throne, appointed the Tyrwhitt's as governor and governess of the household.

In 1548 he was granted a Crown property at Mortlake where he and his wife chose to live in preference to their Huntingdonshire home. When Elizabeth I ascended the throne, in 1558, she deprived Tyrwhitt of the dwelling which had once been a residence of King Edward III. Sir Robert, wisely perhaps, decided to retire to his estates in Huntingdonshire. When he died in 1572, having outlived his only child named Katherine, he was buried quietly at Leighton Bromsgrove.

Table Identifying the Men and Women who Raised Tudor Princes and Princesses

	Lady mistress or governess	Nursery staff	Guardian, governor or mentor	Tutor	Significant other
Parents: Edmund Tudor, 1st Earl of Richmond, 7th creation of the earldom (c.1430–3 — November 1456) = Lady Margaret Beaufort, Countess of Richmond and Derby (31 May 1443 — 29 June 1509)					
Henry Tudor b.28 January 1457 later King Henry VII ruled from 21 August 1485 d.21 April 1509	Anne Herbert, Countess of Pembroke	unknown	Jasper Tudor, 1st Earl of Pembroke, 7th creation of the earldom, and Duke of Bedford William Herbert, 1st Earl of Pembroke, 8th creation of the earldom	Edward Haseley Sir Hugh Johnys Andrew Scot	Francis I, Duke of Brittany Jean de Rieux, Marshal of Brittany
Parents: King Henry VII (28 January 1457 — 21 April 1509) = Elizabeth of York, Queen of England (11 February 1466 — 11 February 1503)					
Arthur, **Prince of Wales** b.19/20 September 1486 d.2 April 1502	Elizabeth Haute	Katherine Gibbs (wetnurse) Agnes Butler (rocker) Alice Bywimble (rocker) Eveleyn Hobbes (rocker) William Wangham (servant) John Hoo (servant)	Peter Courtenay, Bishop of Winchester	Bernard André John Argentine John Burton Giles D'Ewes Thomas Wriothesley	Lady Margaret Beaufort The Council of Wales Senior household officers at Ludlow

	Lady mistress or governess	Nursery staff	Guardian, governor or mentor	Tutor	Significant other
Margaret b. November 1489 later Queen of Scotland 8 August 1503–9 — September 1513 married secondly, Archibald Douglas, 6th Earl of Angus d.1541	Jane Guildford	Alice Davy (wetnurse) Alice Bywimble (day-wife) Anne Mayland (rocker) Margaret Troughton (rocker) Margery Gower (rocker)		Giles D'Ewes Jane Popincourt	Lady Margaret Beaufort
Henry b.28 June 1491 later King Henry VIII ruled from 22 April 1509 d.28 January 1547	Elizabeth Denton Jane Guildford	Anne Oxenbridge/Luke (wetnurse) Margery Gower (rocker) Frideswide Puttenham (rocker) Margaret Troughton (rocker) Elizabeth Bailey Jane Chace Avice Skidmore	William Blount, 4th Baron Mountjoy (mentor) Arthur Plantagenet, Lord Lisle (mentor)	Giles D'Ewes John Holt William Hone John Skeleton Sir William Tyler Thomas Wriothesley	Lady Margaret Beaufort Senior members of his household staff at Eltham
Mary b.18 March 1496 Queen of France 13 August 1514 —1515 married secondly, Charles Brandon, Duke of Suffolk d.25 June 1533	Anne Cromer Jane Guildford			Giles D'Ewes William Hone John Palsgrave Jane Popincourt	Lady Margaret Beaufort

	Lady mistress or governess	Nursery staff	Guardian, governor or mentor	Tutor	Significant other
Parents: King Henry VIII = Katherine of Aragon, Queen of England (1485–1536) — marriage annulled in 1533					
Mary b.18 February 1516 later Queen Mary I ruled from 19 July 1553 m. Philip II King of Spain d.17 November 1558	Lady Margaret Bryan Jane Calthorpe Alice Clere Elizabeth Denton Lady Margaret Pole, Countess of Salisbury Anne Shelton	Catherine Pole (wetnurse) Alice Baker (dry nurse)		Giles D'Ewes Richard Featherstone Thomas Linacre John Palsgrave Henry Rowle	Sir Philip Calthorpe Sir John Shelton Juan Luis Vives John Veysey, Bishop of Exeter
Acknowledged illegitimate son **Parents:** King Henry VIII and Bessie Blount (d.c.1539–1541). Elizabeth Blount afterwards married Gilbert, Lord Tailboys of Kyme					
Henry FitzRoy Duke of Richmond and Somerset b.15 June 1519 d.23 July 1536	Lady Margaret Bryan	Agnes Partridge (dry nurse)	Cardinal Wolsey Henry Howard, Earl of Surrey (mentor)	Richard Croke John Palsgrave	Senior household officers at his household in Sheriff Hutton The Council of the North
Parents: Henry VIII = Anne Boleyn, Queen of England (1500–1536) — Anne attainted of treason and executed					
Elizabeth b.7 September 1533 later Queen Elizabeth I ruled from 17 November 1553 d.24 March 1603	Katherine Ashley Isabel Baynton Lady Margaret Bryan Joan Denny Blanche Herbert, Lady Troy Anne Shelton Elizabeth Tyrwhitt	Mrs Pendred (wetnurse) Blanche Parry	Sir Walter Buckler Sir Anthony Denny Sir Henry Parker Sir John Shelton Sir Robert Tyrwhitt	Roger Ascham John Belmain Giovanni Battista Castiglione Kat Champernowne later Ashley William Grindal John Picton	Sir Edward Baynton Katherine Parr, Queen of England Thomas Seymour, 1st Baron Seymour of Sudeley

	Lady mistress or governess	Nursery staff	Guardian, governor or mentor	Tutor	Significant other
Parents: King Henry VIII = Jane Seymour, Queen of England (1507/1508–1537) Died from complications following childbirth					
Edward b.12 October 1537 later King Edward VI ruled from 28 January 1547 d.6 July 1553	Lady Margaret Bryan Anne Sidney	Mother Jack (wetnurse) Sybil Penn (dry nurse)	John Dudley, Duke of Northumberland Edward Seymour, Duke of Somerset Sir Richard Page	John Astley John Belmain William Buckley Giovanni Battista Castiglione John Cheke Richard Cox William Thomas Philip van de Wilder	Sir John Cornwallis Sir Thomas Darcy Sir John Gates Sir Richard Page Katherine Parr, Queen of England Sir William Sidney
Parents: Lady Frances Brandon, the eldest daughter of Mary, Queen of France and her second husband Charles Brandon, Duke of Suffolk (1517–1559) = Henry Grey, Marquess of Dorset (1517–1554)					
Lady Jane Grey b. October 1537 m. Guildford Dudley 25 May 1553 The Nine Days Queen ruled from 10 July 1553 — 19 July 1533 d.12 February 1554		Mrs Ellen (nurse)	Thomas Seymour, 1st Baron Seymour of Sudeley	Dr Thomas Harding John Aylmer	Katherine Parr, Queen of England

Notes

All the authors referenced in the notes have their works listed in the bibliography at the end.

Introduction: From Knaves to Kings and Renaissance Princes

1. Beattie, Andrew, p.146.
2. Ibid., p.147.
3. Guy: 2011, p.99.
4. Hilton, p.4.
5. Ibid.
6. Ibid.
7. Dowling, p.30.
8. Weir, 2002, p.466.
9. Bushnel, p.123.
10. Mynors and Dalzell, p.103.
11. Machiavelli, p.93.

Chapter One: The Rise of the Tudors

1. Roberts, online.
2. The Penal Laws, II, p.19.
3. Sayles, G.O., 'The Royal Marriages Act of 1428' in *Scripta Diversa* (London, 1982), pp.285–289. Cited in Griffiths p.1013.
4. Rot. Parl. 10 Henry VI. p.415.
5. For a fuller exploration of illicit marriages and legitimacy see Ashdown-Hill.
6. Breverton, 2017, p.163.
7. Calendar Patent Rolls, p.344.

Chapter Two: Battle for the Crown

1. Breverton, 2017, pp.188–189.
2. Alberge, Dalya, 16 September 2018 *The Guardian.*
3. C.P.R. 1461–1467, p.114. Cited in Chrimes, p.15.
4. Ellis (ed.), p.134. Cited in Chrimes, fn 4, p.16.

Chapter Three: Henry Tudor — A Fifteenth-Century Aristocratic Education

1. Breverton, 2014, p.130.
2. Chrimes, p.16 fn 4.
3. Richardson, p.22.

4. Bentley, *Henry VII's Privy Purse expenses*, item 9, p.103.
5. Chrimes, pp.16–17 n.5; C.P.R. 1485–1495, 332.
6. Bliss, p.4.
7. Hickey, 2023, p.117.
8. Condon and Jones, p.1 fn 6.
9. Ibid.
10. Hickey: 2023, p.69.
11. Kenyon, p.10.
12. Jones, p.48.
13. Ibid.
14. Jones, p.49.

Chapter Four: From Lancastrian 'Imp' to King of England

1. Ellis (ed.), *Polydore Vergil*, pp.127–128; and Edward Hall, pp.273–274.
2. Ellis (ed.), *Polydore Vergil*, p.135.
3. Breverton, 2014, p.172.
4. Ibid.
5. Ellis (ed.), *Polydore Vergil*, p.155; and Edward Hall p.302.
6. Breverton, 2014, p.172.
7. Hall, p.305.
8. Ibid.
9. Margaret Beaufort was married as a child to her guardian's son, John de la Pole before she was 3 years old. This union was annulled and Margaret never recognised it as a valid marriage. She referred to Edmund Tudor as her first husband.
10. Ellis (ed.), *Polydore Vergil*, p.164.
11. Cal. S.P. Milan, August 30 1497 no. 537 p.322.
12. Ibid.
13. Ibid., May 17 1499 no. 617 p.375.
14. Ibid., August 30 1497 no. 537 p.322.
15. Ellis (ed.), *Polydore Vergil*, p.194 for promise of marriage prior to declaration at Rennes and p.203 for description of oath.
16. Ibid., p.205.
17. BL. Harleian Ms. 787 cited in Horrox, p.155.
18. Ibid., p.212.

Chapter Five: A Royal Family

1. Jones and Underwood, p. 80.
2. Ibid., p.92.
3. Licence, p.157.
4. Jones and Underwood, p.73.
5. Leland's *Collectanea* indicated that the ordinances that governed the household were drawn up by Margaret, pp 179–184.
6. Tallis, 2019, p.186.
7. Harleian Library (no. 6079).

8. Ibid., p.186.
9. Licence, p.134.
10. St John's College, Cambridge (MS N.24). Cited in Tallis, 2019, p.187.
11. Weir, Alison, 2014, p.236.
12. Calendar Patent Rolls Henry VII, vol. 1, p.306. Cited in Cunningham, p.vii and Weir, 2014, p.235.
13. Gunn, p.11.
14. Oxford English Dictionary, Marl-Z, volume 2.
15. Borman, p.12.
16 Tallis, 2019, p.122.
17. Langley, fn 9, p.50.
18. CPR 1476–1485, p.241. Cited in Orme, p.13.
19. Streeter, p.51.
20. Pollnitz, p.22.
21. Gunn, p.7.
22. Cunningham, pp.34–35 citing CPR (Calendar of Patent Rolls) 1476–1485, p.241.
23. Ibid., p.43.
24. Furdell, p.20; and Strickland, p.60.
25. Orme, 2001, p.202.
26. Leyland's *Collectanea*, volume 4, p.250.
27. Strickland, p.5.
28. Ibid.
29. Weir, 2015, p.434.
30. Cunningham, p.32.
31. Levin *et al.* p.466.
32. Dryburgh, pp.26–28.
33. Leyland's *Collectanea*, vol. 5, p.234.
34. Breverton, 2016 p.258.
35. *Excertpa Historica*, p.117.
36. Weir, 2014, p.331.
37. Bentley, *Henry VII Privy Purse expenses*, item 28, p.124.
38. Account Book of Elizabeth of York, p.1.
39. Account Book of Elizabeth of York, p.29.
40. Bentley, *Henry VII Privy Purse expenses*, p.125.
41. Ibid., p.133.
42. Green, p.55. Citing Wardrobe Accounts. 15. Henry VII, ff. 16, 24, A. vi, 25, Chapter House Documents, Rolls House.
43. Borman, p.40.
44. Hutchinson, p.36.
45. Borman, p.40
46. Ibid.
47. Cited in Norton, p.175.
48. Ibid.
49. Cal. S.P. Spain, vol. 1, p.176. Cited in Tallis, 2019, p.247.

50. Grummitt, online.
51. Watkins, p.12.
52. Ibid., p.18.
53. Byrne (ed.), p.xi.

Chapter Six: Prince Arthur

1. Cunningham, p.37.
2. Erler, p.508.
3. Ibid., pp.39–40.
4. Streeter, p.52.
5. thomasmorestudies.org/Pageant_Life (pdf).
6. Bentley (ed.), *Henry VII Privy Purse expenses*, item 24, p.88.
7. Cunningham, p.52.
8. Ibid., p.255.
9. Bentley,(ed.), *Henry VII Privy purse expenses*, item 20, p.109.
10. Cal. S.P. Milan, September 8 1497, no. 539, p.322.
11. Pollnitz, p36. N.127.
12. Cited in Gunn, p.8.
13. Cited in Pollnitz, p.41.
14. Fuller, p.128.
15. Corbet, p.307.
16. Ibid., p.189.
17. Halliwell, p.138, in the letter of 28 September 1473 entitled 'Ordinances, touching the guiding of our said Son's person, which we commit to the said Earl Rivers', pp.136–144.
18. Cited in Nichols,1854, p.vii.
19. Ibid.
20. Cunningham, p.vii.
21. Hicks, *Richard III*, p.268.
22. Cited in Pollnitz, p.26.
23. Rayner, p.28.
24. Stephen, Leslie, (ed.), *Dictionary of National Biography*, Volume 53, (London: Smith, Elder and Co,1895) p.140.
25. Ibid.
26. Churton, p.64.
27. Mercer, p.117.
28. Ibid, p.121.
29. C.P.R. 1476–1485, p.520.
30. C.P.R. 1476–1485, p.572.
31. Gower p.40.
32. Surrey Archaeological Society, vol. 3, 1865, pp.103–104.
33. Thornton, p.144 and fn 6.
34. Cal SP Spanish, 11 January 1500, no. 249 p.213.
35. Ibid., 19 May 1499 no. 241 p.209.

36. Ibid., 5 Oct 1499, no. 246 p.212.
37. Ibid.
38. Gairdner, J. (ed.), 1863, volume 2, pp.101–102.
39. Cited in Cunningham, p.vii and Taylor, p.16.
40. Nicholas (ed.), *Privy Purse expenses of Elizabeth of York*, p.25. The provisions delivered to Margaret Cotton for the Courtenay children includes a note identifying a household composed of the children, their governess, two female servants and a groom. The cost of the household amounted to 31s each year, p.219.
41. Weir, 2014 p.371.
42. Ibid., p.375.
43. Croyland Chronicle Continuations, (Pronay and Cox eds.), pp.170–171.
44. Nicholas (ed.), *Privy Purse expenses of Elizabeth of York*, p.103.
45. Croft, p.43.
46. Nicholas (ed.), *Privy Purse expenses of Elizabeth of York* details the queen's summer progress beginning with a journey from Greenwich to Richmond. She began by making a gift at the high altar to Saint George. On 22 August she gave her an offering to Saint Anne in the Wood (p.42) and having travelled to Raglan and the Marches returned via Caversham where she made an offering to the Virgin Mary p.50.

Chapter Seven: Henry VIII — The Education of a Christian Prince

1. Calendar of the Close Rolls, 1500–1509, (HMSO, 1963) p.160 and Calendar of the Patent Rolls 1494–1509, (London 1916) p.583.
2. Cited in Guy, p.134.
3. Calendar of the Patent Rolls, p.46.
4. Transactions of the Essex Archaeological Society, vol. 3, 1865 pp1–16, p.6.
5. Penn, p.172.
6. Wooden and Watson, p.40.
7. Preserved Smith, *Erasmus*, (New York 1923) cp.62. Cited in Walker p.40.
8. British Library, Add.26,787.
9. Scarisbrick, p.5.
10. Edwards,1949, pp.288–289.
11. Bientenholz and Deutscher, p.198.
12. Ibid. Holt's will was proved on 14 June 1504.
13. Ibid., p.6.
14. Loades, p.16.
15. Folger Shakespeare Library, PA6295.A3 1502 Cage.
16. British Library Royal MS 2A XVI, f.98v.
17. Carley, p.100.
18. David Starkey, *The Inventory of Henry VIII. Society of Antiquaries MS 129 and British Library MS Harley 1419: The Transcript* (London: Society of Antiquaries, 1998).
19. Pollard (ed.) p.232 (vol. II).

20. Weir, 2002, p.111.
21. Guy, p.16.
22. Aslet, p.56–57.
23. Bentley, *Henry VII Privy Purse expenses*, item 14, p.123.
24. Wedgewood and Holt, pp.888–889.
25 Report of Sebastian Giustinian, *Henry VIII: July 1519, 16–29, Letters and Papers, Foreign and Domestic*, Volume 3, no. 402. p.142.
26. Edward Hall, *Chronicles*, p.674.
27. In 1494, for instance, the king's expenses include payment of a gambling debt made to Sir Charles Somerset for the loss of a tennis match. Bentley, item 14, p.98.
28. Report of Sebastian Giustinian *Henry VIII: July 1519, 16–29, Letters and Papers, Foreign and Domestic*, Volume 3, no. 402. p.142.
29. Thurley, p.179.
30. Correspondence of Fuensalida, p.449. Cited in Scarisbrick, p.6.
31. Penn, p.283.
32. Hutchinson, p.95.
33. Sloane MS 104.
34. Carlson, p.253.
35. Weir, 2002, p.6.
36. *Hall's Chronicle.* p.515.
37. Sidney Lee, *Dictionary of National Biography* (London: MacMillan and Co., 1896) p.437.
38. Exploration of Henry VII's income in Breverton, 2016, p.310. Mackie estimated that during the last five years of his reign, Henry's income averaged about £142,000, p.218.

Chapter Eight: Mary Tudor and Henry FitzRoy

1. In 1513 he was in receipt of £6 13s 4d as an annual wage for his role as school master. The King's Book of Payments in Brewer, p.1459.
2. Jones, Philippa, p.72.
3. Letter from Mary, Queen of France to Henry VIII dated 12 October 1514 in Brewer; Letters and Papers, Foreign and Domestic, Henry VIII, vol. 1, item 5488, p.899.
4. Letter from Mary, Queen of France to Wolsey dated 12 October 1514, Ellis's Historical Letters, vol. 2, p.243. Cited in Strickland, p.16. It is also reprinted in Galt, Letter III, pp.255–256 and Brewer, item 5489, pp.899–900.
5. Cited in Chapman, p.173.
6. Strickland, p.16.
7. Wood, 1846, p.149.
8. Ridley, p.18.
9. Patent Rolls, 2 July 1517 — an annuity of £20 paid to 'Catherine, wife of Leonard Pole, Esq'. Cited in Madden, p.xxi.

10. Henry VIII gave orders that Lady Bryan was to have the annuity of 40 marks as lady mistress after the death of Elizabeth Denton who was to retain the fee during her lifetime. 19 November 1518, in Brewer, vol. 2, item 3802, p.1191.
11. The appointment of Lady Bryan was confirmed in a letter from Cromwell, MS. Cott. Otho C.x.f.230. Cited in Madden *Privy Purse Expenses*, p.xx.
12. Porter, p.28 and Madden, *Privy Purse Expenses* p.xx who records that the chaplain received 6d a day.
13. Giustinian to the Doge, 6 June 1518, item 4213, in Brewer, vol. 2, p.1305.
14. Giustinian to the Doge, 10 November 1518, item 4568, in Brewer vol. 2, p.1399.
15. Ellis's Original Letters, vol. 1, p.175. Cited in Madden p.xxiii.
16. 13 October 1521, Pace to Wolsey in Brewer, vol. 3, p.697.
17. Tremlett, p.47.
18. Printed in Madden, pp.clxxiii-clxxiv.
19. Vives, p.59.
20. Vives, in Watson, p.147.
21. Madden, p.xxxii.
22. Porter, p.27.
23. Guy, p.45.
24. Bushnell, p.39.
25. Two letters to Henry VIII and Cardinal Wolsey written by Henry FitzRoy, and dated 31 January 1527–1528, requesting a suit of armour as a New Year's gift. Reproduced in Nichols, 1855 pp.xlviii–xlix.
26. Nichols, 1855, p.xlvi–xlvii.
27. Cal. S.P. Spanish, 18 March, 39, p.123.
28. Tremlett, p.252.
29. Porter, p.38–39.
30. Porter, p.40 and Wroe, pp.464–465. Katherine Gordon married three more times after her marriage to Perkin Warbeck. In 1512 she married James Strangeways and in 1518, after the death of her second husband, she married Matthew Cradock, the Earl of Worcester's deputy in South Wales. After his death in 1531, she married Christopher Ashton.
31. Ms. Cott. Vit. C.i f. 24.b printed in Madden pp.xli-xlii.
32. Cal. S. P. Spanish, 1–3 May 1527 no. 62, p.173.
33. Ridley, p.31.
34. Childs, p.56.
35. Cal. S.P. Milan, June 28 1530, no. 816, p.519.
36. Ibid.
37. Cal. S.P. Milan, 16 December 1530, no. 838, p.533.
38. Ibid., 25 July 1531, no. 873, p.546.
39. Cal. S.P. Milan, October 1 1533, no. 925, p.563.
40. Sim, p.76.
41. Letter from Katherine of Aragon to Mary, undated, printed in Gairdner, vol. 6, no. 1126, p.472.
42. Chapuys, letter dated 15 September 1533, Gairdner, vol. 6, pp.471–472.

43. Nichols, 1855, p.lxii.
44. Chapuys, letter dated 23 December 1533, Gairdner, vol. 6, p.629.
45. Chapuys, 16 December 1533, in Gairdner, vol. 6, no 1528, p.617.
46. Cited in Ridley, p.47.
47. Anne Hussey's statement survives as part of the fire damaged Cotton collection, MS. Cott. Otho. C.x.f.254 Cited in Madden, p.lxii.
48. Cited in Ridley, p.65.
49. Cal. S.P. Milan, 12 August 1536, no. 970, p.578.
50. Cromwell to Gardiner, 5 July 1536, item 29, pp.16–17.

Chapter Nine: Elizabeth and Edward

1. Cal. S.P. Milan, 17 August 1536, no. 971, p.579.
2. Cited in Angus, p.93.
3. Letter from Lady Bryan to Thomas Cromwell, no. 203 in Gairdner,1888, p.90; and printed in Watkins, p.33–34.
4. Ibid.
5. Letter from Mary to Henry VIII dated 21 July 1536, in Gairdner,1888, no. 132, pp.34–35.
6. Sir John Shelton to Cromwell, dated 16 August 1536, in Gairdner, 1888, no.312, p.181.
7. Letter from Lady Bryan to Thomas Cromwell, in Gairdner, 1892, no. 1290. Cited in Loach.
8. The Lisle Letters, vol. 5, p.79 (letter no 1130). Cited in Loach, p.9.
9. Brennan, p. xxi.
10. Wallace, p.5.
11. Madden, *Privy Purse Expenses*, p.54.
12. Porter makes a similar point when discussing the moral imperative of Vives' curriculum for Mary, p.34.
13. Ascham, *The Schoolmaster*, pp.6–7.
14. Tucker in de Mause (ed.), p.246.
15. Letter from Cox to Sir William Paget, 10 December 1544, Letters and Papers Henry VIII, vol. 19, no 726, p.438.
16. Levi, p.218.
17. Richardson, p.44.
18. Ibid., pp. 44–45.
19. Will of Sir John Cornwallis, proved 9 July 1544, in Nichols, 1826, pp.714–715.
20. An annuity was paid to Sir Richard Page on 11 May 1544, no. 436, in Gairdner and Brodie, 1901, p.260.
21. Page was responsible for designing Henry FitzRoy's armorial bearings.
22. Prosa, p.50.
23. Loach, p.12.
24. Loades, 2004, p. 60.
25. Loach, p.13.
26. Dumitrescu, pp.83–86.

27. Ibid.
28. Edward's *Chronicle*, p.73. Cited in Loach, p.15.
29. Dumitrescu, pp.83–86.
30. Guy, p.111.
31. Pryor, p.41
32. Elizabeth's letter to Katherine Parr, 31 December 1544, L.P. Henry VIII, vol. 19, part 2, no. 794, p.466.
33. Ibid.
34. Thompson Cooper, 'Buckley, William' (1518/18–1571), in ODNB online.
35. Watkins, p.61.
36. Watkins, p.7.
37. British Library Royal MS 7 D.10.

Chapter Ten: Hard Lessons

1. Cited in Loach, p.55.
2. Guy, p.116.
3. Edward's *Chronicle*, pp.8–9.
4. Skidmore, p.79.
5. Edward's *Chronicle*, p.9.
6. Mendleson, p.4.
7. Norton, p.81.
8. Confessions of Katherine Ashley, Chadwick, p.29.
9. Guy, 2014, pp.118–119.
10. Loach, p.56 and Norton p.101.
11. Cited in Porter, p.306.
12. Letter from Ascham to Sturm, 4 April 1550, in Giles, volume1, part 2, p.lxiv.
13. Ascham, *The Schoolmaster*, p.266.
14. Ibid.
15. Ibid., p.242.
16. Ibid.
17. Ibid., p.216.
18. Ibid., p.190.
19. Thirsk, p.7.
20. Confessions of Thomas Parry, in Chadwick, p.25.
21. Pollnitz, p.222.
22. Strickland, p.106.
23. Ascham, *The Schoolmaster*, p.40.
24. Sil, p.55.
25. East Hertfordshire Archaeological Society Transactions, vol. 3, 1906, p.202.
26. Letter from Ascham to Sir Anthony Denny, March 29 1549, in Giles, vol. 1, part 1, p.132.
27. Norton, p.138.
28. Ibid., p.136.
29. Loades, 2006, p.41.

30. Porter, p.257.
31. Letter from Elizabeth to Katherine Parr, written at Cheshunt, 31 July 1548, in Mueller *et al.*, no 10, p.20.
32. Confessions of Katherine Ashley, Chadwick, p.30.
33. Ibid.
34. Ibid., p.29.
35. Confessions of Thomas Parry, Chadwick, p.24.
36. L.P. Domestic Edward, vol. 1, January; Confessions of John Fowler, p.13.
37. Cal S P, Spain, volume 9, 1547–1549, p.332.
38. Porter, p.165.
39. Haynes, pp.103–104. The original is now lost.
40. Letter from Elizabeth to Protector Somerset, written at Hatfield 28 January 1549, in Chadwick, p.23 and Mueller *et al.*, letter 13, pp.22–24.
41. Cited in Norton, p.263.

Chapter Eleven: Final lessons

1. Howard, pp.68–69.
2. Letter from Elizabeth to King Edward VI, with a Present of her Portrait, 15 May 1549, p.35. Cited in Loades (Elizabeth I), p.73.
3. Edward's *Chronicle*. Cited in Loach, p.91.
4. Edward's *Chronicle*, pp.61–62.
5. Edward's *Chronicle*, p.18. Cited in Loach, p.94.
6. Loach, p.15.
7. Ibid., p.98.
8. Letter from Robert Tyrwitt in Haynes, p.104. Cited in Brace, ODNB online and Starkey, p.75.
9. British Museum, 1894, 0729.1.
10. Clarke *et al.*, John Nichols, p.9.
11. Coros, historyofparliamentonline, 1509–1558.
12. Ascham, letter XC, To William Ireland, Cheshunt, 8 July 1549, *The Whole Works*, vol. 1, part 1, p.lvii.
13. Ascham, *The Schoolmaster*, pp.201–202.
14. Ascham, *The Whole Works*, vol. 1, p.xcii.
15. Letter from Ascham to Cheke written at Augsberg, 11 November 1550, *The Whole Works*, p.216.
16. Letter from Ascham to Cecil, written at Speyer, 27 September 1552, in Giles, vol. 2, pp.330–334.
17. Add. M.S., B.M., 4724, ff.104-6.
18. Literary Remains, vol. 2, p.ccxvii.
19. Edward's *Chronicle*, p.37.
20. Literary Remains, vol. 2, p.ccxx. Also described in Loach pp.154–155.
21. Literary Remains, vol. 2, p. ccxxii.
22. Skidmore, p.4.
23. CS Spain Vol. 10, pp.209–212. Cited in Loach p.131 and described in Edward's *Chronicle*, p.36.

24. Ibid.
25. Bryson, A. & Evans, M., 2017, 'Seven rediscovered letters of Princess Elizabeth Tudor' in *Historical Research*, vol. 90, no. 250, pp.829–858, pp. 832–833.
26. Loades, *Elizabeth I: A Life*, p.76.
27. Harris, p.18.
28. Letter from the Duke of Northumberland to the Duke of Suffolk, April or May 1553, in Taylor, (ed.) pp.16–17.
29. Letter from Duke of Suffolk to Duke of Northumberland, in Taylor, (ed.) p.19.
30. Loades, *Elizabeth 1: A Life*, p.84.

A Who's Who of Lady Mistresses and Governesses Who Raised the Tudors

Katherine Ashley (Champernowne)

1. Burke, p. 271–272.
2. O Day, p.157.
3. Loades, 2006, p.41.

Isabel Baynton

1. Russell, p.33.
2. Baker, ODNB.
3. Madden, p.143.

Lady Margaret Bryan, 1st Baroness Bryan

1. Margaret Bryan was the half-sister of Thomas Howard, 3rd Duke of Norfolk, and of Elizabeth Howard, who would be better remembered by history as Anne Boleyn's mother. She was also Catherine Howard's aunt.
2. Harris, Barbara, p. 219. Jenkins book, *The Kings Chamberlain*, 2021, identifies John's wife as Margaret Howard.
3. Jones, 2009 p.295.
4. Ibid.

Jane (Amata, Amy or Anne) Calthorpe

1. Jane's sister-in-law, Elizabeth Howard, was Margaret's half-sister.
2. Brewer, vol. 13, Windsor, 13 Oct 1521; Pace to Wolsey, no. 1673; and Record Commission, Correspondence between the king and Cardinal Wolsey, 1518–1530, part 2 (London: J. Murray, 1830), p.71.
3. Letter from Pace on behalf of Henry VIII to Wolsey, Ibid., p.48.
4. Gairdner (ed.), 1890, vol. 12, part 1, p.531.
5. Madden, p.143.

Alice Clere

1. Hilton, p.26.
2. Will of Dame Alice Clere reprinted in *Visitation to Norfolk* 1563, Dashwood and Bulwer (eds.), p.319.
3. Emerson, p.646.

Anne Cromer

1. Weir, 2014, p.448.
2. Richardson, p.566.
3. Ibid., p.602.

Elizabeth Darcy

1. Metcalfe, p.111.
2. Hicks, Jan 1988, p.89.
3. King, H. W., pp.1–24.
4. Weir, 2014, p.49.
5. Hampton, p.214.
6. Higginbottom, p.124.

Elizabeth Denton

1. Richardson, p.512.
2. Suckling, p.105.
3. O Day, p.466.
4. Seymour, pp.692–693.
5. Strype, p.222.

Jane Guildford

1. Myers, p.405.
2. TNA PRO< C81/863/4673.
3. British Library digitised manuscripts, Add MS 17012, f.20v.
4. https://blogs.bl.uk/digitisedmanuscripts/2023/03/a-tudor-autograph-book.html.
5. Wood, pp.158–159.
6. White, p.80.

Lady Anne Herbert, Countess of Pembroke

1. The online *Dictionary of Welsh Biography* offers a date of 1459 for the marriage.
2. Royal 18 D. II f.6.
3. Kren and McKendrick, item 130, p.431–432.
4. *The Book of Margery Kempe*, Lynne Staley (ed), TEAMS Middle English Texts Series (Kalamazoo: Medieval Institute Publications, 1996), 1, pp.773–783. Cited in Sauer, p.94.
5. Robinson, 2008, p.310 and Griffiths, p.248.
6. Sauer, p.94.
7. Marsh, p.189.
8. Bernard, p.60.
9. Ibid., p.59–60.
10. Griffiths, pp. 41–42.
11. Robinson, 2008, p.313.
12. Jones and Underwood, p.162.
13. Robinson, 2011, p.23.

Blanche Herbert, Lady Troy

1. Richardson, p.40.
2. Ibid., p.41.
3. Ibid., p.49.

Anne Shelton

1. British Library, Add. MS 17492.
2. Chapuys to Charles V, 11 February 1534, no. 10, in De Gayangos, p.34.
3. Chapuys to Charles V, 14 May 1534, Letters and Papers, no. 57, in De Gayangos, p.155.
4. Chapuys to Charles V, 18 November 1534, no. 111 in De Gayangos, p.329.
5. Cited in Jones, 2009, p.243.

Elizabeth Tyrwhitt

1. Ryrie, p.296.
2. Haynes, p.103–104.

A Who's Who of Governors, Mentors and Household Officers Who Raised the Tudors

William Blount, 4th Baron Mountjoy

1. Carley, ODNB.

Sir Walter Buckler

1. 'Henry VIII: December 1546, 26–31', in *Letters and Papers, Foreign and Domestic, Henry VIII, Volume 21 Part 2, September 1546–January 1547*, (ed.) James Gairdner and R. H. Brodie (London, 1910), pp.313–348. Online.
2. Guy, p.134.
3. Goding, pp.71–72.

Sir Philip Calthorpe

1. James, pp.1–19.
2. The Rushall Manor, p.128.
3. Wedgewood and Holt, p.148, fn 8.
4. Ibid., p.148.
5. Weir, 2012, p.134.

Peter Courtenay, Bishop of Winchester

1. Cherry, p.77.
2. Ibid., p.96.
3. Thomson, J. A. F., pp.230–246.

William Herbert, 1st Earl of Pembroke

1. Kent, p.18.
2. Ibid., p.22.
3. Robinson, David, pp.17, 38 and Taylor, John, p.40.

Sir Richard Page

1. Davies, ODNB online.
2. Guy and Fox, p.356.
3. Davies, ODNB online.
4. Madden, p.30.
5. Ibid., p.31.

Sir John Shelton

1. Block, ODNB online.

Jasper Tudor, Earl of Pembroke and Duke of Bedford

1. Chrimes, p.15, nn. 3.
2. Forster, p.2.
3. Thomas Tonge, Norray King of Arms, pp.35–36.

Bibliography

Primary Sources

Andreas, Bernard, *Historia Regis Henrici deptimi, a Bernardo Andrea. Tholosate Conscripta*, Gairdner, James (ed.). (Cambridge: Cambridge University Press, 1858 reprinted 2012.)

Anon, *The Gentleman's Magazine and Historical Review*. July 1852.

Ascham, Roger and Giles. J. A. (ed.), *The Whole Works of Roger Ascham*. 1864.

Ascham, Roger, *The Scholemaster*. (1570, republished online by Gutenberg.org, 1999, updated 2020.)

Ascham, Roger, *Toxophilus, The School of Shooting, in Two Books*. (London: John Russell Smith, 1866.)

Bentley, Samuel, *Excerpta Historica, Or Illustrations of English History*. (London: Richard Bentley, 1833.)

Bergenroth, G. A., *Calendar of Letters, Despatches and State Papers Relating to the Negotiations between England and Spain Preserved in the Archives at Simancas and Elsewhere: Henry VII, 1586–1509*, Volume 1. (London: Longman, Green and Roberts, 1862.)

Bergenroth, G. A., *Calendar of Letters, Despatches and State Papers Relating to the Negotiations between England and Spain Preserved in the Archives at Simancas and Elsewhere: Henry VIII, 1509–1546*. (London: Longman, Green and Roberts, 1862.)

Brewer, J. S. (ed.), *Letters and Papers, Foreign and Domestic, Henry VIII, Volume 2, 1515–1518*. (London: Longman, 1864.)

Brewer, J. S. (ed.), *Letters and Papers, Foreign and Domestic, Henry VIII, Volume 3, part 1 1519–1523*. (London: Longman, 1867.)

Brewer, J. S. (ed.), *Letters and Papers, Foreign and Domestic, Henry VIII*, Volume 13.

Bryne, Murial St Claire, (ed.), *The Lisle Letters An Abridgement*. (London: Secker and Warburg, 1983.)

Chadwick, Charles, *Recollections of Royalty From the Death of William Rufus, in 1100, to that of the Cardinal of York, the Last Lineal Descendant of the Stuarts, in 1807*, Volume 2. (London: Saunders and Otley, 1828.)

Clarke, Elizabeth, Goldring Elizabeth, Eales Faith *et al.* (eds.), *John Nichols's The Progresses and Public Processions of Queen Elizabeth: Volume V.* (Oxford: Oxford University Press, 2014.)

Condon, M., & Jones, E., *Bristol 1465: Particulars of Account of Thomas Gibbes and John Senecle*, customers, 29 September to 28 September 1465. Bristol Customs Account, 22 January 2016. (bristolcustoms1465database.)

Dashwood, G. H., and Bulwer, E. E. G. (eds.), *Harvey William, Clarenceux King of Arms, The Visitation of Norfolk in the Year 1563*, Volume 2. (Norwich: College of Arms and Norwich and Norfolk Archaeological Society, 1895.)

De Gayangos, Pascual, *Calendar of Letters, Despatches, and State Papers, relating to the Negotiations Between England and Spain, preserved in the Archives at Simancas and Elsewhere, Henry VIII, 1534–1535*, Volume 5, part 1. (London: Longman, 1886.)

Ellis, Henry, Sir (ed.), *Polydore Vergil's English History Comprising the Reigns of Henry VI, Edward IV and Richard III.* (London: The Camden Society, 1844.)

Gairdner, James (ed.), *Letters and Papers Illustrative of the Reigns of Richard III and Henry VII*, Rolls Series 24. (London: Longman, 1863.)

Gairdner, James (ed.), *Historia Regis Henrici Septimi, a Bernardo Andrea Tholosate Conscripta.* (Cambridge: Cambridge University Press, 2012.)

Gairdner, James (ed.), *Letter and Papers, Foreign and Domestic, of the Reign of Henry VIII*, Volume 6. (London: Longmans, 1890.)

Gairdner, James (ed.), *Letter and Papers, Foreign and Domestic, of the Reign of Henry VIII*, Volume 11. (London: Longmans, 1888.)

Gairdner, James (ed.), *Letter and Papers, Foreign and Domestic, of the Reign of Henry VIII*, Volume 12. (London: Longmans, 1888.)

Gairdner, James and Brodie, R. H. (eds.), *Letters and Papers, Foreign and Domestic, of the Reign of Henry VIII*, Volume, 19, part 2. (London: HMSO, 1905.)

Hall, Edward, *Hall's Chronicle; Containing The History of England During the Reign of Henry the Fourth and the Succeeding Monarchs, to the End of the Reign of Henry the Eight.* (London: G. Woodfall, 1809.)

Halliwell, James-Orchard, *Letters of the Kings of England, Now First Collected from Royal Archives*, Volume 1. (London: Henry Colburn, 1848.)

Haynes, Samuel, '*A Collection of State Papers, Relating to Affairs. From the Year 1542–1570, Transcribed from Original Letters and other Authentick Memorials, Never before Publish'd, Left by William Cecill Lord Burghley, and Now remaining at Hatfield House in the Library of the Right Honourable the present Earl of Salisbury.*' (London, 1740.)

Hinds, Allen, B (ed.), *Calendar of State Papers and Manuscripts, existing in the collection of Milan*, Volume 1. (London: HMSO, 1912.)

Machiavelli, Niccoló, *The Prince.* (Norderstedt: Books on Demand, 2023.)

Madden, Frederick (ed.), *Privy Purse Expenses of the Princess Mary, Daughter of King Henry VIII, afterwards Queen Mary.* (London, William Pickering, 1831.)

Marcus, Leah S., Mueller, Janel, and Rose, Mary Beth (eds.), *Elizabeth I Collected Works.* (Chicago and London: University of Chicago, 1992.)

Murray Jones, Peter, 'Argentine, John (c.1443–1508)'. (ODNB online, September 2004.)

Mynors, R. A. B. and Dalzell, Alexander (trans.), *The Correspondence of Erasmus, letters from 1356 to 1534, 1523 to 1524.* (Toronto: University of Toronto Press, 1992.)

Nicolas, Sir Nicholas Harris, *Testamenta Vetusta, Being Illustrations from Wills, of Manners, Customs, Et, as well as of the Descents and Possessions of Many Distinguished Families from the Reign of Henry the Second to the Accession of Queen Elizabeth*, Volumes 1–2. (London: Nichols & Son, 1826.)

Nicolas, Sir Nicholas Harris, *Privy Purse Expenses of Elizabeth of York: Wardrobe Accounts of Edward IV, With a Memoir of Elizabeth of York, and Notes.* (London: William Pickering, 1830.)
Nichols, John Gough (ed.), *Grants Etc. From the Crown During the Reign of Edward The Fifth.* (London: The Camden Society, 1854.)
Nichols, John Gough (ed.), *Inventories of the Wardrobes, Et of Henry Fitzroy, Duke of Richmond, and of Katherine Princess Dowager at Baynard's Castle.* (London: The Camden Society, 1855.)
Nichols, John Gough (ed.) *Literary Remains of King Edward the Sixth.* (London: Roxburghe Club, 1857.)
Public Record Office, *List of Early Chancery Proceedings, Lists and Indexes*, No. 29, Volume IV. (London: PRO, 1963.)
Sauer, Michelle M., 'The meaning of Russet: A Note on Vowesses and Clothing' in *Early Middle English*, Volume 2, No. 2, 2020, pp.91–97.
Skidmore, Chris, *Edward VI: The Lost King of England.* (London: Orion, 2011.)
Starkey, David, *The Inventory of Henry VIII. Society of Antiquaries MS 129 and British Library MS Harley 1419: The Transcript.* (London: Society of Antiquaries, 1998.)
Taylor, James D., *Documents of Lady Jane Grey Nine Days Queen of England, 1553.* (New York: Agora Publishing, 2004.)
Thompson, Edward Maunde (ed. and trans.), *Chronicon Adam De Usk, A.D. 1377–1404.* (London: John Murray, 1876.)
Tonge, Thomas, Norroy King of Arms, *Heraldic Visitation of the Northern Counties in 1530.* (Durham: The Surtees Society, 1863.)

Secondary Sources

Anon, 'Analytical Account of Ascham's "Schoolmaster", with a Biographical Note of Roger Ascham and Wolsey's Letter to the Master of Ipswich School' in *The Schoolmaster: Essays on Practical Education from the Quarterly Journal of Education*, Volume. 1. (London: Charles Knight, 1836) pp.1–105.
Amin, Nathen, *The House of Beaufort: The Bastard Line That Captured The Throne.* (Stroud: Amberley Press, 2017.)
Ashdown-Hill, John, *Royal Marriage Secrets: Consorts and Concubines, Bigamists and Bastards.* (Cheltenham: The History Press, 2013.)
Aslet, Clive, *The Story of Greenwich.* (Harvard: Harvard University Press, 1999.)
Baker, T. F. T., 'Baynton, Sir Edward (1495–1544)'. (ODNB online, 1993.)
Beattie, Andrew, *Henry VIII: A History of his Most Important Places and Events.* (Barnsley: Pen and Sword, 2023.)
Bernard, G. W. (ed.), *The Tudor Nobility.* (Manchester: Manchester University Press, 1992.)
Bientenholz, Peter G. and Deutscher, Thomas Brian, *Contemporaries of Erasmus, A Biographical Register of the Renaissance and the Reformation*, Volume 1. (Toronto: University of Toronto, 1985.)
Bliss, Thomas, *Some Account of Sir H. Johnys, Deputy Knight Marshal of Engand, temp. Henry VI and Edward IV, and of the monumental brass to Sir Hugh and*

Dame Cradock his wife in the chancel of St Mary's Church, Swansea. (Swansea: John Williams, 1845.)
Block, Joseph, S., 'Shelton family, (per. 1504–1558)'. (ODNB online, 2006.)
Borman, Tracy, *The Private Lives of the Tudors, Uncovering the Secrets of Britain's Greatest Dynasty.* (New York, Grove Press, 2016.)
Brace, Patricia, 'Tyrwit (nee Oxenbridge), Elizabeth, Lady Tyrwhit, (d.1578)'. (ODNB online, 2004.)
Bradley, Stuart, *John Morton: Adversary of Richard III, Power Behind the Tudors.* (Stroud: Amberley, 2019.)
Brennan, M. and Kinnamon, N., *A Sidney Chronology: 1554–1654.* (London: Palgrave MacMillan, 2003.)
Breverton, Terry, *Henry VII, The Maligned Tudor King.* (Stroud: Amberley Press, 2016.)
Breverton, Terry, *Jasper Tudor, Dynasty Maker.* (Stroud: Amberley Press, 2017.)
Breverton, Terry, *Owen Tudor: Founding Father of the Tudor Dynasty.* (Stroud: Amberley Press, 2017.)
Brigdon, Sarah, 'Bryan, Sir Francis [called the Vicar of Hell] (d.1550)'. (ODNB online, 2004.)
Buckley, Will, 'Why Henry VIII loved sport more than women' in *The Observer*, Sunday 3 May, 2009.
Burke, John, *A Genealogical and Heraldic History of the Commoners of Great Britain and Ireland, Enjoying Territorial Possessions or High Official Rank*, Volume 2. (London: Henry Colburn, 1835.)
Bushnell, Rebecca W., *A Culture of Teaching, Early Modern Humanism in Theory and Practice.* (USA: Cornell University Press, 1996.)
Carley, James P., *The Books of King Henry VIII and his Wives.* (London: The British Library, 2004.)
Carlson, 'Andre (Andreas), Bernard, (c.1450–1522)'. (ODNB online, 23 September 2004.)
Chapman, Hester W., *The Thistle and the Rose*, reprint of *The King's Sisters.* (New York: Coward, McCann and Gheoghegan, 1971.)
Cherry, M., 'The Courtenay Earls of Devon: The Formation and Disintegration of a Late Medieval Aristocratic Affinity' in *Southern History*, Volume 1 (1979) pp.71–97.
Chrimes, S.B., *Henry VII.* (London: Methuen, 1972.)
Churton, Ralph, *The Lives of William Smyth Bishop of Lincoln and Sir Richard Stutton Knight, Founders of Brase Nose College; Chiefly Compiled from registers and Other Authentic Evidences: with an Appendix of Letters and Papers Never Before Printed.* (London: University Press, 1800.)
Clegg, Melanie, *Margaret Tudor, The Life of Henry VIII's Sister.* (Barnsley: Pen and Sword, 2018.)
Clive & Heale Martin (eds.), *The Late Medieval English College and its Context.* (York: York Medieval Press, 2008) pp.231–253.
Cooper, Thompson, revised by McConnell, Anita, 'Buckley, William (1518/18–1551/1552)'. (ODNB online, 2004.)
Corbet, Anthony, *Edward IV, England's Forgotten Warrior King: His Life, His People and His Legacy.* (Bloomington: iUniverse, 2015.)

Corbett, W. J. and Tindal Method, T., 'The Rise and Devolution of the Manors in Hepworth, Suffolk' in *The Suffolk Institute of Archaeology and History*, Volume 10, part 2 (1899) pp.125–143.
Coros, D. F., 'Parker, Sir Henry (by 1514–52), of Morely Hall, Hingham, Norf. And Furneux Pelham, Herts'. (historyofparliamntonline.org, volume 1509–1558.)
Croft, O. G. S., *The House of Croft of Croft Castle*. (Hereford: E.J. Thurston, 1833.)
Cunningham, Sean, *Prince Arthur, The Tudor King who Never Was*. (Stroud: Amberley Press, 2016.)
Davies, Catherine, 'Page, Sir Richard, (d.1548)'. (ODNB online, 2004.)
Dowling, Maria, *Humanism in the Age of Henry VIII*. (London: Croom Helm, 1986.)
Dryburgh, Paul, 'Living in the Shadows: John of Eltham, Earl of Cornwall (1316–36)' in Dodd, Gwyllym and Bothwell, James (eds.), *Fourteenth Century England IX*, Volume 14. (Woodbridge: Boydell Press, 2016) pp.23–49.
Dumitrescu, Theodor, *The Early Tudor Court and International Musical Relations*. (London: Taylor and Francis, 2017.)
Edwards, H. L. R., *Skelton: The Life and Times of an Early Tudor Poet*. (London: Jonathan Cape, 1949.)
Edwards, John, *Archbishop Pole*. (London: Taylor and Francis, 2016.)
Elton, G. R., *The Tudor Revolution in Government*. (Cambridge: Cambridge University Press, 2010.)
Emerson, Kathy Lynn, *A Who's Who of Tudor Women*. (Kindle edition, 2020.)
Emerson, Kathy Lynn, *The Writer's Guide to Everyday Life in Renaissance England*. (Cincinnati: Writers Digest, 1996.)
Erler, Mary C., 'Devotional literature' in Hellinga Lotte, and Trapp, J. B. (eds.), *The Cambridge History of the Book in Britain*, Volume 3, 1400–1557. (Cambridge: Cambridge University Press, 1999) pp.495–526.
Fonge, Charles (ed.), *The Cartulary of St Mary's Collegiate Church, Warwick, Studies in the History of Medieval Religion*. (Woodbridge: Boydell Press, 2004.)
Forster, J, *Eminent British Statesmen: Oliver Cromwell*. (London: Longman *et al.*, 1847.)
Fox-Davies, *The Art of Heraldry: an encyclopaedia of armory*. (London: T. C. & E. C. Jack, 1904.)
Fuller, Thomas, *The History of Cambridge And of Waltham Abbey, With the Appeal of Injured Innocence*. (London: T. Tegg, 1840.)
Furdell, Elizabeth Lane, *The Royal Doctors, 1485–1714: Medical Personnel at the Tudor and Stuart Courts*. (New York: University of Rochester Press, 2001.)
Galt, John, *Life of Cardinal Wolsey*. (London: D. Bogue, 1846.)
Goding, John, *Norman's History of Cheltenham*. (London: Longman Green, 1868.)
Gower, Granville W. G. L., *Notices of the Family of Uvedale of Titsey, Surrey, and Wickham, Hants*. (London: Cox, 1865.)
Green, D. H., *Women Readers in the Middle Ages*. (Cambridge: Cambridge University Press, 2007.)
Green, Mary Anne Everett, *Lives of the Princesses of England*, Volume 4. (London: Henry Colburn, 1852.)

Green, Mary Anne Everett, *Lives of the Princesses of England*, Volume 5. (London: Longman, 1857.)

Griffiths, R. A., 'Queen Katherine of Valois and a Missing Statute of the Realm' in *King and Country: England and Wales in the Fifteenth Century* (London, 1991) pp.103–115.

Griffiths, R. A., *Sir Rhys ap Thomas and his Family: A Study in the Wars of the Roses and Early Tudor Politics.* (Cardiff: University of Wales, 1993.)

Grummitt, David, 'Plantagenet, Arthur, Viscount Lisle'. (ODNB online, 2004.)

Gunn, Steven, J., *Henry VII's New Men and the Making of Tudor England.* (Oxford: Oxford University Press, 2016.)

Guy, John, *The Children of Henry VIII.* (Oxford: Oxford University Press, 2013.)

Guy, John and Fox, Julia, *Hunting the Falcon: Henry VIII, Anne Boleyn and the Marriage that Shook Europe.* (London: Bloomsbury Publishing, 2023.)

Hampton, W. E., 'Sir James Tyrell, with some notes on the Austen Friars London and those buried there' in Petre, J. (ed.), *Richard III: Crown and People.* (Gloucester: Alan Sutton Publishing, 1985) pp.204–224.

Harris, Barbara J., *English Aristocratic Women, 1450–1550.* (Oxford: Oxford University Press, 2002.)

Harris, Jonathan, *The End of Byzantium.* (New Haven and London: Yale University Press, 2010.)

Harwood, Winifred A., 'The College as School: The Case of Winchester College' in Burgess, Clive and Heale, Martin (eds.), *The Late Medieval English College and its Contexts.* (London: Boydell and Brewer, 2008) pp.230–252.

Hedges, John Kirby, *The History of Wallingford*, Volume 2. (London: William Clowes & Sons, 1881.)

Hickey, Julia, *The Kingmaker's Women.* (Barnsley: Pen and Sword, 2023.)

Hicks, M. A., 'The last days of Elizabeth Countess of Oxford' in *English Historical Review*, Jan 1988, Volume 103, no. 406, pp.76–95.

Higginbotham, Susan, *The Woodvilles, The Wars of the Roses and England's Most Infamous Family.* (Cheltenham: The History Press, 2013.)

Hilton, Lisa, *Elizabeth, Renaissance Prince.* (New York: Houghton Mifflin Harcourt, 2015.)

Horrox, Rosemary, 'Henry Tudor's Letters to England during Richard III's Reign' in *The Ricardian* 80 (1983), pp.155–158.

Hutchinson, Robert, *Young Henry: The Rise of Henry VIII.* (London: Pheonix, 2011.)

James, Lee Warner, 'The Calthorps of Burnham' in *Norfolk Archaeology*, Volume IX. (Norwich: A.H. Goose & Co., 1884) pp.1–19.

Jones, Michael K., 'For My Lord of Richmond, a pourpoint…and a palfrey: Brief Remarks on the Financial Evidence for Henry Tudor's Exile in Brittany 1471–1484' in *The Ricardian* 13, (2003) pp.283–293.

Jones, Michael K. and Underwood, Malcolm G., *The King's Mother Lady Margaret Beaufort, Countess of Richmond and Derby.* (Cambridge: Cambridge University Press, 1992.)

Jones, Philippa, *The Other Tudors, Henry VIII's Mistresses and Bastards.* (London, New Holland, 2009.)

Kent, G. H. R., 'The Estates of the Herbert Family in the Mid Fifteenth Century'. Unpublished Keele PHD thesis (1973).

Kenyon, John, R., *Raglan Castle.* (Cardiff: Cadw, 2003.)

Kilne, Stephanie, *Edward VI, Henry VIII's Overshadowed Son.* (Barnsley: Pen and Sword, 2023.)

King, H. W., 'Ancient Wills' in *Transactions of the Essex Archaeological Society*, Volume 4. (Colchester: Essex and West Suffolk Gazette, 1869) pp.1–24.

Kipling Gordon, 'Duwes (Dewes), Giles, (pseud. Aegidius de Vadis)'. (ODNB online, 2004.)

Kirby, John, *The Suffolk Traveller, or, A Journey through Suffolk.* (Ipswich, John Bagnall, 1735.)

Kren, Thomas and McKendrick, Scot, *The Triumph of Flemish Manuscript Painting in Europe.* (Los Angeles: The J. Paul Getty Museum, 2003.)

Langley, Phillippa, 'The Tyrell Confession: Fact of Fiction' in *Ricardian Bulletin*, June 2021, pp.44–53.

Lehmberg, Stanford, 'Carew, Sir Nicholas, (b.in or before 1496, d.1539)'. (ODNB online, 2004.)

Le Neve, John, *Fasti Ecclesiæ Anglicanæ: Or, An Essay Towards Deducing a Regular Succession of All the Principal Dignitaries in Each Cathedral, Collegiate Church Or Chapel (now in Being) in Those Parts in Great Britain Called England and Wales, from the First Erection Thereof to this Present Year 1715.* (London: J. Nutt, 1716.)

Lewis, J. M., *Welsh Monumental Brasses.* (Cardiff: National Museum of Wales, 1974.)

Licence, Amy, *In Bed with the Tudors.* (Stroud: Amberley Press, 2012.)

Licence, Amy, *Elizabeth of York.* (Stroud: Amberley Press, 2013.)

Loach, Jennifer, *Edward VI.* (New Haven and London: Yale University Press, 1999.)

Loades, D. M., *Intrigue and Treason: The Tudor Court, 1547–1558.* (London: Longman, 2004.)

Loades, David, *Elizabeth I: A Life.* (London: Bloomsbury Academic, 2006.)

Loades, David, *Henry VIII, Court, Church and Conflict.* (London: Bloomsbury, 2009.)

McKitterick, David *et al.* (eds.), *The Cambridge History of the Book in Britain*, Volume 3. (Cambridge: Cambridge University Press, 1999.)

Mackie, J.D., *The Earlier Tudors, 1485–1558.* (Oxford: Clarendon Press, 1952, this edition, 1991.)

Marsh, John Fitchett, *Annals of Chepstow Castle.* (Exeter: William Pollard, 1883.)

Maurice, Howard, *The Tudor Image.* (UK: Penshurst Press, 1995.)

Mendleson, Sera, *Women in Early Modern England 1550–1720.* (Oxford: Oxford University Press, 2020.)

Mercer, Malcolm, *The Medieval Gentry: Power, Leadership and Choice During the Wars of the Roses.* (London: Bloomsbury Publishing, 2010.)

Miller, William E., 'Double Translation in English Humanistic Education' in *Studies in Renaissance*, Volume 10 (1963), pp.163–174.

Myers, A. R., 'The Household of Queen Margaret of Anjou, 1452–1453' part 2 in *Bulletin of the John Rylands Library*, Volume 40 (2), 1957 pp.391–431.

Noble, Mark, *A History of the College of Arms: and the Lives of All the Kings, Heralds, and Pursuivants from the Reign of Richard III, Founder of the College, Until the Present Time.* (1805.)

Norton, Elizabeth, *Margaret Beaufort, Mother of the Tudor Dynasty*. (Stroud: Amberley Press, 2011.)

Norton, Elizabeth, *The Temptation of Elizabeth Tudor*. (London: Head of Zeus, 2015.)

O'Day, Rosemary, *The Routledge Companion to the Tudor Age*. (London: Routledge, 2010.)

Orme, Nicholas, *Going to Church in Medieval England*. (New Haven and London, Yale University Press.)

Orme, Nicholas, *Tudor Children*. (New Haven and London: Yale University Press, 2023.)

Penn, Thomas, *Winter King, The Dawn of Tudor England*. (London: Penguin, 2011.)

Pollnitz, Aysha, *Princely Education in Early Modern Britain*. (Cambridge: Cambridge University Press, 2015.)

Porter, Linda, *Mary Tudor, The First Queen*. (London: Piatkus, 2010.)

Porter, Linda, *The Remarkable Life of Katherine Parr*. (London: MacMillan, 2010.)

Pryor, Felix, *Elizabeth I, Her Life in Letters*. (California: University of California Press, 2003.)

Rayner, Simeon, *The History and Antiquities of Haddon Hall*. (London: Robert Moseley, 1836.)

Richardson, Douglas, *Plantagenet Ancestry*, 2nd edition, Volume 1. (Salt Lake City: Douglas Richardson, 2011.)

Richardson, Ruth Elizabeth, *Mistress Blanche, Queen Elizabeth's Confidante*. (Woonton Almeley: Logaston Press, 2007.)

Ridley, Jasper, *The Life and Times of Mary Tudor*. (London: George Weidenfeld & Nicholson Ltd, 1973.)

Roberts, Glyn, 'Ednyfed Fychan (Ednyfed ap Cynwrig) and his descendants' in *Dictionary of Welsh Biography*. (National Library of Wales, 1959, online.)

Robinson, David. M., *Tintern Abbey*, 5th edition. (Cardiff: Cadw, 2011.)

Robinson, R. B., 'Sir Hugh Johnys: A Fifteenth-century Welsh Knight' in *Morgannwg* 14, 1970, pp.5–34.

Robinson, W. R. B. 'The Early Tudors', in R.A. Griffiths *et al.* (eds.), *The Gwent County History, Volume 2: The Age of the Marcher Lords,* c.*1070–1536*. (Cardiff: University of Wales 2008), pp.309–336.

Roger, Euan Cameron: Unpublished thesis, *St George's College, Windsor Castle, in the Late- Fifteenth and Early-Sixteenth Centuries*. (Department of History, Royal Holloway University of London, 2015.)

Royle, Trevor, *The Road to Bosworth Field*. (London: Little Brown, 2009.)

Russell, Gareth, *Young and Damned and Fair, The Life and Tragedy of Catherine Howard at the Court of Henry VIII*. (London: William Collins, 2017.)

Ryrie, Alec, *Being Protestant in Reformation Britain*. (Oxford: Oxford University Press, 2013.)

Salter Elizabeth, *Six Renaissance Men and Women*. (Aldershot: Ashgate Publishing, 2007.)

Salter, F.M., 'Skelton's Speculum Principis' in *Speculum*, Volume 9, no. 1 (January 1934), pp.25–37.

Scarisbrick, J. J., *Henry VIII.* (Berkeley and Los Angeles: University of California, 1968.)

Seymour, Robert, *A Survey of the Cities of London and Westminster, Borough of Southwark, and Parts Adjacent,* Volume 1. (London: T. Read, 1733.)

Sil, Narasingha Prosad, *Tudor Placement and Statesmen: Select Case Histories.* (London: Rosemont Publishing, 2001.)

Skidmore, Chris, *The Rise of the Tudors: The Family that Changed History.* (New York: St Martin's Press, 2013.)

Sobecki, S. (2020), 'New Life Records for John Skelton as Rector of Diss, Norfolk (1514 and 1516)' in *Huntington Library Quarterly, Studies in English and American History and Literature,* 83(2), pp.395–400.

Spring, Matthew, *The Lute in Britain: A History of the Instrument and its Music.* (Oxford: Oxford University Press, 2001.)

Starkey, David, *Elizabeth: Apprenticeship.* (London: Vintage Books, 2001.)

Streeter, Gareth, *Arthur, Prince of Wales: Henry VIII's Lost Brother.* (Barnsley: Pen and Sword, 2023.)

Strickland, Agnes, *Lives of the Tudor and Stuart Princesses.* (London: W. Blackwood, 1850.)

Strype, John, *John Strype's Survey of the Cities of London and Westminster,* (1720). (hriOnline, Sheffield: Online.)

Suckling, Alfred, *The History and Antiquities of the County of Suffolk,* Volume 1. (London: John Weale, 1846.)

Surrey Archaeological Society, *Surrey Archaeological Collections Relating to the History and the Antiquities of the County.* Volume 3. (London: Lovell Reeve and Co., 1865.)

Tallis, Nichola, *Crown of Blood, The Deadly Inheritance of Lady Jane Grey.* (London: Michael O'Mara Books Ltd., 2016.)

Tallis, Nichola, *Uncrowned Queen: The Fateful Life of Margaret Beaufort, Tudor Matriarch.* (London: Michael O'Mara Books Ltd., 2019.)

Taylor, James D., *Complete State Trials of the Tudor Era.* (New York: Algora Publishing, 2019.)

Taylor, John, *Tintern Abbey and Its Founders Comprising a Revision and Correction of Preceeding Accounts, with Numerous Additional Particulars Hitherto Uncollected, including the Dates of the Various Buildings.* (London: Houlston & Wright, 1869.)

Thirsk, Joan, *Horses in Early Modern England: For Service, for Pleasure, for Power,* Issue 11 of Stenton Lecture S. (Reading: University of Reading, 1978.)

Thomson, J. A. F., 'The Courtenay Family in the Yorkist Period' in *Bulletin of the Institute of Historical Research,* Volume 45, Issue 112, November 1972, pp.230–246.

Thornton, Tim, *Cheshire and the Tudor State 1480–1560.* (London: Royal Historical Society, 2000.)

Thurley, S. *The Royal Palaces of Tudor England.* (New Haven and London: Yale University Press, 1993.)

Tremlett, Giles, *Catherine of Aragon, Henry's Spanish Queen.* (London: Faber and Faber, 2010.)

Tucker, M. J., in 'The child as beginning and end' in DeMause, Lloyd (ed.), *The History of Childhood.* (USA: Roman and Littlefield, 1995) pp.229–258.

Walker, Greg, *John Skelton and the Politics of the 1520s*. (Cambridge: Cambridge University press, 2018.)
Wallace, Malcolm William, *The Life of Sir Philip Sidney*. (Cambridge: Cambridge University Press, 2011.)
Warnicke, Retha M., *Elizabeth of York and Her Six Daughters-in-Law, Fashioning Tudor Queenship, 1485–1547*. (London: Palgrave MacMillan, 2017.)
Watkins, Sarah-Beth, *Sir Francis Bryan, Henry VIII's Most Notorious Ambassador*. (Alresford: Chronos Books, 2019.)
Wedgewood, J. C. and Holt, A.D. (eds.), *History of parliament 1439–1500*, Volume 1. (Oxford: Oxford University Press, 1936.)
Weir, Alison, *The Children of Henry VIII*. (London: Jonathan Cape, 1996.)
Weir, Alison, *Henry VIII: The King and His Court*. (London, Ballantine Books, 2002.)
Weir, Alison, *Mary Boleyn: The Great and Infamous Whore*. (London: Vintage, 2012.)
Weir, Alison, *Elizabeth of York, The First Tudor Queen*. (London: Vintage Books, 2014.)
Weir, Alison, *The Lost Tudor Princess, A Life of Margaret Douglas, Countess of Lennox*. (London: Jonathan Cape, 2015.)
White, J. G., *The Churches and Chapels of Old London, With a Short Account of Those Who have Ministered In Them* [1901]. (London: Legare Street Press, 2023.)
Wooden, Warren W. and Watson, Jean, *Children's Literature in the English Renaissance*. (Kentucky: University of Kentucky, 1986.)
Wroe, Ann, *Perkin, A Story of Deception*. (London: Jonathan Cape, 2003.)
Yorke, Robert, 'Wriothesley [formerly Writhe], Sir Thomas, (d.1534)'. (ODNB online, September 2004.)

Index

Aberystwyth Castle, Wales 11, 12
address, forms of 136–137
Aesop, fables of 51, 103, 108
Agincourt, Battle of (1415) 2
Alcock, John, Bishop of Ely and Lord Chancellor 39, 53, 54, 55
almsgiving *see* charity
alphabet, learning the 44, 45
André, Bernard 19–20, 51, 52, 59, 65, 67, 186
Anglesey, Wales 1
Anne of Cleves, Queen of England 103, 105, 106, 141, 152
Anne of York 29
annotations 45, 69
Ap John, Sir Hugh 20, 186
Ap Nicholas, Gruffydd 11, 14
Ap Thomas, Sir Gruffydd ap Rhys 62
Ap Tudur, Goronwy 1
Aquinas, Thomas 84, 153, 156
archery 50, 109
Argentine, John 55, 186
aristocracy xii, xiii, 1, 44, 46, 51, 54, 86, 93, 120, 133, 158
Aristotle 36
arms *see* training at arms
Arthur, Prince of Wales ix, 35, 36, 37, 38, 49–64, 65, 186
  burial of 62–63
  death and funeral of 62
  education of xi, 40, 49, 50–52, 53–54, 56, 59
  guardian of 173–174
  household of xi–xii, 36, 37, 49, 52–53, 54, 55, 57, 63, 66, 67
  letters to Katherine of Aragon 59
  marriage to Katherine of Aragon 59, 60, 61, 155, 156
Ascham, Roger xiv, 106, 109, 110, 117, 118, 119, 121, 122, 124, 128, 130, 131, 188
  on Jane Grey 130–131
  praise of Elizabeth I 118
  The Schoolmaster 131
  Toxophilus 109
Ashley, John *see* Astley, John
Ashley, Katherine 104, 105, 107, 109, 115–117, 119, 121, 122, 124, 125, 126, 127
Askew, Anne 122–123, 152, 167, 175
Astley, John 104, 114, 116, 124, 137, 189
astronomy 45, 74, 106, 110, 111, 131
astronomical clock 173
attainder 14, 25, 130, 154, 172, 174
Aylmer, John 120, 121, 189
Bacton, Herefordshire 162
Bailey, Elizabeth 65, 187
Baker, Alice 88, 188
baptism 34, 79
  of Bridget of York 37
  of Prince Arthur 34, 35, 49
  of Margaret Tudor 39
  of Mary Tudor 78–79
  of Elizabeth I 92
  of Edward VI 101, 104, 140, 146
Barking Abbey 6
Barnet, Battle of (1471) 26, 27, 57, 141, 182
Barton Blount, Derbyshire 170
Baskerville, Jane 160
Baynton, Lady Isabel 105, 138–141, 188
Baynton, Sir Edward 105, 138–141, 188
beating *see* corporal punishment
Beauchamp, Eleanor 4
Beauchamp, Margaret 145
Beauchamp, Richard, 13th Earl of Warwick 3
Beaufort family 3, 7, 26, 30–31
Beaufort, Edmund, 2nd Duke of Somerset 3, 7, 10, 31
Beaufort, Edmund, 4th Duke of Somerset 26
Beaufort, Henry, 3rd Duke of Somerset 11, 25
Beaufort, Henry, Cardinal 4, 7
Beaufort, Joan 31
Beaufort, John, 1st Duke of Somerset 8
Beaufort, John, 1st Earl of Somerset 3
Beaufort, Lady Margaret, Countess of Richmond and Derby viii, x, xi, xii, xiv, 8, 13, 17, 21, 22, 30, 31, 33, 34, 35, 37, 38, 39, 41, 43, 45, 46, 47, 52, 55, 56, 57, 58, 62, 64, 65, 66, 67, 68, 69, 70, 73, 76, 77, 81, 130, 142, 144, 145, 153, 157, 158, 160, 162, 174, 183, 184, 185, 186
  Mirror of Gold for the Sinful Soul, translated into English, 41, 111
behaviour, rules for 43, 46, 47, 81, 84; *see also* manners
Belmain, John 108, 109, 110, 188, 189
Bergavenny, Lord *see* Neville, George
Bermondsey Abbey 4
Berners, 2nd Baron *see* Bourchier, John
Bess of Hardwick 121
Bewdley, Worcestershire 56, 59, 62
Bibbesworth, Walter de 36
Bible, study of xiii, 85, 118
Bishop's Stortford, Hertfordshire 42
bishopping *see* baptism
Blackfriars, London 90
Blackheath, London 42, 171

Bletsoe Castle, Bedfordshire 10
Blickling Hall, Norfolk 147, 164
Blount, Elizabeth 'Bessie', later Tailboys 80, 144, 188
Blount, William, 4th Baron Mountjoy xi, 46, 67, 68, 170, 187
Boleyn, Anne *see* Shelton, Lady Anne
Boleyn, Anne, Queen of England xiv, 69, 88, 90, 91, 92, 93, 101, 104, 108, 111, 116, 126, 145, 146, 155, 161, 178, 180, 188
Boleyn, Alice *see* Clere, Lady Alice
Boleyn, Amata *see* Calthorpe, Lady Jane
Boleyn, George 126, 130, 140, 149, 165
Boleyn, Jane *see* Calthorpe, Lady Jane
Boleyn, Mary 97, 111–112
Boleyn, Sir Thomas 82, 144, 171
Boleyn, William 147, 149
Book of Common Prayer (1549) 132
books 19, 41, 43, 44–45, 49, 51, 52, 53, 68, 69, 70, 71, 73, 74, 83, 85, 92, 103, 108, 109, 110, 110, 112, 120, 123, 130, 143, 155–156, 157, 162, 174
Books of Hours 35, 45, 49, 69, 155–156
Bosworth, Battle of (1485) ix, 33, 58, 66, 142, 159, 174, 183, 184,
Bothe, Charles 56
Bourchier, John, 2nd Baron Berners 80, 143
  The Castle of Love 143
Bradgate Park, Leicestershire 119, 120, 123, 131
Brandon, Charles, 1st Duke of Suffolk 73, 78, 101, 104, 123, 156, 187
Brandon, Eleanor 134
Brandon, Frances, Duchess of Suffolk xiv, 83, 118, 120, 121, 131, 134, 189
Brandon, Henry 109
Brasenose College, Oxford 55
Bray, Sir Reginald 24, 25, 30, 58, 155
breastfeeding 35–36, 92
Bridget of York 37, 41, 56
Bristol 20, 177
Brittany ix, xiii, 26, 27, 28, 30, 31, 155, 159, 182, 183
Bryan, Elizabeth see *Carew*, Elizabeth
Bryan, Sir Francis 79, 101, 143, 146–147, 174, 175
Bryan, Lady Margaret xii, xv, 79, 80, 81, 97, 100, 101, 102, 104, 105, 137, 139, 141–147, 148, 153, 164, 169, 180, 188
Buckingham, Duke of *see* Stafford, Edward; Stafford, Humphrey; Stafford, Henry
Buckingham's Rebellion 30–31, 37, 58, 155, 173
Buckler, Sir Walter 130, 170–171, 188
Burbage, Cecily 42
Burton, John 55, 186
Butler, Agnes 36, 186
Butts, Dr William 96, 108
Bywimble, Alice 36, 39, 186, 187

Cade's Rebellion 149
Caesar, Julius 87
Calais 14, 15, 23, 47, 67, 172–173, 176, 178
  Captain of Calais 9, 14, 179
Caldicot Castle, Wales 11
Calthorpe, Elizabeth 148
Calthorpe, Lady Jane 82, 88, 91, 147–148, 163, 188
Calthorpe, Sir Philip 82, 88, 92, 163, 171, 188
Cambridge University 41, 46, 53, 68, 86, 103, 108, 110, 117, 120, 122, 132, 166, 170, 174
Campeggio, Cardinal Lorenzo 90
canon law 8
Canterbury, archbishops of *see* Cranmer, Thomas; Morton, John
Canterbury Cathedral 35, 39
Carew, Elizabeth 144, 147
Carew, Sir Nicholas 105, 143, 146
Carey, Henry 111–112, 145
Carey, Katherine 105, 111–112, 145
Carey, William 111, 144, 171
Carmarthen Castle, Wales 11–12, 19, 22, 157, 175
Carreg Cennen Castle, Wales 11, 58
Castiglione, Giovanni 71, 110, 189
  Book of the Courtier 71
Castillon, Battle of (1453) 8
Catherine of Valois 2, 3, 4, 5, 7, 11
Catherine of York 37, 56, 61, 64, 78
Catholicism 105, 113, 123, 127, 132, 133, 141, 146, 153, 178
Caxton, William 41, 43, 45, 52, 54
  Book of the Knight of the Tower 43
Cecil, William 131, 133
Chace, Jane 65, 187
Champernowne family 137, 152
Champernowne, Katherine *see* Ashley, Katherine
chastity 90, 158
  oath of perpetual chastity 158–159
chaplains xii, xiii, 10, 19, 31, 49, 55, 56, 74, 80, 85, 88, 104, 108, 120, 132, 133, 170
Chapuys, Eustace, Imperial ambassador 92, 94, 95, 96, 97, 99, 100, 155, 164, 165
charity 63, 85
Charles V, Holy Roman Emperor and King of Spain 81, 88, 92, 96, 97
Charles VI, King of France 2
Charles VIII, King of France 31
Charles d'Orléans, Duc de Longueville 77
Chateau de Josselin, Brittany 28
Chateau de Suscinio, Brittany 27
Chateau L'Hermine, Brittany 29
Chatsworth House, Derbyshire 45
Cheddington, Buckinghamshire 147
Chelsea Manor xv, 116, 119, 121, 125, 137
Cheke, John 108, 109, 110, 114, 117, 122, 131, 132, 189
Chester 58
Chester herald *see* Whiting, Thomas
Chichester Cathedral School 68
childbirth 10, 34, 35, 38, 39, 63, 101
child marriage viii, 8, 46–47, 60
chivalric education *see* training at arms
chivalric literature 90
Chronicon Angliae 3
churching of women 35
Cicero 51, 52, 59, 85, 118
  De Officilis 52, 68
Civilitie of Childhood 103
classical languages, study of 68, 86, 90, 111, 112, 177; *see also* Greek language; Hebrew; Latin
Clarence, Duke of *see* George, Duke of Clarence

clocks 122
Clere, Lady Alice 95–96, 97, 149, 164, 180, 188
Clifford, John, 9th Baron Clifford 15
Clifford, Lady Margaret 135
Clifford, Thomas, 8th Baron Clifford 10, 15
clothing 2, 6, 29, 33, 34, 61, 84, 94, 100, 102, 140, 148
Codnor Castle, Derbyshire 65
coinage 128, 129
Coldharbour, Surrey 40, 153
Coldingham, Scotland 89
Colet, John 170, 174
Collectanea 34,
College of Physicians 72–73
Collyweston, Northamptonshire 41, 71
Commentaries on the Lord's Prayer xiv
Companions xiii, 48, 53, 66, 83, 87, 90, 104, 129, 132, 143, 155, 167, 178
Company of Barbers and Surgeons 73
Confraternity of the Holy Trinity, Knaresborough 21
consent x, 3, 124, 126, 155
consumption *see* tuberculosis
Conway, Sir Hugh 30
Cope, John 62
Corbet, Sir Richard 24, 158
Cornwall, duchy of 38
Cornwallis, Sir John 101, 107, 189
coronation:
of Elizabeth of York 33, 38, 81, 155
of Henry VI 2
of Henry VII 174
of Henry VIII and Katherine of Aragon 66, 76, 180
of Richard III 30, 31, 142
corporal punishment 94, 103, 108, 165
Corpus Christi College, Oxford, 33
Cotton, George 87
Cotton, Margaret 61, 194
Cotton, Sir Robert 50
Council of the Marches *see* Council of Wales
Council of the North xi, 86, 170, 188
Council of Wales xi, xii, 53, 54, 56, 58, 87
Court of Augmentations 133
Court of Wards and Liveries ix
Courtenay, Lady Catherine *see* Catherine of York
Courtenay, Edward, son of Catherine of York 61, 63
Courtenay, Edward, 1st Earl of Devon, grandson of Catherine of York 138
Courtenay, Henry, 1st Marquis of Exeter 61, 146
Courtenay, John, 7th/15th Earl of Devon 26
Courtenay, Margaret, Baroness Herbert 61
Courtenay, Peter, Bishop of Winchester 36, 40, 172–174, 186
Courtenay, Thomas, 6th/14th Earl of Devon 172
Courtenay, William, 1st Earl of Devon 61–62
courtly behaviour 47, 51, 81, 121, 143
counsel 33, 46, 67, 69, 95–96
Cox, Richard 103, 108, 189
Craddock, Lady Katherine *see* Gordon, Lady Katherine
cradles 34, 36, 39, 63, 79
Cranmer, Thomas, Archbishop of Canterbury 141
Croft, Sir Richard 56–57, 63
Croke, Richard 86–87, 88, 90, 178, 188
Cromer, Anne 42, 149, 150, 187
Cromwell, Thomas, 1st Earl of Essex ix, xii, 79, 92, 97, 100, 101, 102, 105, 106, 136, 137, 140, 145, 146, 147, 148, 166, 169, 170, 175, 180, 184
Croyland Chronicle 62 173
Culpeper, Joyce 138, 139
Culpeper, Thomas 141

D'Ewes, Giles 44, 46, 68, 69, 80, 88, 109, 186, 187, 188
Dagenham Manor, Essex 61
dancing xiii, 2, 43, 44, 73, 82, 86, 88, 106, 115, 120, 168
Darcy, Sir Thomas 99, 129
Daventry, Northamptonshire 5, 6
Davy, Alice 39–40
Dee, John 111, 131–132
De la Pole, Edmund, 3rd Duke of Suffolk 61
De la Pole, Katherine, Abbess 6
De la Pole, John, 1st Earl of Lincoln 38, 184
De la Pole, John, 2nd Duke of Suffolk 8
De la Pole, William, 3rd Earl of Suffolk, later 1st Duke of Suffolk viii, 5
Denbigh, Wales 22
Denny, Sir Anthony xv, 108, 109, 113, 121–122, 124, 129, 130, 170, 174–175, 188
Denny, Joan 123, 124, 137, 152
Denton, Elizabeth xi, 40, 42, 47, 65, 71, 79, 144, 152–153, 157
Derby, Earl of *see* Stanley, Thomas
Devereux family 18, 49
Devereux, Anne *see* Herbert, Anne, Countess of Pembroke
Devereux, Elizabeth 24
Devereux, Walter 12, 19
Devereux, Walter, 8th Baron Ferrers of Chartley 22, 24
Devise for the Succession 134
Devon, earls of *see* Courtenay, John; Courtenay, Thomas; Courtenay, William; Stafford, Humphrey
Devonshire Manuscript 164
disease 36, 41, 42, 72
Diss, Norfolk 67
dissolution of the monasteries 16, 99, 100, 109, 156, 160, 174, 181, 185
Ditton Park, Bedfordshire 83
Dogmersfield, Hampshire 60
domestic skills, training for xiv, 84, 85, 166
Dormer, Jane 167
Dorset, Marquis of *see* Grey, Thomas
double translation 19, 118
Douglas, Archibald, 6th Earl of Angus 89, 187
Douglas, Margaret 39–40, 89, 90, 91, 93, 99, 164
legitimacy of 89
dower rights 158
Drayton, Michael 2
Dudley, Andrew 129, 134

Dudley, Edmund 73
Dudley, Guildford 134
Dudley, John, Earl of Warwick later 1st Duke of Northumberland x, 113, 128, 189
Dudley, Mary *see* Sidney, Mary
Dudley, Robert 129, 138
Dudley Conspiracy 138
Dunstable, Bedfordshire 91
Durham House, London 63, 71, 86, 124

Edgecote, Battle of (1469) 23, 24, 25, 158, 177
Edmund, Earl of Rutland 15
Edward, 2nd Duke of York:
The Mayster of Game 70
Edward, Earl of March *see* Edward IV
Edward I, King of England 61, 142
Edward II, King of England 1, 41
Edward III, King of England 1, 3, 82, 141, 185
Edward IV, King of England viii, 15, 16, 17, 18, 22, 23, 24, 25, 26, 27, 28, 29, 53, 54, 56, 57, 58, 142, 150, 151, 154, 157, 158, 159, 160, 162, 172, 173, 176, 177, 183
Edward of Lancaster *see* Edward, Prince of Wales, son of Henry VI
Edward of Middleham, son of Richard III, 20, 31
Edward, Prince of Wales, son of Edward IV *see* Edward V
Edward, Prince of Wales, son of Henry VI 9, 10, 11, 15, 26, 56, 154, 182
Edward V, uncrowned king of England x, 30, 37, 47, 50, 51, 52, 53, 54, 55, 57, 151, 169, 184
Edward VI, King of England x, 129, 133, 135, 136–137, 146, 147, 175, 179
and Elizabeth I 128
and Jane Grey 120, 123, 134
and Katherine Parr 119
and Mary I 132
and Thomas Seymour 117, 122–123, 125, 127
Chronicle of, 114, 129
education of xv, 103, 108, 109, 110, 111, 117, 131, 132
In Defence of Astronomy 131
regency council of x, 113, 114, 115, 129
Edward the Confessor 179
Elizabeth I, Queen of England
and Edward VI 101, 108, 128, 134, 135
and Katherine Parr 106, 110, 111, 113, 115, 119, 121, 122, 123
and Mary I 94, 95, 97, 98, 100, 102, 115, 135, 138
and Thomas Seymour 114, 116, 119, 121, 124, 125, 126, 138, 168, 185
birth and baptism 92, 161
education of xiii, xiv, xv, 103–104, 105, 109, 110, 111, 112, 117, 118, 121, 131, 132, 133, 137
household xii, 92, 93, 94, 100, 101, 104, 105, 106, 107, 122, 124, 125, 126, 127, 130, 133, 137, 138, 140, 145, 146, 149, 161, 162, 164, 166, 168, 171, 185, 188
legitimacy of 93, 94, 95, 97, 100, 145
succession to the throne 133–134, 181, 185
Elizabeth of York, Queen of England x, xii, 28, 30, 33, 34, 35, 37, 38, 39, 40, 41, 43, 44, 45, 47, 54, 59, 61, 62, 63, 64, 68, 81, 142, 150, 155, 170, 186, 187
Eltham Palace 41
Elton, G.R. ix
embroidery, training in 44, 85, 104, 106, 111
Englefield, Sir Thomas 56, 58
Erasmus, Desiderius xiii, xiv, 46, 47, 52, 66, 67, 68, 72, 73, 83, 84, 85, 86, 88, 103, 110, 170, 174
Education of a Christian Prince 85
esquires of the body 66, 101
etiquette *see* manners
Eucharist 122
Exeter, bishops of *see* Courtenay, Peter; Veysey, John
Exeter Conspiracy 105, 146, 163

falconry, training in 21, 70, 85–86, 120
Farnham Castle, Surrey 36, 38, 39, 40, 49, 150
Featherstone, Richard 85, 88, 93, 188
female sovereignty xiv, 80, 81, 84, 87
feminine virtues 44, 85, 106, 121
feudal dues viii, 1, 181
Ferch Tomos, Marged 1
Ferdinand II of Aragon 59, 63, 72
Field of the Cloth of Gold (1520) 82
First Battle of St Albans (1455) 10, 11, 13, 181
Fisher, John, Bishop of Rochester 10, 41, 45, 68
FitzPatrick, Barnaby 109
FitzRoy, Henry, Duke of Richmond and Somerset xi–xii, 80–81, 86, 87, 90, 91, 93, 94, 100, 101, 107, 144, 178, 188
Flodden, Battle of 101, 168
Florio, Michelangelo 120
foreign policy 2, 21, 80, 88, 104
Anglo-French marriage treaties 77, 78, 80, 81, 82, 88
Anglo-Scottish marriage treaties 12, 46, 60, 61, 71, 114
Anglo-Spanish marriage treaties 59, 71, 81, 174
fostering viii, 137
four humours 36, 72
Fowler, John 114, 125
Foxe, Richard, Bishop of Winchester 33, 69, 71, 174
Framlingham Castle, Norfolk 100, 135
France ix, xiii, 1, 2, 7, 18, 27, 28, 31, 77, 80, 81, 82, 88, 101, 141, 159, 175, 182, 185
Francis II, Duke of Brittany ix, 26, 27, 29, 31
Francis I, King of France 75, 78, 80, 84
French language, study of 19, 28, 46, 68, 69, 77, 80, 83, 84, 86, 88, 108, 109, 110, 112, 120, 132, 154, 177
Froissart's Chronicle 80
Fychan, Ednyfed 1

gambling 102, 131, 139
games 47, 50, 118
Gardiner, Stephen, Bishop of Winchester 86, 97, 122, 123, 184
Gates, Sir John 128–129, 189

Geoffrey of Monmouth 35
Gemini, Thomas 131
George, Duke of Clarence 16, 23, 24, 54, 55, 59, 70, 82, 105, 162, 172, 173, 177, 182
Geraldini, Alessandro 83
Geraldini, Antonio 83
Gibbs, Katherine 36, 186
Giles's Latin Chronicle see Chronicon Angliae
Giosafat, Barbaro:
  Travels to Tana and Persia 129
Giustinian, Sebastian, Venetian ambassador 70–71, 80
glossaries as an aid for learning 85
Glyndwr, Owain 1
Glyndwr's Rebellion 19
godparents, responsibilities of 39
Gordon, Lady Katherine 87, 196
Gower, Margery 65, 187
grammar, study of xiii, 19, 20, 46, 51, 53, 66, 67–68, 108, 118, 120
grammar schools 53, 56
Great Chronicle of London 71
Greek language, study of xiii, xiv, 52, 86, 87, 88, 108, 110, 117, 118, 120, 131, 132
Green, Maud *see* Parr, Lady Maud
Greenwich Palace 40, 41, 42, 62, 69, 70, 76, 78, 79, 92, 102, 135, 139, 164
Gregory's Chronicle 22
Grey, Henry 3rd Marquis of Dorset, later Duke of Suffolk 120, 121, 123, 131, 134
Grey, Lady Jane xv, 119, 120, 123, 124, 134, 135
Grey, Lady Katherine 119, 120
Grey, Lady Mary 119, 120
Grey, Thomas, 1st Marquis of Dorset 31
Greyfriars Church, Hereford 16
Grice, John 63
Grindal, William 110, 117, 128, 188
Grosseteste, Robert 43
Gruffydd, Elis, 'Soldier of Calais' 2
guardianship viii–ix, x, xi, xii, 8, 120–121, 133
Guildford, Sir Henry 48, 66, 143, 155
Guildford, Joan 39, 48, 49, 77, 143, 154–155
Guildford, Sir Richard 155
Guillemeau, Jacques 92
Guto'r Glyn 58

Haddon Hall, Derbyshire 55
Hall, Edward 25, 27, 56, 73
Hammes Castle, Calais 32, 183
Hampton Court Palace ix, 71, 74, 91, 101, 106, 110, 125, 134, 140, 141, 166
handwriting *see* italic handwriting
Harlech Castle, Wales 18, 22, 54, 176
Harvel, Edmund, English Ambassador 170
Haseley, Edward 20, 186
Hatfield, Old Palace 5, 70, 92, 93, 94, 109, 122, 124–125, 130, 135, 145, 161, 164, 165, 168, 180
Haute family 150
Haute, Alice 150
Haute, Elizabeth, Lady Darcy 37–38, 50, 71, 150–152, 186
Haute, Richard 37, 151–152
hawking *see* falconry
Hebrew 112, 120
henchmen 49, 102
Henry IV, King of England 1, 4
Henry VI, King of England viii, 2, 3
  Regency Council of 2, 3, 4, 5
Henry VII, King of England
  betrothals 16, 24, 30
  birth viii, 11, 12, 13, 47
  education ix, xiii, 13, 16, 18–22, 24, 29, 45, 49
  guardianship of 13, 16, 17, 18, 19, 25, 26
  household 49
  in exile xiii, 27, 28, 29, 31, 32, 55
  marriage to Elizabeth of York 30, 33
  succession fears x, 50, 54, 59, 62, 65
Henry VIII, King of England ix, x
  and Sir Thomas More 47
  as Duke of York ix, 43, 45, 60
  birth and baptism 40
  break with Rome 90, 92, 93–94
  divorce from Katherine of Aragon 61, 80, 88, 89, 90, 91, 94
  education 43, 44, 45, 46, 48, 5, 65–68, 69, 70, 75
  household 40, 42, 70, 72, 75, 78, 155, 187
  illegitimate children 83, 87, 94, 97, 99, 112
  interests 71, 72, 73, 74, 109
  inventory of belongings 69
  mistresses 77, 80, 95, 112, 143
  regency council x
  succession fears x, xiv, 81, 82, 87, 90, 92, 134, 139–140, 146
  will x, 113
  wives 71, 76, 79, 88, 91, 93, 98, 101, 103, 105, 106, 110, 139, 141, 145
Henry VIII's Book of Medicines 73
Henry VIII Psalter 68
Henry of Burgundy 103
Hepburn, Patrick, Earl of Bothwell 89
heraldry 51, 76, 179
Herbert family 19, 20, 104
Herbert, Anne, Countess of Pembroke viii, 16, 17, 19, 24, 25, 136, 157–160
Herbert, Blanche, Lady Troy xv, 104, 137, 160–162, 188
Herbert, Maud viii–ix, 16, 21, 24, 157
Herbert, William, 1st Earl of Pembroke viii–ix, 12, 15, 16, 17, 18, 21, 22, 23, 24, 158, 175–177, 182, 186
Herbert, William, 2nd Earl of Pembroke, later 1st Earl of Huntingdon 21, 134, 160
Hereford 12, 15, 16, 175
Hertford, Earl of *see* Seymour, Edward
Hexham, Battle of (1464) 17, 25
history, study of xiii, 51, 53, 54, 66–67, 85, 106, 120
Hobbes, Evelyn 36, 186
Holbein, Hans 73, 74, 75, 132, 164
Holland, Henry, 3rd Duke of Exeter 28
Holt, John 67–68, 187
  Lac Puerorum (Milk for Children) 67
Homer:
  The Odyssey 51
Hone, William 68, 187

Hoo, John 37, 186
Hoppar, Isabel 89
horn books 44, 45
horses 21, 50, 53, 70, 86, 118, 132, 162
Hours of Henry VII 45
Hours of Henry VIII 45
households x–xi, xi, xii, xv, 1, 2, 21, 35, 36, 37, 39, 40, 42, 47, 49, 53, 54, 55, 57, 60, 61, 63, 65, 66, 67, 68, 69, 77, 79, 82, 86, 87, 88, 92, 93, 94, 95, 96, 97, 98, 100, 101, 102, 103–104, 105, 106, 115, 117, 120, 121, 123, 125, 128–129, 130, 139, 143, 144, 145, 148, 149, 151, 152, 155, 161–162, 166, 169, 170, 171
Household ordinances of Edward IV xi, 38, 53
Household ordinances of Henry VII 34
Howard, Catherine, Queen of England 105, 106, 127, 130, 139, 141
Howard, Edmund 138–139
Howard, Elizabeth 144, 147
Howard, Henry, 3rd Duke of Norfolk xii, 93, 100, 141
Howard, Henry, Earl of Surrey 90, 101, 122, 177–179, 188
Howard, Sir John 142
Howard, Mary 93, 164, 178
Howard, Thomas 99
Howard, Thomas, 2nd Duke of Norfolk 139
Howell, Richard 49
humanism xiii, 47, 51, 53, 66–67, 72–73, 81, 86, 152, 163, 170
Humphrey, Duke of Gloucester 2, 3, 5
Hundred Years War 2, 3, 7, 8
Hungerford, Sir Walter, 1st Baron Hungerford 1, 2, 5, 6,
Hunsdon, Hertfordshire 97, 135
hunting 21, 27, 50, 69, 70, 71, 85–86, 87, 90, 91, 118
Hussey, Lady Anne 95, 99
Hussey, Sir John 92, 99

Ightham Mote, Kent 151–152
Isabella I of Castile 83
Isocrates 118
italic handwriting 87, 85, 109–110, 120

James IV, King of Scotland 12, 71, 153
James V, King of Scotland 89
Jesus College, Cambridge 53
John of Gaunt, 1st Duke of Lancaster 3, 28, 30, 31, 59, 183
John, Duke of Bedford 5
jousting *see* tournaments
Julius II, Pope 76
Julius Caesar:
  Commentaries 87

Katherine of Aragon, Queen of England
  children 76, 77, 78, 82, 87, 153
  death 96
  divorce from Henry VIII 61, 80, 89, 91, 92
  dowry 63
  education 44, 83, 85
  household 40, 80, 162, 170, 185
  influence over Queen Mary I's education xiv, 79, 83, 144
  ladies-in-waiting 62, 77, 99, 101, 110, 143
  marriage to Henry VIII 71, 76
  marriage to Arthur, Prince of Wales 59, 60, 61, 82, 92, 155, 156
  pregnancies 77, 80, 88
  widowhood 63, 71
  wifely virtues 44, 85, 91
Kenilworth Castle, Warwickshire 38
Kenninghall, Norfolk 93, 115, 181
Kett's Rebellion 128, 175
King Arthur 35, 90
kingship ix, 52, 65, 103–104, 131–132
King's Great Matter 90
King's Mother *see* Beaufort, Lady Margaret
Kingston, Mary 105, 140
Knollys, Robert 49
Knollys, Sir Francis 106
Knowsley Hall, Liverpool 55
Kratzer, Nicholas 74

lady mistresses of the royal nursery xi, xii, xiv, 37, 47, 71, 77, 107, 122, 136–137
Lambeth Palace 60, 68, 139
Landais, Pierre 31
languages, study of 118, 120, 167
Largoet, Elven 28
Latin xiii, 19, 28, 46, 49, 51, 52, 59, 60, 67, 80, 81, 83, 84, 85, 86, 87, 88, 95, 103, 108, 110, 112, 118, 120, 131, 132, 156, 167, 174
Laws:
  of citizenship 1
  pertaining to marriage viii, 8, 10–11
  relating to remarriage of dowager queens of England 4
Layer Marney House, Essex 66
lying-in *see* childbirth
legitimacy 4, 5, 8, 26, 29, 37, 81, 86, 87, 89, 90, 91, 93, 97, 99, 163, 165
Leland, Thomas 34, 62, 191
letters and correspondence 27, 38, 59, 68, 77, 87, 110, 112, 115, 122, 123, 156, 179
Letters Patent 134
Leviticus 61
Lincoln, Earl of *see* De la Pole, John
Linacre, Thomas 52, 67, 72, 73, 81, 188
  De sphaera 52
  Rudiments of the Latin Language 81
Little Missenden, Buckinghamshire 102
livery 37, 51, 53, 92
Livy 51
Llywelyn, Fawr, Prince of Wales 1
logic 19, 54
London 1, 5, 11, 14, 15, 21, 23, 24, 25, 29–30, 36, 41, 60, 62, 63, 76, 86, 90, 101, 113, 124, 126, 131, 135, 151, 160, 171, 175, 176, 178, 180, 184
London, Treaty of (1518) 81
Longueville, Duc de see Charles d'Orléans
Louis XI, King of France 26, 27, 182
Louis XII, King of France 77–78, 156

Ludlow Castle xii, 14, 52–54, 55, 56, 57, 60, 61, 62, 65, 87–88, 90, 144, 148, 151, 160, 162, 163, 169, 171, 174, 176
Ludford Bridge, Battle of (1459) 14
Luke, Anne *see* Oxenbridge, Anne
Luther, Martin 68, 123
Lydgate, John:
Siege of Thebes 157
Table Manners for Children 43
Troy Book 157

Machiavelli, Niccolò:
The Prince xv
Magdalen College, Oxford 67, 68
Malory, Sir Thomas 35
Mancini, Dominic 55
manners, acquisition of 20, 43, 49, 80, 103, 106, 166
maps and map making 74, 111
Margaret of Anjou, Queen of England 7, 8, 9, 11, 16, 18, 25, 26, 154, 176, 181, 182
Margaret, Duchess of Burgundy 45
Marney, Henry 66
Marney Grace 66
Marney, Sir Henry 66, 69
marriage viii, xii, 8, 10–11, 46, 119, 120–121, 133
martial sports *see* training at arms
Mary Herbert 18
Mary, Queen of France, daughter of Henry VII *see* Tudor, Mary, Queen of France and Duchess of Suffolk
Mary I, Queen of England:
and Edward VI 101, 132
and Elizabeth I 93, 94, 95, 96, 97, 100, 102, 115, 138, 140, 145
and Henry FitzRoy 80–81, 87, 93
and Katherine Parr 106, 115
and religious beliefs 81, 84–85, 95, 97, 132, 133
and succession to the throne 80, 87, 90, 135, 181
birth of 78, 81
education of xiii, xiv, 80, 81, 83, 84, 85, 86, 88, 90, 91, 108, 109
household of xii, 81, 82, 83, 78–79, 88, 89, 91, 92, 93, 98, 99, 131, 140, 144, 148, 149, 163, 171
legitimacy 87, 88–89, 90, 91, 92, 93, 145
marriage betrothals 81–82, 88, 114
Mary, Queen of France *see* Tudor, Mary
Margaret of Navarre:
The Mirror or Glass of the Sinful Soul 111
Margaret, Queen of Scots *see* Tudor, Margaret, Queen of Scotland
Mary, Queen of Scots 114, 120, 123
Massey, Alice 39, 63
mathematics, study of 19, 73, 74, 111, 131, 132
Matilda, Empress, uncrowned queen of England 81
Mayland, Anne 39, 187
Mazzoni, Guido 74
medicine, study of 72–73
Medina del Campo, Treaty of 59
memorisation 51, 67, 85, 103
Mendoza, Iòiogo de, Spanish Ambassador 87
mentors and mentoring xiii, 46, 47, 50, 51, 67, 68, 69, 90, 131, 170
Meredith, Owen *see* Tudor, Owen
midwives 35, 39, 63
Milanese ambassador 28, 29, 52, 91, 92, 97, 132
Milbourne, Blanche *see* Herbert, Blanche, Lady Troy
Milford Haven 32, 58, 70, 183
milk production, medical theory of 38
minority monarchy 10–11
modern languages, study of 28, 41, 45, 46, 68, 83, 84, 88, 109, 110, 112, 120, 154, 177
moral character xiii, 84–85
moral stories 45, 51
More, Sir Thomas xiii, xiv, 30, 45, 46, 47, 50, 54, 67, 68, 72, 74, 80, 81, 85, 86, 88, 96, 110, 118, 151, 167, 170, 174
Pageant Verses 50
Prosopopoeia Britanniae 47
Utopia 72, 85
Morgan, Anne 104, 111
Morgannwg, Lewys 161
Mortimer family 14, 56
Mortimer, Anne 14
Mortimer, Edmund, 5th Earl of March
Mortimer, Eleanor 56
Mortimer, Sir Hugh 56
Mortimer's Cross, Battle of (1461) 15–16, 56, 176, 182, 183, 184
Morton, John, Archbishop of Canterbury and Bishop of Ely 31, 39, 56, 68
Moryson, Sir Richard 131
mothers viii, xii, xiv, 19, 40, 43, 44, 70, 115
Mother Guildford *see* Guildford, Joan
Mother Jack 102, 137, 189
Mowbray, dukes of Norfolk 142, 179
Mowbray, Anne, Duchess of York 142
Mrs Pendred 104, 188
Much Hadham, Hertfordshire 5
music xiii, 44, 53, 69, 82, 85, 86, 118
musicians 46, 69, 97, 102, 109
musical instruments 46, 53, 84, 88, 109, 120, 143, 180

natural order 84, 118, 133
Neville family 9, 10, 14, 17, 181
Neville, Anne, Queen of England 31, 142, 154
Neville, Cecily, Duchess of York 35, 150, 158
Neville, Sir Henry 129
Neville, George, Archbishop of York 21, 177
Neville, George, 3rd Baron Bergavenny 86
Neville, Isabel, Duchess of Clarence 23, 162
Neville, Margaret 110
Neville, Richard, 5th Earl of Salisbury 14, 163
Neville, Richard, 16th Earl of Warwick 10, 14, 22, 23, 81, 158, 177, 182
Newgate Prison 6
New learning *see* humanism
New Testament, study of xiii, 85, 118
Newton, Sir Peter 56

Norfolk, dukes of see Howard, Henry; Howard, Thomas
Nonsuch Palace ix
Norham Castle, Northumberland 89
Northampton, Battle of (1460) 15
Northumberland, earls of see, Percy Henry
Northumberland, Duke of *see* Dudley, John
Nottingham 23, 177
Nursery:
of Catherine of York's children 61
of Edward IV's children xi, 37, 38, 41
of Edward VI 101–103, 166, 167
of Elizabeth I 107
of Henry VII's younger children 41, 42–45, 46, 47
of Mary I 78, 79–80
of Prince Arthur xi, 38

Oath of Succession 96
Old Testament, study of xiii, 85
ordinances xi, 34, 38, 53, 64, 144, 150
original sin 35
Orleans, Charles d', Duc de Longueville 77
Oxenbridge, Anne 40, 66, 187
Oxenbridge, Elizabeth *see* Tyrwhitt, Elizabeth
Oxenbridge, Geoffrey 66
Oxford, earls of *see* Vere, John de
Oxford University 33, 41, 46, 55, 56, 66, 67, 68, 74, 83, 108, 170, 172, 179
Oystermouth Castle, Wales 20

Page, Sir Richard 107–108, 114–115, 140, 175, 179–180, 189
pages 2, 19, 20, 22, 172; *see also* squires
paintings and portraits xiii, 48, 61, 74, 75, 128, 164
Palsgrave, John 77, 80, 86, 87, 178, 187, 188
papal dispensations 13, 59, 78, 93, 97
Parker, Henry, Lord Morley 68, 130, 171, 181, 188
parliament 3, 8, 9, 10, 26, 58, 117, 134, 145, 171, 176, 181, 185
Parr, Katherine, Queen of England xii, xiii, xv, 106, 110, 113, 115, 116, 119, 121, 122, 123, 124, 125, 126, 127, 130, 132, 137, 138, 141, 152, 167, 170, 171, 175, 185, 188, 189
Prayers or Mediations 112
Psalms or Prayers 106
The Queen's Prayers 130
Parr, Lady Maud 110
Parr, Sir William xi, 87, 154
Parry, Blanche 104, 107, 138, 161–162, 188
Parry, Thomas 122, 124, 125, 126, 130, 185
Partridge, Agnes 86, 188
patronage 13, 50, 52, 67, 74, 83, 120–121, 122, 131, 147, 172, 179
Pembroke Castle, Wales 9, 11, 12, 13, 14, 16, 18, 26, 176, 183, 184
Pembroke, earls of *see* Herbert, William; Tudor, Jasper
penal laws 4
Penn, Mary 102
Penn, Sybil 102, 189
Percy family 9, 181
Percy Henry, 2nd Earl of Northumberland 10
Percy Henry, 4th Earl of Northumberland 19, 24
Perpetual Peace, Treaty of 60
Penshurst Place, Kent 102
Phillips, Sir David 56
philosophy, study of xiv, 54, 74, 110
Picquigny, Treaty of (1475) 28, 29, 154
Picton, John 109, 188
piety xiii, 43, 44, 85, 88
pilgrimages 20, 77, 155
Pilgrimage of Grace 99, 146, 178
Plantagenet, Arthur, Lord Lisle xi, 47, 48, 70, 179
Plantagenet, Edward, 17th Earl of Warwick 59, 82, 162, 184
Plantagenet, Margaret *see* Pole, Margaret, Countess of Salisbury
Plato 85, 131
Pliny 59
Plymouth, Devon 60
poetry 43, 46, 47, 58, 66, 67, 84, 89, 90, 112, 118, 130, 164, 168, 178
Pole, Arthur 163
Pole, Catherine 79, 188
Pole, Eleanor 54
Pole, Geoffrey 162, 163
Pole, Henry 105
Pole, Margaret, Countess of Salisbury 54, 79, 81, 82, 87, 88, 89, 92–93, 96, 105, 109, 144, 148, 162–164, 188
Pole, Cardinal Reginald 105, 146, 162, 163
Pole, Sir Richard 54, 62, 162
Pole, Ursula 162
Pontefract Castle, Yorkshire 15, 99, 151
Popincourt, Jane 46, 77, 187
Poyntz, Anthony 155
Poyntz, Thomas 49
prayers 19, 39, 44, 49, 80, 84, 103, 106, 112, 119, 130, 156, 158
Princes in the Tower x, 10, 30
Proculus 52
protestantism *see* reformers
Psalter 19, 45, 68
Pudsey, Ralph 66
Puebla, Roderigo de, Spanish Ambassador 59
Puttenham, Frideswide 65, 187

quintain *see* training at arms

Raglan Castle, Wales 12, 16, 18–19, 21, 24, 63, 157, 159, 175, 176
Readeption 25–26
Record, Robert:
First Principles of Geometrie 131
Rede, John 40, 51, 52, 59
Reformers (Protestant) xiii, 103, 108, 120, 121, 122, 123, 127, 129, 130, 132, 134, 146, 152, 167, 175
Regents and protectors:
of Edward V 29
of Edward VI 113–114
of Henry VI 2, 3, 8–9, 11
of Henry VIII x

regency council:
 Edward V 30
 Edward VI 113, 114, 124, 178
 Henry VI 2, 3, 4, 5
religious education 19, 84, 85, 104, 120, 132
Renaissance xii–xiii, xv, 12–13, 65, 72, 75, 76, 109–110, 178
Regnéville, France 7
Rennes Cathedral, France 31
rhetoric, study of xii, 46, 51, 59, 66, 67, 84, 118
Richard II, King of England 26
Richard, Duke of Gloucester, later Richard III, King of England 17, 25, 29
Richard, 3rd Duke of York 7–8, 9, 10, 11, 12, 13, 14, 15
Richard, Duke of York, son of Edward IV x, 27–28
Richmond, Duke of *see* FitzRoy, Henry
Richmond, earls of see Tudor, Edmund; Henry VII
Richmond Palace 42, 61, 63, 69, 71, 76, 79, 80, 82, 91, 138
Rieux, Jean de 28, 186
Robin Dhu 6,
Robin of Redesdale 23, 177
Robins, John 74
rockers 36, 39, 61, 79, 186, 187
role models *see* mentors and mentoring
romances 84, 143
Roper, Margaret xiv, 45, 110
Rough Wooing 114–115
Rowle, Henry 80, 188
Royal Book 36, 37, 38, 39, 150
royal nurseries:
 pensions xi, 36, 38, 66, 78, 155, 161
 staff xii, 36, 37, 39, 40, 41, 49
 routine 38, 42, 43, 45, 50, 69, 117, 119
 wages 40, 44, 93
running rings *see* training at arms

St David's Cathedral, Pembrokeshire 12
St George's Chapel, Windsor 72, 74
St John, Catherine 62
St Laurence's Church, Ludlow 62
St Malo, Brittany 28–29
St Paul's Cathedral School 174
Sandal Castle, Yorkshire 15
Sawston Manor, Cambridgeshire 135
Scarpinello, Augustino, Milanese Ambassador 91
Scotus, Andrew 20
Scudamore, Sir John 18
Seymour, Edward, 1st Earl of Hertford, later Duke of Somerset x, xv, 101, 107, 113, 114, 126, 127, 128, 178, 180, 185, 188
Seymour, Jane, Queen of England 98, 101, 105, 140, 146, 167, 178
Seymour, Thomas, 1st Baron Seymour xv, 113, 114, 115–117, 119, 120–121, 122, 123, 124, 125, 127, 167, 189
Sforza, Ludovico, Duke of Milan 28, 92
Shelton, Lady Anne xiv, 94, 95, 96, 105, 148, 149, 164–166
Shelton, Sir John xii, 97, 100, 105, 145, 180–181, 188
Shelton, Madge 95, 165
Shelton, Mary 95, 165
Sheriff Hutton, Yorkshire xi, 86, 179, 188
Sidney family 166–167
Sidney, Lady Anne 166–167
Sidney, Sir Henry 129
Sidney, Mary 166–167
Sidney, Sir William 101–102, 107, 189
Sidonius 85
Simnel, Lambert 44, 184
Simpson, Thomas 70
Skelton, John 46, 66, 67, 68
 Speculum Principis 46, 66
Skern, Anne 42
Skidmore, Avice 65, 187
Smeaton, Mark 97
Smith, William, Bishop of Lincoln 55–56, 63
Somerset, Elizabeth, Countess of Worcester 104, 160, 161, 162
Sophicles 118
South Wales 9, 11, 12, 16, 18, 21, 56, 58, 88, 157, 159, 176, 181, 182, 183
Spain 20, 59, 71, 81, 174
sport xiii, 46, 48, 69, 70, 71, 74, 109, 178
squires 2, 19, 22, 53; *see also* pages
Stafford, Edward, 3rd Duke of Buckingham 37, 82, 163, 176, 179
Stafford, Henry, 2nd Duke of Buckingham 30, 31, 151, 184
Stafford, Henry, 1st Baron Stafford 163
Stafford, Henry, Sir 13
Stafford, Humphrey, 1st Duke of Buckingham 13, 15
Stafford, Humphrey, 1st Earl of Devon 23, 24
Stanhope, Anne, Duchess of Somerset 107, 108, 119, 125, 180
Stanhope, Elizabeth 180
Stanley family 33, 58, 108
Stanley, Thomas, 2nd Baron Stanley, later 1st Earl of Derby 27, 29, 30, 31 55, 158
Stanley, Sir William 56
Stewart, James 89
Stoke Field, Battle of (1487) 38
Stony Stratford, Buckinghamshire 151
Strangeways, Sir Thomas 90
Succession, Acts of 93, 95, 120, 134, 165
Succession, Oath of 93, 96
sweating sickness 62, 72
Swynford, Katherine, Duchess of Lancaster 3, 26
Syon Abbey 99, 111, 141, 162

Tacitus 51
Tailboys, Gilbert 80, 144, 188
Talbot, Anne 55
Talbot, Elizabeth, Duchess of Norfolk 39
Talbot, John, 1st Earl of Shrewsbury 8, 55
Tantallon Castle, Scotland 89
taxation 9, 73, 181
Tempest, Sir Thomas xi
Tenby, Wales 18, 183, 184
tennis 69, 71, 90, 132, 157

Tewkesbury Abbey, Gloucestershire 26, 56, 150, 151, 154, 159, 182, 183
Tewkesbury, Battle of (1471) 26, 56, 150, 151, 154, 159, 182, 183
Thomas, William 66, 129
Thucydides 51
Tickenhill Manor, Worcestershire 59, 61
Tilney, Agnes, Duchess of Norfolk 141
Tilney, Elizabeth, Duchess of Norfolk 139, 142
Titus Livius 118
Torrigiano, Pietro 76
tournaments 22, 43, 50, 57, 61, 70, 77, 78, 92, 132, 146
Tours, Treaty of (1444) 7
Tower of London 9, 26, 29, 30, 42, 59, 61, 63, 66, 89, 95, 96, 99, 105, 126, 128, 138, 140, 142, 154, 163, 164, 166, 179
Towton, Battle of (1461) viii, 16, 56, 57, 172, 182
training at arms 70, 90
Trollope, Sir Andrew 14
Trussell, Elizabeth, Countess of Oxford 82
Tuberculosis 62, 134
Tudor family:
  coat of arms 4, 5
  claim to the throne 26
  family origins 1
  legitimacy 5, 8
  succession 93, 95, 96, 99, 120, 134, 135, 146
  suspected relationship to the Beaufort family 4, 5
Tudor, David 14
Tudor, Edmund, 1st Earl of Richmond viii, 5, 6, 8, 9, 11, 12, 19, 157
Tudor, Edmund, Duke of Somerset, son of Henry VII 42, 47
Tudor, Edward, son of Henry VII 42
Tudor, Elizabeth, daughter of Henry VII 42
Tudor, Jasper, 1st Earl of Pembroke, later Duke of Bedford viii, ix, 4, 5, 6, 8, 9, 10, 11, 12, 13–14, 15, 16, 17, 18, 21, 22, 25, 26, 27, 28, 29, 30, 31, 32, 56, 159, 176, 181–185, 186
Tudor, Katherine, daughter of Henry VII 63–64
Tudor, Margaret, daughter of Catherine of Valois 5
Tudor, Margaret, Queen of Scotland:
  betrothal and marriage to James IV of Scotland 46, 47, 60, 61, 153
  birth and baptism 39, 142
  divorce from Archibald Douglas 89
  education of xiv, 43–44, 45, 46
  household 40, 42, 43, 65, 154, 187
Tudor, Mary, Queen of France and Duchess of Suffolk:
  betrothal and marriage to Louis XII of France 77, 78
  birth and baptism 42
  children of 78, 120
  education of xiv, 43, 44, 45, 46, 68, 69
  household 42, 43, 60, 77, 78, 91, 154, 187
  marriage to Charles Brandon 78
Tudor, Owen 1–2, 4, 5, 6, 7, 8, 14, 15, 16, 172, 183
Tudor, Owen, son of Catherine of Valois 5
Twt Hill, Battle of (1461) 22, 176, 182
Tyler, Sir William 70, 187
Tyrell, Lady Elizabeth *see* Haute, Elizabeth, Lady Darcy
Tyrell, Sir James 63, 151
Tyrell, Sir John 150
Tyrell, William 150
Tyrwhitt, Sir Robert 107, 126, 130, 167, 168, 171, 185, 188
Tyrwhitt, Elizabeth 123, 126, 127, 130, 167–168, 188
  Morning and Evening Praiers, with Divers Psalmes Himnes and Meditations 130

Urswick, Christopher 31
Usk, Lordship of 12, 157, 175
Uvedale, Sir William 56, 57, 63

Van der Delft, François, Imperial Ambassador 125
Van de Wilder, Philip 109, 189
Vannes, Brittany 29, 31, 173
Vaughan family 18, 20, 159
Vaughan, Roger 26, 183
Vaux, Joan *see* Guildford, Joan
Vaux, Katherine 155
Vaux, William, 154
Venetian ambassadors, observations by, 70, 71, 78, 80, 87
Vere, John de, 13th Earl of Oxford 32
Vere, John de, 12th Earl of Oxford 151
Vergil, Polydore 16, 25, 183
Verney, Ralph 54
Vernon, Sir Henry 55, 59
Veysey, John, Bishop of Exeter 87, 188
Virgil:
  The Aeneid 51, 52, 84
Vives, Juan Luis xiii, xiv, 83–86, 89, 108, 110, 115, 188
  The Education of a Christian Woman xiv, 83–84

Wakefield, Battle of (1460) 15, 56
Wales xi, 1, 4, 5, 6, 8, 9, 11, 12, 13, 14, 16, 18, 21, 22, 25, 26, 28, 30, 31, 53, 54, 56, 57, 58, 87, 88, 89, 157, 159, 162, 176, 177, 181, 182, 183
Wallingford Castle, Oxfordshire 2, 3
Wallingford Pursuivant 51
Walsingham, Norfolk 77
Wangham, William 37, 186
Warbeck, Perkin 42, 46, 59, 87, 196
wards and wardship viii, ix–x, 8, 19
Wars of the Roses 7, 8, 9, 10, 11, 12, 13, 14, 15, 16, 17, 18, 22, 25, 26, 28, 30, 31, 32, 33, 38
Waynflete, William, Bishop of Winchester 57, 174
weaning 35, 39, 42
weapons handling *see* training at arms
Weobley Castle, Wales 24, 158
Westbury, Maurice 41, 56
Westminster Abbey 5, 30, 39, 41, 42, 64, 76, 184
Westminster Palace 3, 14, 15, 38, 50, 60, 70, 76
wetnurse 35–36, 92
  of Edmund Tudor, son of Henry VII 42
  of Elizabeth I 92, 104, 161, 188
  of Elizabeth Tudor, daughter of Henry VII 39

of King Edward VI 102, 189
of King Henry VIII 40, 42; 66, 187
of Margaret Tudor 42, 187
of Mary I 79, 188
of Mary Tudor 42, 188
of Prince Arthur 36, 186
Whiting, Thomas 28
Wilson, John 56
Winchelsea, Hampshire 66
Winchester, Hampshire 35
Cathedral 49, 174
College 40, 57
Windsor Castle xi, 3, 6, 43, 60, 63, 72, 74, 82–83, 90–91, 103, 178
Windsor Commission 103
Woking, Surrey 17, 38
Wolsey, Thomas, Cardinal ix, xi, xii, 77, 78, 82, 83, 86, 87, 90, 144, 148, 156, 178, 179, 188
Woodstock, Oxfordshire 52, 61
Woodville family 30, 35, 150, 151, 155, 169
Woodville, Anthony, 2nd Earl Rivers 53, 54, 155, 169
Woodville, Catherine, Duchess of Buckingham 184, 185
Woodville, Elizabeth, Queen of England 23, 27, 30, 31, 33, 34, 37, 42, 44, 142
Woodville, Joan 151
Woodville, Mary 21, 160
Worcester Cathedral vi, 62, 63
Worde, Wynkyn de 41
Wortley, Sir Thomas 151
Wriothesley, Thomas 51, 186, 187
Wyatt, Thomas 108, 140, 178

York, dukes of see Edward, 2nd Duke of; Richard, 3rd Duke of; Richard (younger son of Edward IV); Henry VIII

Zouche family 145